RESOURCES FOR TEACHING

A WORLD OF IDEAS

ESSENTIAL READINGS
FOR COLLEGE WRITERS

NINTH EDITION

Lee A. Jacobus
University of Connecticut

BEDFORD/ST. MARTIN'S ◆ Boston/New York

Instructors who have adopted *A World of Ideas: Essential Readings for College Writers,* Ninth Edition, as a textbook for a course are authorized to duplicate portions of this manual for their students.

Manufactured in the United States of America.

8   7   6   5   4   3
f   e   d   c   b   a

For information, write: Bedford/St. Martin's, 75 Arlington Street, Boston, MA 02116 (617-399-4000)

ISBN 978-1-4576-0444-7

PREFACE

This book is designed for first-year college English instruction in composition, the level at which I use these essays for my own students. I am well aware of the problems involved in trying to teach something other than writing while teaching writing. We usually ask our students to read compositions while they are learning to write them, and I have found that using essays by significant writers is one of the best ways to help students to write and keep writing. I do have to teach the essays, it is true. And I am sure that you, too, will have to devote class time to a discussion of each of the essays you choose to teach. But I am convinced that it is important time spent well. I find it exhilarating to discuss Freud, Arendt, and Darwin with first-year college students. They sense that these are writers they ought to know. And because they feel that way, I find it easier to hold their attention and show them how to learn about writing—while learning about other things—from a discussion of the prose before them.

These *Resources* are arranged in three sections. The first section includes discussions of all fifty-six readings in *A World of Ideas* and provides additional writing suggestions to supplement those in the book. The second section consists of sentence outlines; each selection is outlined to ensure that the main ideas stand out clearly. You should feel free to photocopy or download these sentence outlines and hand them out to students as an aid to understanding. (I am grateful to Carol Verburg, Ellen Troutman, Ellen Darion, Mike Hennessy, and Jon Marc Smith for preparing the sentence outlines.) The third section includes alphabetically arranged bibliographies of all of the writers represented in the book. If students wish to read more by and about these writers, you may want to distribute photocopies of these as well. Finally, I include in an appendix two student papers written in response to essays in *A World of Ideas*. You might want to use these as models or as prompts for discussion.

This manual is designed not to get in your way. I can't pretend to explain these essays the way you should explain them to your class. Students are all so different that no two discussions of, say, Machiavelli are ever the same. Even principal areas of focus change from discussion to discussion. Therefore, you probably will not want to use all of the materials—discussion topics, writing assignments, sentence outlines, and bibliographies—for each essay that you teach. But you may appreciate knowing that all these options are available, particularly if some of the essays turn out to be more difficult than you thought.

Using this book with first-year students implies that we respect their native intelligence. The Brunerian hypothesis—that students who are treated as if they were geniuses will perform as such—may not withstand the proof of experience, but I have found that even the most difficult students in an average class can derive benefit from assignments on this kind of material. Not every first-year class can handle this approach. I have had extensive experience in remedial English and understand some of the reading problems that even an average class contains. Yet I have been warmed by the enthusiasm my students have shown for the approach I recommend here. Granted, one must work hard to help them understand the ideas and grasp the basic rhetorical principles that they must apply. But I find the work is well rewarded.

One genuine reward is the quality of class discussions. I am pleased with the ways my students will pursue lines of argument or implications of a thought and then try to make sense of the essays they have read. I find, for instance, that it is very interesting to discuss Machiavelli's questions concerning ends and means, particularly in a world in which the justification of certain means is still a primary subject.

Another reward of this approach is the belief that I am contributing to the education of beginning students. Because most composition classes demand that some reading material be used for discussion and models of good writing, I consider it important to provide the best there is. In this case, the best thinkers, talking about some of the most vital ideas of all time, represent the best stimuli and models for writing. It is surprising to see how each of these authors does provide a model.

Whether the essay posits an argument, employs image or metaphor, or examines a single idea from many points of view, it remains a model with teaching potential for beginning students. Contemporary journalistic essays of the sort that appear in most anthologies available today are easy and fun reading for my students. But they are also insubstantial in many cases and often do not really offer the kind of model for writing that is truly useful. Most of the essays in this category—by Joan Didion, Tom Wolfe, E. B. White, Joseph Wood Krutch, and other fine writers—fascinate the reader because of their style. It is not the invention or the organization that stands out. It is style. And style is the one element that first-year students simply cannot learn from such models. These students can learn in their first semester how to use methods of development to help invention. They can also learn about argumentation, narrative, and other organizational principles. But they cannot hope to imitate or learn directly from a mature polished style. That comes only with time. Meanwhile, the kinds of essays included here have a great deal to offer beginning students of writing. I have tried to make the going as simple as I can to maintain morale and give students the chance to make the most of this valuable opportunity.

The contents of this manual may be downloaded from bedfordstmartins.com/worldofideas.

CONTENTS

PART ONE

DEMOCRACY

PART TWO

GOVERNMENT

PART THREE

ETHICS AND MORALITY

PART EIGHT

DISCOVERIES AND THE MIND

EVALUATING IDEAS
AND
WRITING ABOUT IDEAS

Evaluating Ideas

The first section of the text, "Evaluating Ideas," treats the question of critical reading. I know that some of the essays in this book are not easy for many students to read, and sentence outlines for all the selections are available at the end of this manual to help students cope with demanding material during the first difficult stages. Reports travel to me from great distances, as well as from teaching assistants down the hall, about how students begin to learn to read these essays well. I have heard that students in two-year colleges as well as four-year colleges of all kinds are able to master the material. It takes time, but student confidence eventually builds, and class discussions help many people learn to read critically.

You might include some opportunity for students to read aloud in your first experiments with the text in class. I recommend beginning with Machiavelli, in part because it is so accessible and in part because most students hold strong opinions on the issues that Machiavelli raises. I have never been disappointed using this essay.

Begin with paraphrasing in order to gain a sense of the extent to which your students understand the immediate meaning of what they are reading. Then proceed to the level of questioning. Encourage students to develop questions from the text, and then show them how some of the questions can be developed and how implications can be widened by applying questions to various kinds of experience.

I have divided the stages of critical reading into five relatively obvious and traditional steps:

1. Prereading
2. Annotating
3. Questioning
4. Reviewing
5. Forming your own ideas

I have been around long enough to know that few if any students will actually follow these five steps—or let's say few will follow all of them. But that is no reason to ignore them. I think that annotating and questioning are the two most important, and I observe my class early in the term to ensure that students are marking up the margins of their books. Many students resist writing in books, so a good lesson or two can help them. I would suggest you photocopy a few pages of your own text and show them how it is done.

Underlining a text is important for later recall, but I also think that writing commentary in the margin is even more so. You might mention points that seem obvious to teachers but not to students: when you comment on a passage in class, the students should mark it for future examination. If the passage is important enough to comment on, then surely it is important enough to be remembered.

Suggestion

Give your students a chance to annotate the rest of Machiavelli in class, and have them break into groups of three and discuss with one another the ways in which they annotated passages. They can learn fairly quickly from one another, especially if you provide them with initial suggestions and advice.

The kinds of questions that emerge out of annotating depend on many factors, but you will probably find related questions for discussion in your class. It helps to select a few questions that were developed by your own students and then offer them for examination by the class. You can remind your students that in their discussion they are carrying on a dialogue with the text, with one another, and with you. And that dialogue is a model for critical thinking.

FORMING YOUR OWN IDEAS

I hope it is clear from "Evaluating Ideas" that one of my principal purposes is to help students develop some ideas of their own. I do not want them to be passive receptors when they are reading these writers. I know from the experience of reading student responses from all over the country that many students fiercely disagree with some of these authors. I have added some authors in this ninth edition who will provoke even more disagreement. But controversy notwithstanding, it is essential that students be given the opportunity to initiate their own thoughts and their own responses to the ideas in this text. I want students to be participants in the quest for truth. For that reason, I end this section with a stimulus to thought. The point of this book is to encourage students to think on an intellectual level that is worthy of them.

Writing about Ideas

The second section, "Writing about Ideas," begins on page 13. The sample essay that offers one way to approach Machiavelli appears in the text on page 47. It continues the discussion of Machiavelli that is begun at the front of the book in "Evaluating Ideas." If you choose, you could assign both the first and second sections of the text at the same time. Or you could wait for students to read one or two of the selections and then assign the section titled "Writing about Ideas."

You know best what kinds of essays or responses you want from your students after they have read some of this material. I have found that I can direct my students toward writing that is personal and revealing or toward writing that is more formal and objective. Some of the suggestions for writing invite a personal response, and for certain students, this is the best kind of response. But for other students, a more reasoned and detached response might be desirable. What kind of response to aim toward lies with you, and the text is flexible enough to allow you to decide.

I have suggested in earlier versions of this manual that you hold some discussions with your students about your expectations and discuss openly with them what their expectations in the course are and what kind of writing they feel they need to do. I feel that self-expressive writing is appropriate for some students, but I also feel that most students at the first-year level should attempt less self-expressive writing and should instead practice writing that asks them to reason well, to think clearly, and to work with ideas that are mature and demanding. For that reason, you will find that most of the assignments direct students toward a kind of writing that is similar to the material they are reading—discursive, demanding, thoughtful, and rooted in the universal human experience.

Suggestions
1. Hold an open discussion with your students on why they ought to write about these essays instead of just discuss them. Ask them what they think the difference is, for example, between writing an essay and taking an examination on Plato's selection. I think you will uncover some interesting attitudes and be able to help your students understand the differences between these two processes.
2. In the course of discussing an essay—Machiavelli should do nicely—you might ask your students to make some observations about the author's tone or attitude toward the audience. These are important issues, and discussing them at an early stage can help you clarify some points. You can also explore with your students the kinds of choices they can make to control tone and use it to their best advantage.
3. It may be dangerously subjective—but also exceptionally human—to ask your students to comment on what they think about the author they are working with. How much of Machiavelli comes through, and in which passages? Or you may prefer to ask your students to decide on the attitude the authors assume. For example, is Lao-tzu cynical? Is Machiavelli cynical? What about Jefferson or Arendt? Or Douglass, King, and Marx?

4. Spend some time in your class discussions on the question of what students might write about. Suggest topics as they occur to you, and ask students to recommend and refine topics for essays. The virtue of this approach is that it encourages students to start thinking about writing topics early on, which in turn motivates them as they read.

GENERATING TOPICS FOR WRITING

You may regard the suggestions for writing at the end of the selections as a last resort for your students. But people tell me that the suggestions work. In fact, when I asked one user of the book what I could do to improve it, she recommended only that I include more suggestions for writing, which this edition does accomplish.

My students come up with ideas as they discuss the essays, but many also rely on the suggestions for writing and the questions that are intended to stimulate class discussion. Most students appreciate these suggestions, and students produce surprisingly varied papers based on what they choose.

Thinking Critically: Asking a Question

Education consists largely of learning how to ask the right questions. It is very important to point out that the authors in the text are often answering questions in their essays. The questions posed by students based on Machiavelli's essay are only a fraction of those that could be asked.

Suggestions

1. Ask your students to come up with as many questions as there are in the text. None of these questions is actually developed into an essay in the introduction, but all are indirectly relevant. Coming up with more questions can be very useful in discussing how to find ideas for writing. You might use some of the questions as vehicles for your students' writing.
2. This is a good place to develop thesis statements and to discuss the ways in which a thesis statement emerges from questions. If you use this book with a rhetoric text, you can introduce such material as is relevant.
3. Go over some sample arguments in class. When I do this, I usually link them with the methods of development (see text p. 29) and show how each method of development can yield an appropriate thesis statement from the same or similar concerns. Students need drilling in this, and no matter how many times you go over it, you will find students proposing theses that are too broad, too narrow, or too obvious for an essay. Sometimes no thesis statement at all will surface. If you feel this is important, you should allow some time for it in the opening days of the course.

Working up questions on the text is a good beginning exercise in class. You can begin by proposing some questions and then show how they can be answered in an essay. To me, the important issue is to teach how to raise questions of depth and complexity. I try to steer students away from any questions that require too simple a response. If the question is deep enough, the student will need to think carefully, and that will help produce an essay that might even surprise the student. This has happened often to me, and it is rewarding.

I ask two basic types of questions. One kind limits itself to the author of the material and to what might be called internal issues. That means dealing with the way an author works with an idea by articulating a concept and then examining it. Other questions examine life and experience outside the text. You probably will want to stress one kind of question on some occasions and another kind on others.

Using Suggestions for Writing

In addition to suggestions for writing after each selection, there are more suggestions in this manual. I often take one of the suggestions from the manual, photocopy it for the class, and use it to discuss possible strategies for essay topics. This helps students become accustomed to the approaches that you will find in the "Suggestions for Critical Writing" sections.

One tip for the first papers is not to let them be too long. I am particularly finicky about the first set of papers. I urge even my best students to write no more than three pages, but I really think two pages for the first paper is acceptable. That way you can go over the paper in detail and inform your students about what kind of performance you expect. If you review the first papers carefully, you should have a better experience with the second papers.

Developing Ideas in Writing

Methods of Development

Users of earlier editions will recognize my reference to methods of development as allusions to many common topics. The use of definition, comparison and contrast, causal analysis, and discussion of circumstances can be important initial issues for most students. I work with my students very closely on these matters, and I find that it helps them think more clearly and write more confidently.

If you agree with me about the usefulness of studying these methods of development, especially as such methods are evident in the selections, then I suggest that you try my approach of having your students develop single-paragraph essays guided by one of the methods of development. I often ask my students, once they have gotten used to thinking in terms of the methods of development, to write an essay using each method in turn. That is the structure of the sample essay at the end of "Writing about Ideas."

Suggestions

1. Assign the class the job of writing a single paragraph using any one of the methods of development. Give your students a choice to ensure some variety in your reading. Be sure to ask them to identify at the beginning of the essay which method they are using. If you would prefer that everyone use the same method of development, try causal analysis or analysis of circumstance. Or for one that is less difficult, try definition, which is important for freshmen.
2. Assign a one-paragraph essay, but do not allow students to identify the method they used. Read some aloud in class (or photocopy them), and see if the class can identify them.
3. Request an essay, like the sample essay that uses a different method of development in each paragraph.

This type of assignment may not appeal to you. However, you will see that it serves the important purpose of connecting the act of writing to the act of reading the essays in a way that is helpful for improving your students' writing. I feel that these methods of invention can be learned from watching how good writers work, even when the writers are formidable thinkers. The final result is that your students think much more about how they write something. Not only should their writing styles improve, but their thoughts about the subject at hand should deepen. The suggestions I have made have produced some probing essays and have also given some of the most problematic student writers approaches they never knew before. Often such students show the most rapid progress.

Sample Essay

Give your students a chance to go over the sample essay with you. You may find it contains elements that you do not want your students to repeat. If so, give the essay a thorough critique. Your students will want to critique it on their own terms, and they should be given a chance to do so.

Suggestion

I make an agreement with my students. They hand in each essay on time, and I grade it and give it back in the next meeting. This helps build morale. Students know how well they did almost immediately, and I know what needs to be done to have them writing at the level I think appropriate for them. The reward for turning in the essay on time is that if the student truly underperforms, I permit the student to resubmit the revised essay for a better grade. This works.

My most helpful practice is to photocopy some samples from my students' work and offer critiques of them in class. The rule is that no one knows whose work is being discussed, and there is to

Nov. 21	Thursday:	Read Chomsky, "New Horizons in the Study of Language," pp. 843–855.
Nov. 26	Tuesday:	Read Baldwin, "If Black English Isn't a Language, Then Tell Me, What Is?," pp. 795–803. **7th essay due.**
		ASSIGNMENT: Write an essay using principles of argumentation.
Nov. 28	Thursday:	THANKSGIVING
Dec. 3	Tuesday:	Read Greer, "Masculinity," pp. 725–737.
Dec. 5	Thursday:	Read Butler, from *Undoing Gender*, pp. 739–760.
Dec. 10	Tuesday:	Read Mill, "The Subjection of Women," pp. 669–687. **8th essay due.**
		ASSIGNMENT: Write an essay that uses both principles of argumentation and principles of research.
Dec. 12	Thursday:	Read and discuss an essay of your choice.

NOTE: Prompt completion of essays is crucial in this course. If you feel you cannot keep the pace we have set, you need to see me. All late essays, except those made late by *real* problems, will suffer a grade reduction.

Completed essays are due on the following days:

1. September 10
2. September 24
3. October 8
4. October 22
5. November 5
6. November 19
7. November 26
8. December 10

SUGGESTED PAIRINGS OF ESSAYS

Many instructors look for useful connections between two or more essays; if you are interested in trying that approach, you might consider the following groupings. In "Suggestions for Critical Writing" following each selection, the "Connections" items also make concrete suggestions for pairings.

1. Madison and Nyerere: The question of how to control power in any government is central to these selections.
2. The Constitution of the United States contrasts well with Tocqueville's view of democracy as he saw it at work.
3. Jefferson and Rousseau: Trace the influence of Rousseau in Jefferson. Also, try Rousseau and Lao Tzu together.
4. Nyerere and Bhutto are interesting to consider in relation to Becker. Democracy is central to all of them.
5. Machiavelli, Arendt, and Jefferson (and even Marx) read together will produce some interesting insights. The questions of oppression and striking out for freedom as well as the question of maintaining power are very strong here.
6. Carnegie, Galbraith, and Reich offer an interesting progression. The issue of poverty contrasts with the issue of the freedom of the individual to pursue wealth.
7. Douglass and Thoreau cover obedience and disobedience, just laws and unjust laws. These selections work well together and will also work well with King.
8. Wollstonecraft and Woolf deal with the same issues.
9. Greer and Butler both tackle basic questions of gender marking, and both will be very controversial and stimulating.
10. Woodson, Baldwin, and Kozol are a natural combination. These selections are likely to stir interesting responses in class.
11. Carter's online selection, "The Separation of Church and State," can be paired with any essay in the "Democracy" section.

12. Cicero's online selection, "The Defense of Injustice," pairs with any essay in the "Government" section.

13. Milton and Rose Friedman's online selection, "Created Equal," pairs with any essay in the "Wealth and Poverty" section.

14. Aristotle's online essay, "The Aim of Man," works with all the essays in the "Ethics and Morality" section.

15. Emerson's online essay, "On Education," naturally connects with any essay in the "Education" section.

16. Horney's online essay, "The Distrust between the Sexes," pairs well with the essays in the "Gender and Culture" section.

17. Pope's online poem, "An Essay on Criticism," connects to the essays in the "Language" section.

18. Descartes' online "Fourth Meditation" connects well with the essays in the "Discoveries and the Mind" section.

DEMOCRACY

The eight selections in Part One treat the issues of democracy as it was developed in the ancient world and as it has been enacted in modern times. Because democracy is not a simple idea, nor is there only one form of democracy, we need to examine some of its roots and some of the struggles to reinvent it in modern times. We need to avoid a simplistic approach to democracy and understand its complexities, its significance for developing nations as well as its promise for the modern industrialized nations. Because the United States Constitution has served as the model for democracy in many nations, we need to see exactly what kind of democracy it guarantees.

ARISTOTLE
Democracy and Oligarchy (pp. 59–73)

The style of this piece is not bright or flashy, as I mention in the introduction to the selection. But the rhetorical usefulness of the categorical method that Aristotle uses has not lessened in modern times. The concept of analyzing government in terms of genus, species, and individual is the basic approach that Aristotle uses for most of his discussions. Analyzing individual species of government, such as democracy and oligarchy, offers him a great opportunity to discuss his subject in detail.

You might want to point your students to discussing the reasons why Aristotle reduces the many forms of government he mentions to just two: democracy and oligarchy. According to his view, this distinction is based on the issue of wealth and poverty. He sees that if the wealthy minority rules the poor majority, the result is oligarchy. If the majority poor rule, then the result is democracy. Your students will probably be able to see that this distinction is not as clear-cut as it seems. One of the problems with categorical thinking is that not everything fits the categories with as much certainty as writers sometimes think.

Aristotle mentions the demagogue in connection with democracy, and I usually feel it is useful to raise the question of how the demagogue can dominate a given government. We have had interesting experiences with dangerous people, such as Senator Joseph McCarthy, who raised demagoguery to a serious level in the 1950s. The point is that even in a relatively open democracy such as in the United States, the demagogue can raise fears and suspicions that can undo the beneficial qualities of a democratic state.

Certain distinctions in this selection merit close attention. For example, there is relatively little mention of monarchy, whereas the history of the world after Aristotle is marked by a succession of monarchs. Perhaps Aristotle thought this a simple form of oligarchy, since in most cases the monarch is the richest or one of the richest people in the state. Also, the constitutional forms of government are mentioned by Aristotle but not given much weight. Your students might ask why, particularly in light of the fact that the United States Constitution is the next selection in Part One.

Of course, one discussion you will probably have in class with your students will center on whether or not the current system of government that we enjoy is in fact a democracy or an oligarchy. It will be interesting to see what kinds of evidence or testimony your students bring to this question, especially if many of them are politically minded. This is one of the key issues that we all have to face, especially in view of the fact that one ambition of modern times is to spread democracy. What will that really mean?

SUGGESTIONS FOR CLASS DISCUSSION

1. When is majority rule a potential problem in a modern democracy?
2. Is a state that holds regular elections in danger of becoming an oligarchy when the wealth is concentrated in a very small percentage of the population?
3. Is our form of government a democracy or an oligarchy?

SUGGESTIONS FOR BRIEF ESSAYS

1. Aristotle talks about the ways in which people qualify for a voice in government. In Athens, property ownership and freeborn status permitted citizens to vote. Taking into account social issues, gender issues, and wealth distribution, determine what the qualifications are for citizens today to be able to have a voice in government. What would impede people from taking part in the democratic process?
2. Aristotle discusses the relationship of laws to democracy in paragraph 6 and elsewhere. What would Henry David Thoreau contribute to his discussion? IIow would Thoreau react to the idea that the laws are above the community? Would Thoreau feel that he lived in an Aristotelian-style democracy?
3. Some nations that describe themselves as democratic seem to be governed by military statesmen. Since Aristotle takes care to mention the warrior "element" of a society as its most important, would he agree that such democracies are indeed democratic?

SUGGESTIONS FOR LONGER ESSAYS

1. After reading and considering Aristotle's discussion of democracy and oligarchy, how do you view the status of democracy in your country today? What forces seem to be pushing the state toward oligarchy? What forces are pushing it toward democracy? Is the state today easily categorized as a democracy? What are your concerns for the future of democracy?
2. Aristotle sees that there is not just one form of democracy, but several. What do you see as the basic characteristics of democracy? What variants do you see in our own government? What variants do you see in other governments? What do you see as the ideal form of democratic government?
3. When Aristotle discusses various forms of government in paragraph 11, he mentions aristocracy, by which he means government by the aristocrats. He defines aristocrats as the best people in the society. Plato regarded the best government as one headed by the best people. To what extent do you agree or disagree with Plato's view? Why would Aristotle think the aristocrats are the best people? Has aristocratic government been tried and succeeded? Or has it failed?
4. In paragraph 17, Aristotle talks about a government that could be a fusion of democracy and oligarchy. Clarify his thinking on this issue, and then argue the case for either the likely success or the likely failure of such a fusion to produce a happy government.
5. In paragraph 14, Aristotle discusses distributing the important offices of government according to merit. He also says this is a characteristic of aristocracy. Do you feel that it is appropriate to award the important offices of government on the basis of merit? Is this a natural characteristic of a democratic government? Have you observed this pattern of distribution of offices of government in your own government? Is this idea limited to aristocracy? Is it impossible in an oligarchy?

SENTENCE OUTLINE: See p. 102 of this manual.

BIBLIOGRAPHY: See p. 170 of this manual.

THE FOUNDING FATHERS

The Constitution of the United States of America (pp. 75–107)

One discussion that may come up in class concerns the difference between a pure democracy and a republic. For Madison and Hamilton, a republic implied a government without a king or queen. It was a government in which elected people exercised the power given to them by the people who elected them. In other words, in terms of a democracy, it is an indirect (rather than impure) democracy, because the people who are elected represent the wishes of their constituents but can also represent what they see as the best interests of the people in general. You will probably have a lively discussion about how satisfying it is for some of your students to feel they must settle for an indirect democratic government. But even Aristotle points out the difficulties of pure democracy in a state with a large population.

There is no question but that the framers of the Constitution feared a completely democratic government. They saw the general population as unready to bear the burdens of government in part because the people seemed unruly in their views and enthusiasms. The class distinctions that held in England were not transferred intact to the United States, but there was still a very strong feeling among the framers that the gentry were the most qualified to rule. Since, as Aristotle implied, the gentry were not the majority, they had to develop a government that protected them while still guaranteeing the rights of most of the people.

The question of slavery was on the minds of most people drafting the Constitution. The northern states were willing and anxious to put an end to slavery. However, the southern states relied heavily on slave labor. So while Pennsylvania and other states abolished slavery within their borders, the slave states continued until the Civil War in 1865. The fact that the Constitution does not use the word *slave* or *slavery* until the Thirteenth and Fourteenth Amendments—after the Civil War—implies that at least some of the original framers were ashamed enough of the practice that they could not utter its name. Surely this will be an issue that will interest most of your students.

Along the same line, and in light of contemporary political concerns, your students may well be interested in discussing the entire question of limiting states' rights in order to form "a more perfect union." The Articles of Confederation were very loose, equivalent to an agreement to hold together as long as it satisfied the needs of any given state. In a way, it treated the states as individual governments of the kind that existed in eighteenth-century Italy or France—for instance, Savoy, Lombardy, Romagna, Swabia, Tuscany, and the Papal States. Some states, such as Georgia, ignored their obligations to the Confederation almost entirely. In other words, no federal powers could be brought to bear on any state in the Confederation if the state did not adhere to the laws of the Confederation. By contrast, the Constitution established the laws of the entire nation and contained the powers to enforce them across state lines. The question of states' rights was paramount during the struggle to end slavery before the Civil War. Today the question of states' rights is still uppermost in some minds. It's worth exploring this issue with your students.

SUGGESTIONS FOR CLASS DISCUSSION

1. To what extent might the Constitution support an oligarchic government? Are there oligarchic elements present in it in its original form?
2. The first ten Amendments guaranteed certain rights. Which ones seem most to guarantee the rights of individual states? Which guarantee the rights of individuals regardless of their state?
3. The Nineteenth Amendment gave the right to vote to women in 1920. How might the Constitution have been changed if women had a hand in its creation? Why do you think men concerned with individual freedoms took so long to provide them to women?

SUGGESTIONS FOR BRIEF ESSAYS

1. Throughout the Constitution there are procedures for various kinds of elections. Some of these procedures have changed. Which ones are now different, and how do they differ? Do you approve of the differences, or do you prefer the original procedures?
2. What are the powers of impeachment, and on whom may they be used? Do a bit of research and describe the ways in which these powers have been used in history. Does the procedure follow the direction of the Constitution?
3. Judging from the text of the Constitution and its Amendments, do the framers seem to have been very religious people? Is the Constitution a Christian document? Could it be construed to have described a Christian nation or a Christian government?

SUGGESTIONS FOR LONGER ESSAYS

1. What are the specific qualities of the Constitution that permit us to call the government a democracy? What is most democratic about the government that the Constitution establishes and permits?

2. The House of Representatives is a branch of Congress that represents the people at large, and the Senate is a branch of Congress that represents the states. What are the separate interests of the people and the states that would demand such a distinction? What do you see as the differences between these two forms of representation? Are their original purposes served as well today as they were in 1788? Are their original purposes served at all? What are their most important differences?

3. After the Civil War, the Thirteenth and Fourteenth Amendments were added to the Constitution. To an extent they are punitive in regard to the states and those individuals who rebelled against the Union. Describe what they propose, and decide to what extent they would have been helpful in salving the wounds caused by the Civil War. Are they still as relevant today as they were in 1870?

4. Examine the two amendments that concern prohibition of liquor: the Nineteenth Amendment (1920), which prohibiting the manufacture and sale of liquor, and the Twenty-first Amendment (1933), which modifies the Nineteenth Amendment. What do these amendments say, and what is the essential difference between them? Was the original amendment an instance of the federal government overreaching? Is it an instance of an invasion of states' rights? What is restored in the Twenty-first Amendment?

5. In Article VI and elsewhere in the Constitution, there are frequent references to limitations on the powers of the states. What are these limitations, and does it seem justified to have them appear in the Constitution? Do any of these limitations significantly reduce the liberty of people living in the states? Do you favor these limitations? What powers of individual states might come in conflict with the Constitution's "Law of the Land"? In what way might limiting the power of specific states help guarantee the democratic values of the nation? Give an example of a conflict between a state's action and the federal interpretation of the Constitution.

SENTENCE OUTLINE: See p. 104 of this manual.

BIBLIOGRAPHY: See p. 177 of this manual.

JAMES MADISON

Federalist No. 51: On the Separation of Departments of Power
(pp. 109–119)

Reading the *Federalist Papers* today is a remarkable experience in part because so much of what Madison, Hamilton, and Jay were concerned with then is still relevant to us today. You will probably not have to stretch too far to get your students talking about the questions of a strong federal government versus a looser government that gives more rights to the states. Moreover, the struggles in recent years between the legislative and executive branches echo so much of what the founding fathers worried over and make this a very timely piece of prose.

I know most students today may not be as politically active as they were in the 1970s, but they are still fairly aware of what is happening politically. The war cries from politicians in the cause of smaller government may seem on the surface to be separate from Madison's issues, but under those cries is the issue of how much government impinges on individual freedoms today. In Madison's day the experience of government was much different than it is today. Even Tocqueville commented on his sense that there was no presence of government at all in most places he visited in America. Because Madison grew up with the colony of Virginia between him and the government in Whitehall, the question of a strong local government was not an issue. But after the Revolutionary War and the incredible uncertainties that followed it—along with the inadequacies of a voluntary confederation that simply did not work—Madison understood that only a federal-style government would keep the states together and form a real nation.

So, with a strong government a virtual certainty, Madison's concerns turned to the means by which that government could be structured to prevent it from becoming so strong as to be oppressive. His defense of the three-part government, something that had not been tried before, is eloquent, but sometimes a bit obscure. This is, after all, a newspaper piece republished later with mild revisions, and it is meant to be read in a context of new ideas and change. In the process of discussion, you will want to try to help students understand the nature of the legislative, executive, and judicial branches—all things they would have learned in high school and possibly in a first-year American History class. If you have some potential history majors in your class, see if you can have them do some research to add to the class discussion of the *Federalist Papers* and Madison's role in the public debate on the Constitution.

One very important concern of Madison in this selection is his fear of a majority somehow oppressing a minority. You may need to clarify the terminology: Madison was not referring to contemporary ideas of minorities, which often fall along ethnic lines. He meant more that factions within society, groups of specifically interested people, would impose their will on others: city-dwellers on farmers, the more numerous uneducated on the educated, the poor on the wealthy. This is more in line with Aristotle's definition of democracy. Madison and others feared pure democracy partly because they knew the power of a mass of people roused by demagogues. Yet Madison constantly praised the people as the fountain of power in any government.

Finally, the style of this piece—formal, with long sentences and sometimes long paragraphs—is very much that of the eighteenth century. Compare it, for instance, with Fielding's *Tom Jones,* and you can help your students begin an appreciation of style. They may not appreciate Madison's style because of its formality and indirection. But they should begin to see what Madison is doing by being able to discuss the choice of words, the use of language, the structure of phrases and clauses, and whatever else you determine is useful for them to know. The contrast with the Constitution is of course marvelous and should help students understand what it means to possess a style and how that style may reflect the age.

SUGGESTIONS FOR CLASS DISCUSSION

1. To what extent are the issues that Madison addresses still important today?
2. What is the significance of the reference to the emoluments (the pay) of people in government in paragraph 3?
3. How might Madison react to the way in which the government he proposes has developed in our time? Would he approve? What suggestions for change would he make?

SUGGESTIONS FOR BRIEF ESSAYS

1. Do political parties supply the "opposite and rival interests" that Madison mentions in paragraph 5? Do they help to balance the powers of individual branches of government? Would the government be best when all three branches consist of members of the same political party?
2. What are the most important methods that will protect the rights of the minority from the oppression of the majority? Oppression by the majority was one of the great fears of those who did not trust pure democracy. Are they right to have been fearful in that way?
3. Is it possible that the executive branch may need to be fortified in order to avoid being oppressed by the power of the legislature? What powers does the executive branch have that help balance powers with the remaining branches?

SUGGESTIONS FOR LONGER ESSAYS

1. In paragraph 10, Madison says, "In a free government, the security for civil rights must be the same as that for religious rights. It consists in the one case in the multiplicity of interests, and in the other, in the multiplicity of sects." Is he correct? Is there such a close connection between civil rights and religious rights that one may indeed depend on the other? Does Madison seem to be deeply religious? If possible, research his biography as an aid to considering this point.
2. In paragraph 10, Madison says, "Different interests necessarily exist in the different classes of citizens. If a majority be united by a common interest, the rights of the minority will be insecure."

What different kinds of interests will there be between different classes of citizens today? What do you think Madison means by the word *classes*? Compare his distinction with Aristotle's description of people of different classes, such as the husbandman, the warrior, etc. How does his sense of class seem to differ from the word as used in common speech today? What interests among groups are in conflict today? Are the rights of any minority group at stake in our government?

3. In paragraph 5, Madison says, "This policy of supplying, by opposite and rival interests, the defect of better motives, might be traced through the whole system of human affairs, private as well as public." Explain how this point fits into his views on balancing the powers of government, then go on to discuss the virtues of supplying rival interests in any walk of life that you choose. Demonstrate how it is a positive force or how it is a destructive force. When does any social organization profit from a conflict of interests? Why should one promote rival interests?

4. In "Federalist No. 51," Madison says a few important things about the power of faction to disable or distort government, but in "Federalist No. 10" he develops the point in much more detail. Read "Federalist No. 10," then explain his position on the question of faction while also defining what he means by faction. Then evaluate his view and decide whether or not you see the operation of faction at work in government today. What is the result of the operation of faction in government? Is it always negative or is it sometimes positive?

5. The entire purpose of "Federalist No. 51" is to convince you that the federal system Madison proposes (and developed in the Constitution) is the most desirable form of government. How completely does Madison convince you? What loose ends does he omit that you consider as important? To what extent are you not convinced by his argument, and what are your alternatives to his view?

SENTENCE OUTLINE: See p. 106 of this manual.

BIBLIOGRAPHY: See p. 185 of this manual.

ALEXIS DE TOCQUEVILLE

Government by Democracy in America (pp. 121–141)

It is a shame that there cannot be much more of Tocqueville in this book. Reading him and responding to his amazement at the success of the experiment in democracy in America are invigorating at a time when the question of spreading democracy is one of the most prominent issues in modern politics. Tocqueville knew that things in France were changing profoundly and that the days of the aristocracy were numbered. His sympathies were with the democratizing wave of the future, and he did what he could to further it. Yet he was, at least in 1835, fearful of the force of the "majority"—the poor people who would enact the laws, as he thought they would. He had more reason to fear that force even than James Madison had, because Tocqueville knew from his parents' firsthand experience how bloodthirsty the poor could be when they got power in the French Revolution. Tocqueville also saw the July Monarchy, the revolution of 1848, and the upheavals in French government and society. Yet he held firm to his beliefs.

If you have a copy of the complete text of *Democracy in America*, you might want to consult his discussion of education and its effects on democracy in Volume 1, Part 2, Chapter 9. Also, his thoughts on the condition and future of the native Indian population and the African slaves are in Chapter 10, "A Few Remarks on the Present-day State and the Probable Future of the Three Races which Live in the Territory of the United States." The selection that appears in this text is from Volume 1, Part 2, Chapter 5, and that chapter continues for another thirty pages or so. If possible, encourage your students to read on in the complete text. If some of your students do so, ask them to contribute their thinking in class.

One thing that interests me and may interest you as well is Tocqueville's certainty in 1835 and 1840 that there could be no civil war in the United States. Even during Andrew Jackson's presidency, Tocqueville felt that the real source of governmental power was in the states and not in the federal government. He reports that he saw very little evidence of the presence of government in America, which is one reason why he must have thought that the federal arm was not long enough to reach all quarters of the nation.

He also notes in several places that the power of individualism is great among the low as well as among the high in the society. He says in Volume 1, Part 2, Chapter 10, "I am, therefore, convinced that, at present, Americans experience fewer natural difficulties in remaining united than they encountered in 1789; the Union has fewer enemies than at that time. Nevertheless, a careful study of the United States history over the last forty-five years readily convinces us that federal power is diminishing." It is difficult to read these words and realize that by 1860, fifteen years after the publication of Volume 2, the nation was on the verge of war. Among other things, it makes us understand the significance of Lincoln's influence on American politics and also helps us understand the negative reactions to Lincoln both during and after the war. The issues that concerned Tocqueville from 1831 to 1840 were central to the function of democracy and federalism then, and in a touch of déjà vu, they seem to have come back to the forefront in the twenty-first century. If you have students who are aware of this, it would be very interesting to see them write about their views and discuss them in class.

Finally, I also find it important to consider Tocqueville's general reaction to the industry of the American citizens. His views on their efforts to produce wealth cause him to decide that the people are very materialistic and that they are driven almost entirely by a love of money. With the expansion of the country, the growth of the population, and the new advantages of overseas trade, it is natural that people could expect to become rich if they work hard enough. In contrast, Tocqueville was also struck by the role of religion in aiding industry. As he says about American preachers: "It is often hard to know from listening to them whether the main intention of religion is to obtain everlasting joy in the next world or prosperity in this" (Volume 2, Part 2, Chapter 9). He believes that self-interest guides the religions of America, but he also says, "Religious insanity is very common in the United States" (Volume 2, Part 2, Chapter 12).

What strikes the reader is how perceptive Tocqueville was of the nation's government in his few months in America. Much of what he determined to be true is still true today.

SUGGESTIONS FOR CLASS DISCUSSION

1. Elsewhere in his book, Tocqueville refers to a potential "tyranny of the majority." What might he mean, and how serious a threat do you think it might be?
2. In paragraph 78, Tocqueville says, "It will always be simple to divide each nation into three classes." What are the classes he refers to, and do you think that what he said is true?
3. Because of the fact that elections introduce new people into office with some frequency, are we threatened by instability of the laws, as Tocqueville thought we might be?

SUGGESTIONS FOR BRIEF ESSAYS

1. Consider what Tocqueville has to say about whether or not democracy is an economical form of government. What are his chief concerns regarding economy in any form of government? Does he feel that democracy is efficient? Does he feel other forms of government are more efficient? What is your position on this issue?
2. In paragraph 91, Tocqueville says of elected officials: "You can guarantee that in the long run, the delegate will always in the end conform to the opinions of his constituents and support their inclinations as well as their interests." Do you agree with this statement or do you think that many delegates will decide not to conform to the opinions of the constituents? How would a delegate know the opinions of the constituents, or how could he or she be certain to know them? Are there times when the delegate should definitely not conform to the opinions of the constituents? If yes, would that abrogate the democratic process?
3. When discussing the failure to elect distinguished people to office, Tocqueville does mention that in times of danger, the nation seems to choose great leaders. Given what you know about American history, consider whether or not this statement is true. How often has government had great leaders during a major crisis?

SUGGESTIONS FOR LONGER ESSAYS

1. One worry that gave Tocqueville pause was the fear that education in the new nation would not be sufficient for the proper government to function. He feared that because education required a great deal of time from the individual, few people could be educated. Yet he knew that education was universal in the United States. Consider what he says and what he implies about education in this selection, and decide whether his concerns and fears were and are justified.

2. Tocqueville was surprised to see that civil servants were just like everybody else. They did not wear special uniforms or conduct themselves in any fashion that made them distinctive. To what extent are his views about civil servants still valid? Consider the issues discussed in his extensive treatment of civil servants. Who was he talking about? Are such people still functioning in government, and is what he said in 1835 pretty much the same as now?

3. Examine what Tocqueville says about the "arbitrary power of magistrates" in the selection from paragraph 54 to 69. Identify the different kinds of magistrates he refers to and the different kinds of governments, such as monarchies and limited monarchies. Clarify his views as best you can, and then go on to either defend them or explain why they may be limited or not effective. At root is the nature of power, which is discussed elsewhere in the essay, and you will need to define the nature of power as Tocqueville interprets it. When you consider power, think, too, of what James Madison says about the nature of power in a democracy.

4. Tocqueville discusses the three classes of people he sees in any nation, starting with paragraph 78. If you can come to an agreement with him about what these classes are and whether you see them as still being in existence today in your own nation, which one class would you want to have making the laws in a democracy? Why? Which class do you feel is currently making the laws? Is the idea of class relevant to a modern democracy? Would Aristotle have agreed with Tocqueville about the nature of social classes in any nation?

SENTENCE OUTLINE: See p. 107 of this manual.

BIBLIOGRAPHY: See p. 194 of this manual.

CARL BECKER

Ideal Democracy (pp. 143–163)

In the suggestions for writing in the text, I mention that Carl Becker was a noted liberal, and it might be useful for you to suggest that the term *liberal* needs definition because it meant something a bit different in 1941 than it does today. Becker was a liberal humanist who felt that the individual should have the freedom to pursue happiness in the manner in which it is mentioned in the Declaration of Independence. Moreover, because he delivers this lecture in Virginia, he calls further attention to himself as a Jeffersonian and an heir to the liberalism that led Jefferson to champion civil rights and personal independence, as well as to personally study liberal arts and ultimately to found a university. The place in which this lecture was delivered was the epicenter of American democracy, and Becker has returned to help restore it to favor and renew its powers.

One of your jobs will probably be to provide a bit of background. Becker is careful to suggest that institutions bear the marks of their time and place, and that is also true of this lecture as well. In the Great Depression of the 1930s, Becker saw that poverty and powerlessness gave the governments of Mussolini and Hitler the opportunity to consolidate power and to undo what had been representative democratic governments. Many of your students will not fully understand what the fascist states stood for and how they operated and why they were anti-democratic even though their officials were elected. The same is true for Stalin's Soviet Russia, which had only recently conducted its wholesale slaughter of Kulaks and other undesirables a few years before Becker wrote. The background you can provide or elicit from your students will help place Becker's essay in a manner that may help students understand why he is concerned about the survival of democracy.

You will probably have some students who are very aware of the current situation in American politics and who are themselves concerned about preserving democracy. It would be useful to see if they can articulate coherent narratives or arguments that will make their own positions clear. As much as possible, ask your students to refer to specific events or circumstances that need to be examined in order to make their views clear. You might scour the newspapers or magazines for issues that seem central to the question of the survival or threat to our democracy. When your students write about their own personal views, be sure to ask them to follow Becker's lead and begin with a careful effort at establishing a working definition of democracy as they understand it functioning today in our world.

It may be a touchy subject, but you may wish to discuss with your students Becker's views on religion. He praises the eighteenth century for its having released modern Europeans from the negative influences of religion. The seventeenth century was dominated by religious wars and religious squabbles that led to governmental overthrows and forced individuals to accept official religions and suffer severe consequences for non-attendance to church and non-allegiance to the official government religion. The eighteenth century introduced the liberal humanism that Becker applauds. You may find yourself having to clarify exactly what that means, since "liberal humanism" has become a dirty term for some people. A close reading of the text should help you establish that Becker's views are not the same as those that are so rigidly condemned by some today.

SUGGESTIONS FOR CLASS DISCUSSION

1. Becker says that democracy flourished originally in very small states. Why would that be true? Does your experience of small groups or limited institutions back up Becker's observation? Why would he feel he can make that statement, and what implication does it have for our own democracy?
2. Communication is a major issue when it comes to maintaining a democracy. To what extent do you think that instant communication devices and techniques, such as cell phones and text messaging, contribute to the creation and maintenance of a democracy?
3. We do not live in the United States of 1941, so some of Becker's ideals may be different for us today. How much does our current political climate alter the definition that you might give democracy?

SUGGESTIONS FOR BRIEF ESSAYS

1. Becker says a minimum requirement for the citizens of a democracy is that they be capable of managing their own affairs. Exactly what would that requirement entail of the average American?
2. Aristotle did not think metics, permanent residents from another city-state, should be permitted to have citizenship in Athens. How does this affect the concept of democracy, and to what extent does Aristotle seem to echo some of the views currently held by some citizens in the United States? Examine Becker's observations in paragraphs 16–19.
3. Democracy is essentially a government by consent of the people in which the majority rule. For a democracy to be truly democratic, how must the concerns of the minority or minorities be considered? Would democracy be different if the minority ruled instead of the majority?

SUGGESTIONS FOR LONGER ESSAYS

1. Aristotle is said to have held that any form of government is neither good nor bad in itself but can be judged only in terms of its ability to promote the happiness of its citizens. Thus, a tyranny might be good, and democracy might be bad. Examine this view and argue both sides of the position in an effort to clarify your own views. You might contrast a monarchy with a dictatorship and with a representative democracy in order to make your thinking on this issue clear. Is it possible that Aristotle is wrong and that democracy is good even if it is not ideal?
2. Democracy is government with the consent of the people. The people vote for their representatives and then permit the representatives to enact laws designed to keep the democracy strong and

healthy. If their representatives fail, the citizens vote them out. What are the requirements, in terms of education especially, of every citizen in order to prevent the election and maintenance of deceptive representatives? Must citizens of a democracy be better educated than citizens of a tyranny?

3. Research Athens and write an essay that specifically clarifies the nature of Greek democracy. What is its character? What is its limitations? How well and for how long did Athenian democracy work? What is ideal about Greek democracy? Is it the same kind of democracy that Becker talks about in his lecture?

4. The term *utopia* refers to an ideal world with an ideal governmental system. What is your idea of utopia? What kind of government would be absolutely the best for you? What qualities would it have and how would it function? Why would it promote your happiness, as in Jefferson's term, "the pursuit of happiness"?

SENTENCE OUTLINE: See p. 109 of this manual.

BIBLIOGRAPHY: See p. 171 of this manual.

JULIUS K. NYERERE
One-Party Government (pp. 165–175)

This essay was published in 1961, just as Tanganyika was being granted its independence and as Nyerere was preparing to take office in the new government. He was thoroughly versed in the British system of government and understood the Western models of representative democracy. He was very idealistic about what could be accomplished in his nation, emphasizing education, public health, and relief from poverty. He fell short in his efforts largely because he could not reduce the levels of poverty that he inherited. But because of his efforts, he voluntarily retired as a well-respected man both in and out of Africa after serving four terms.

Nyerere talks eloquently about the problems besetting a new and essentially impoverished nation and uses the conditions at the time as a basis for his claim that a one-party system can be democratic. You may wish to ask your students to defend or attack this general principle. Why, for example, would a one-party system ever be willing to tolerate another party? There are countless examples of a one-party government refusing to credential another party, thus making it impossible for there to be a counter to any decision that party makes. When considering a second party, Nyerere asks us to think only of opposition parties that are aiming to cause trouble—and from the point of view of the one-party such a possibility would seem unavoidable. Why would any single party encourage opposition? Your students should be able to examine this idea in detail in class. You should ask them if the excuse of a "state of emergency" is enough to warrant the eradication of opposition.

Western governments usually have two parties, often in the pattern of conservative and liberal (or labor and social democrat). What is the advantage in a modern democracy of having two parties hold forth on two almost mutually exclusive positions in governance? Is it possible that some of your students will not see that there are two different positions being defended? Some people say that "there's no difference between the parties." If so, does that help Nyerere's argument? Or would such students feel that if that's true, then there is no democracy at work?

Nyerere's role in the inclusion of the island nation of Zanzibar is interesting because it shows him trying to deal with a troublesome issue. Nyerere went to Catholic schools and was a Roman Catholic. Zanzibar is a Muslim nation, and when it was absorbed into Tanzania it became essentially autonomous. But Nyerere was suspicious of Muslims because he thought they were trying to undermine his government. He is said to have been repressive in his handling of the Muslim minority. One critic asserted that the union of Tanganyika and Zanzibar was instituted to suppress the Muslims, who at that time were thought to be Communist sympathizers. Nyerere was accused of establishing a secular state in Zanzibar against the will of most Muslims. If these charges are true, then it would seem that Nyerere thought of the Muslims as a troublesome opposition party trying to destabilize the new nation.

Ultimately, of course, your students will want to consider the argument in favor of one-party rule and consider Nyerere's position, especially his position as the leader of a new nation whose traditions are very different from those of the West.

SUGGESTIONS FOR CLASS DISCUSSION

1. Why would unity of opinion or unity of political vision be important in creating a democracy in a new nation?
2. Which of Nyerere's definitions of democracy seem most reasonable to you? What is your definition?
3. What would be Nyerere's position if there could be no agreement on a decision even after the elders had sat down and discussed it for days? Nyerere seems to think agreement would always come; what if it does not?

SUGGESTIONS FOR BRIEF ESSAYS

1. Which countries in Africa are considered democratic? Nyerere hoped that the future for democracy in Africa was bright. Was he correct?
2. If your government were to consist of executive, legislative, and judiciary branches all aligned with one party, how could democracy survive? Is it certain that it would fail?
3. According to Nyerere, what are the responsibilities of a government to its people?

SUGGESTIONS FOR LONGER ESSAYS

1. Do some research by looking up the current circumstances in Tanzania. Nyerere ruled for twenty-eight years, and it has been more than twenty years since he left office. What can you determine is the state of democracy in Tanzania? Does the United Nations consider it a modern democracy? Is it governed under a one-party system of rule? Are Nyerere's ideals being respected and to some extent realized?
2. Nyerere says, "True democracy depends far more on the attitude of mind which respects and defends the individual than on the forms it takes" (para. 15). What does he mean by this statement? Is he correct? Do you have any examples from recent governmental decisions that support his argument on the question of attitude? How does attitude express itself on the part of a government? Is this a wise saying, or is it evasive of the facts of government? Why does Nyerere stress the effect on the individual in a democracy?
3. Nyerere offers several definitions of democracy. Comment on the adequacy of each of his definitions, and then go on to offer your own definition. What are the "essentials" of democracy? What must be true about the way a government operates if we are to call it a democracy? What examples of democracy will support your definition? Be sure to consider Aristotle's definitions as you write.
4. Nyerere says, "In the past all that was required of government was merely to maintain law and order within the country, and to protect it from external aggression" (para. 16). However, he says that today this is only part of the government's responsibility. What pressures do you see on nations, whether new or established, that will make it very difficult for a government to serve the needs of its people? What kinds of threats to stability are apparent now that were not apparent when Nyerere was leading Tanzania?
5. How would James Madison have regarded Nyerere's reasons for having a one-party government? What issues does Madison raise that should have concerned Nyerere? The question of balancing three parts of the government—executive, legislative, and judicial—while assuring that they have independent power is central to Madison's views. In Nyerere's view, is the absence of such a system a result of the differences in tradition that Nyerere inherited, or would it have simply impaired his one-party system and thus made it too weak to create the new nation? Would the three-part government function in a one-party system and also guarantee democracy?

SENTENCE OUTLINE: See p. 110 of this manual.

BIBLIOGRAPHY: See p. 189 of this manual.

BENAZIR BHUTTO
Islam and Democracy (pp. 177–194)

Benazir Bhutto was a very complex woman. She was educated in a Christian convent in Pakistan before she went to the United States and Radcliffe College in Harvard University. She focused on comparative governments and then went on to Oxford University to continue her studies in political science. Her father had an immense influence on her thinking, and according to what she has written, his interest in bringing democracy to Pakistan was instrumental in her trying to continue his mission. She suffered greatly from her confinement in prison at the hands of Zia. She wrote about her six and a half years in a stifling cell, living with rats and cockroaches and many other kinds of vermin, suffering boils and terrible skin disorders brought on by heat and the limits of the prison cell's confinement. She was alone save for a twice daily visit from a man who brought her food. She had to beg for water. Being stripped of everything else, she has said, left her only with her Muslim faith, which led her to become extremely devout. She was finally released on medical grounds and possibly in response to international pressures. Apparently this treatment toughened her enough that when she came to power as Prime Minister, she was known as the "Iron Lady" in light of her resolve and willingness to act forcefully.

When she became Prime Minister she sometimes became aggressive, like a man, and has admitted that she went a bit too far at times. She even accused herself of sometimes being a warmonger in her relations with India. But while in office she did a great deal to eradicate polio, to build schools, and to bring electricity to remote areas of Pakistan. The charges of corruption against her and her government are difficult to understand. Her brother, Mir Murtaza, who had a falling out with Bhutto, was instrumental in charging Bhutto's husband, Asif Ali Zardari, with corruption, a charge that may have had some merit to it. But Bhutto herself later complained that she should have attacked corruption in the government early in her career. She recognized that various kinds of corruption had been a staple of the governments of Pakistan. After Mir Murtaza died in a gunfight with police, Bhutto was convicted of corruption and avoided jail time by fleeing to London.

Another issue that may help you understand the complexities of Bhutto's career is that in December 1993 she went to North Korea and negotiated a deal that gave Pakistan missile technology, which helped the country begin to match India's nuclear firepower. At the same time, she adamantly denied that Pakistan traded nuclear technology that would help North Korea achieve nuclear weapons, claiming that she paid in cash, not secrets. Less than three months later, it was learned that Abdul Qadeer Khan, a Pakistani nuclear scientist, had sold nuclear secrets to North Korea, Libya, and Iran. Khan was pardoned by Pervez Mussarraf. While it's nearly impossible to suss out the complete truth from all of this, North Korea soon developed its own nuclear weapons, and Iran is very close if it has not already done so. You might want to ask some students to explore Bhutto's biography in order to give a balanced view of her approach to government.

SUGGESTIONS FOR CLASS DISCUSSION

1. Do you feel it appropriate for religious leaders to have a strong hand in governmental decisions?
2. To what extent has reading Benazir Bhutto's observations about Islam affected your view of that religion?
3. What is your understanding of the word *secular*? Should governments be secular? Why does the term confuse the issues of governance for Muslims? See paragraph 7.

SUGGESTIONS FOR BRIEF ESSAYS

1. In paragraph 15, Bhutto says, "Having the only nuclear-armed Muslim nation fall into chaos would be catastrophic." Consider the rest of what she says in that paragraph in order to write a brief essay that establishes what she might have meant by the term *chaos*. How do you react to the idea of a nuclear-armed Muslim nation's capacity for catastrophe? Would the same fears be raised by a non-Muslim nuclear-armed nation falling into chaos?

2. Consult a copy of the Quran and study it for evidence that Islam promotes diversity and religious tolerance, that it promotes education for both sexes, and that it has the seeds of democracy within it.

3. What is Bhutto's thesis? What are the most effective techniques Bhutto uses to convince you of her argument? Does she seem to be developing an honest argument, or is she ignoring important facts or ideas that might undermine her position if they were taken into account? What can you learn from the methods she uses in this selection?

SUGGESTIONS FOR LONGER ESSAYS

1. Bhutto blames the West for the fact that there are no Muslim democracies. Check on her claim, and develop an argument that relies on examples of Western policies toward a few of the major Muslim nations that have interacted with the West in recent years. Choose Egypt, Libya, Iran, Iraq, or Afghanistan and see to what extent the West may have undermined efforts to create a democracy in that nation.

2. Bhutto claims that the religion of Islam is not a factor in the difficulties Muslim nations may have in becoming democratic. That being the case, what claims can you make for any other religion's effect on creating a democratic form of government if that religion were the official religion of the state and if that religion had a dominant say in the structure and nature of governance? Why might a dominant religion inhibit or enhance democracy in the West? How influential was religion in the considerations of the framers of the United States Constitution? Do you think the separation of church and state in the West was designed to protect religion or protect the state?

3. The West has referred to revolutions and insurrections in Muslim states such as Libya, Egypt, and Syria as an "Arab Spring." What is the state of government in those nations at this time? Did the hopes of the West for free elections and eventual democracy work out? If you feel one or more are democratic governments, do you feel that their form of democracy was what the West would have hoped for?

4. Bhutto goes to great lengths beginning in paragraph 34 to talk about the differences in degree of freedom in Muslim nations. What is the significance of her distinctions between Arab and non-Arab nations? Bhutto herself is non-Arab—does that seem to affect her view of the situation? Given what she says about the Freedom House assessments, what do you feel is the possibility of democracy spreading to the Islamic countries in the near future? What are the forces driving them toward democracy? What are the forces holding them back?

5. In paragraph 43, Bhutto says, "True democracy is defined not only by elections but by the democratic governance that should follow." Assuming that democracy comes to Egypt, Libya, Syria, Pakistan, or another Muslim country, how do you think governance should proceed? What should be the aims of a democratic version of any of these countries? Is it possible that a democratic version of any of these nations would disappoint the hopes of the West? How might a democracy fail to live up to Bhutto's ideals and yet still be a democratic form of government?

SENTENCE OUTLINE: See p. 111 of this manual.

BIBLIOGRAPHY: See p. 172 of this manual.

STEPHEN L. CARTER

The Separation of Church and State
(bedfordstmartins.com/worldofideas/epages)

Carter is himself deeply religious. He participates in the Episcopalian communion, writes regularly for a popular Christian magazine, focuses on issues of law pertaining to religion, and generally shapes his life in a manner consistent with his views. For example, despite his being one of America's most prominent public intellectuals, he finds the time to serve as a Boy Scout leader.

His essay here is the first part of a chapter from his book *The Culture of Disbelief* devoted to the question of how separate the church and state need to be in America. Because this has been a very controversial subject in the past two decades, I felt it was appropriate for students to consider while thinking about the nature of government first in the abstract, then in a more concrete way. The decisions of the courts in recent years have affected all students in one way or another regarding religion in the schools. I myself experienced a daily Bible reading and a prayer and the Pledge of Allegiance every morning in public grade school. It was so routine that I doubt it had much effect on me. I recall being surprised that this procedure was dropped in public high school. Today, of course, public schools omit prayer and the Bible entirely.

Carter begins and ends this selection with a clear statement that guides his entire argument. In the general introduction to the selection I did not discuss the merits of his basic view, but I think it appropriate here to suggest that you consider calling it into question to see how your students react. Carter states, "Simply put, the metaphorical separation of church and state originated in an effort to protect religion from the state, not the state from religion" (para. 2).

It is possible to argue with this premise. For example, events in fundamentalist countries have developed in recent times in such a way as to create states that are close to theocracies. In those cases religion dominates the state, and therefore governing authorities control aspects of people's lives that other governments would ignore. For example, westerners are shocked by the ritual of stoning women to death for adultery in some fundamentalist Islamic countries. In the early years of the Plymouth Colony in Massachusetts, theocratic governments pilloried adulterers. Hawthorne's *The Scarlet Letter* memorializes that era and its government.

The founders of the United States had the English Civil War in their memory. The imposition of religious observances on the part of Anglican Archbishop Laud became so odious to a large number of non-Anglicans that the king had to back off and sacrifice Laud in an effort to make peace with a largely Puritan Parliament. Eventually, the forces of Parliament beheaded Charles I and established a non-Anglican state religion. Years after the Restoration, James II was deposed because he was Catholic, and since then it has been legally impossible for a Catholic monarch to reign in England. The last of the potential revolutions in the name of Bonnie Prince Charlie was less than fifty years before the American Bill of Rights. My sense is that the founders were as worried about the state's being affected by religion as they were about religion's being affected by the state.

One question in contemporary politics concerns what journalists refer to as the religious right's intention to affect the laws that govern all of us. In considering the power of a religious consortium to influence government, one might be concerned to see how the resulting laws might affect the day-to-day behavior of citizens. Religious freedom, which is an essential ingredient of the Establishment Clause, was a basic principle of the founders' purposes in the First Amendment. It is still essential to the concept of freedom of expression. You may find fruitful discussion in class if you and your students explore the current atmosphere of politics and religion as it affects public behavior.

SUGGESTIONS FOR CLASS DISCUSSION

1. The separation of church and state is described as a metaphor. Do you think that implies that the church and the state are not really separate?
2. Should some tenets of science be ignored in public schools if they contradict some religious beliefs?
3. Why is voluntary prayer in public schools generally prohibited by law?
4. Why should a minority population alter the behavior of a majority in a democracy?

SUGGESTIONS FOR BRIEF ESSAYS

1. Religious groups lobby government to ban stem cell research that uses fetal cells. Stem cell research promises cures for several terribly debilitating diseases, such as Parkinson's and Alzheimer's. What is the rationale for the state's adopting the position of the religious lobbyists?

How would you defend this position? How would you defeat it in argument? Where do you stand on these issues?

2. Under what conditions would it be appropriate for local and federal funds to be used to support activities in religious schools? If you feel there are no conditions in which it would be appropriate to spend such funds, establish your argument.

3. What is the most effective portion of Carter's argument? Analyze the process of his argument, and decide which are its strengths and which are its weaknesses. Which portions of his argument are most persuasive to you? Which are not persuasive?

4. Take a stand on the issue of prayer in public schools. If you have a personal story to tell, be sure to include it in your comments and your argument. Try to establish a premise that you feel is secure, and then argue from it. What is your specific reason for supporting or not supporting prayer in public schools?

SUGGESTIONS FOR LONGER ESSAYS

1. Examine the material in paragraph 9 of the selection. Carter says it was right to ban prayer in the schools, but okay to permit a church to hold services on Sunday in a public school. He points out that people have wanted the legend "In God We Trust" struck from our coins and the phrase "under God" struck from the Pledge of Allegiance. He does not approve of those suggestions because he feels they contradict principles of "civil religion." What does he mean by "civil religion"? Is he contradicting himself in this paragraph?

2. One of the large questions about a democracy concerns the responsibility of the state to protect the rights of a minority population. Our democracy does not imply that the will of the majority rules absolutely. If that were true, prayer would be in the schools, gay people would be in the closet, and African Americans, Jews, Arabs, and other groups might be ignored and forced to follow practices abhorrent to them. Feminists can also claim that their rights were ignored by the male power structure. What is the obligation of a democracy to its minorities?

3. At one point, Carter points out that the Constitution does not make it clear whether the Establishment Clause should be administered by the federal government or by individual state governments. Which do you think the case should be? How might different states interpret the Establishment Clause? Why? How would the Plymouth Colony, which existed one hundred fifty years before the Constitution, have interpreted the Establishment Clause?

4. Research the question of banning prayer in public schools. Write an essay that clarifies the controversy and explains the arguments that have been presented both for and against banning prayer in public schools. What harm could religion do in public schools? Examine the arguments of several commentators. Do their arguments convince you of the reasonableness of their case?

SENTENCE OUTLINE: See p. 113 of this manual.

BIBLIOGRAPHY: See p. 173 of this manual.

GOVERNMENT

The seven selections in Part Two focus on the ways in which government shapes itself in response to the interests of the people governed. The selections examine the origins of social order and the results of social experiments such as monarchy and totalitarianism. The relation between the needs of the body politic and questions of power are always part of the concern of these authors.

LAO-TZU

Thoughts from the *Tao-te Ching* (pp. 203–217)

The Book of Tao is difficult for most westerners to understand, and it is risky to offer freshmen this selection as their first text in a discussion of politics. The author, moreover, is reputedly interested less in political issues than in issues that govern individual life. Taoism in its earliest forms conflicted with Confucian thought, much of which originated from Confucius's own desire to be a public officer and a politician. Confucius was concerned with public life and with the virtues essential to serving the people properly. Lao-tzu is said to have mocked Confucius when they met and berated Confucius for his pride. Although the meeting may simply be legend, the way of Tao does represent a much more personal philosophy than Confucianism.

For Lao-tzu, for example, the evil doer should be met with good. Confucius, however, says that the evil doer should be met with justice and the doer of good should be met with good. Confucius's doctrine seems, at least to Western minds, much more worldly, practical, and responsive to the realities in which we live.

I am indebted to Michael Bybee of the University of Oregon, who has used a previous edition of this book with his students. Bybee compared human nature as it is reflected in Lao-tzu's and Machiavelli's discussions of power and the state, and questioned what makes a group of people cohere into a society.

Lao-tzu's text, odd and difficult as it may seem at first, works well with students. They use it to develop ideas of their own, to respond to Lao-tzu's ideas, and to explore issues that are of considerable importance to them. The conflict between the materialism of our culture and the metaphysical views that Lao-tzu promotes is quite palpable to many undergraduates. My experience is that most students are pragmatic, interested in succeeding in the material world and in being well paid when they receive their degrees, but they are also susceptible to idealist viewpoints and have an interest in spiritual values. If you are fortunate enough to teach some students who are attracted by an idealistic outlook, your class discussions may blossom with exciting moments.

What may surprise you is how much discussion may be distilled from small segments of the text. For example, the order of "best" rulers in paragraph 4 is well worth consulting. In any class discussion, students will find many examples of leaders that fit each of the categories.

If you assign the Lao-tzu and Machiavelli selections together, you should stimulate lively debate. For most of my students, Machiavelli holds great appeal. It is wonderful to see them interpret the conflict between these two writers' positions.

SUGGESTIONS FOR CLASS DISCUSSION

1. What are Lao-tzu's views of human nature? Does he seem cynical or optimistic about human nature?
2. What are the chief values that Lao-tzu seems to hold dear? Some are peace, love, wisdom, and benevolence. See how many others your students can find.

3. Ask your students if they would feel comfortable living in a state that is governed in the way Lao-tzu recommends. What problems do they envision a modern American might face?

SUGGESTIONS FOR BRIEF ESSAYS

1. What kinds of individuals would have a difficult time living in the kind of state that Lao-tzu regards as most desirable? Which individuals would find such a state most compatible with their way of life?
2. Taoism has developed into a religion. What religious qualities mark the selection? What qualities are clearly not religious? Is there a conflict between the two? Is it surprising that a book such as the *Tao-te Ching* should now be regarded as religious?
3. What is the role of the military in the state that Lao-tzu praises? How important would the military be, and who would serve in the armies? Which verses indicate the importance of the military? What do they say?

SUGGESTIONS FOR LONGER ESSAYS

1. Examine the way popular advertising in any medium demonstrates the truth of Lao-tzu's contention that "there is no disaster greater than not being content." Show how advertising makes it impossible for anyone who is its victim to be content. What is the result of advertising's success in making people discontented?
2. Choose a text or series of texts that you feel are especially difficult for you to accept as appropriate for either the state or the individual. Examine them in enough detail so that you show why you could not easily accept what they recommend. What would happen to our society if the recommendations were put into effect?
3. Write a series of verses in imitation of Lao-tzu, giving what you feel are the loftiest and wisest principles you can offer on the operation of the state and the proper behavior of its citizens. Use the form that appears in the selections—short declarative sentences that imply more than they say explicitly, verses that include several sections, ideals that can be put into action.
4. Consult the entire *Tao-te Ching*, and collect texts that shed light on what Lao-tzu means by "the way." Consider what recommendations he makes for achieving enlightenment, what enlightenment seems to mean, and how likely you feel it would be to achieve what he recommends. What illumination does the rest of the text provide for Lao-tzu's political views?
5. How would Lao-tzu critique the society in which you live? What would he recommend to you as worthwhile behavior, and what would he condemn? Would you feel it possible to argue against his critique and maintain a worthwhile and virtuous path of behavior for yourself?

SENTENCE OUTLINE: See p. 114 of this manual.

BIBLIOGRAPHY: See p. 184 of this manual.

NICCOLÒ MACHIAVELLI
The Qualities of the Prince (pp. 219–235)

The original Italian word for "qualities," *virtù,* connotes not only strength and force of personality, but also fortune, destiny, and ingrained luck. The term is complex and deserves some opportunity for examination. This excerpt from *The Prince* is one of the most popular selections in *A World of Ideas*, and it is among the easiest to teach. Students seem ready to accept much of what Machiavelli says as being essentially practical and often necessary. One of the best opening gambits is to ask students how they evaluate Machiavelli's advice in terms of its likelihood to produce a successful government.

The question of ends and means—whether the means a prince uses will justify his ends, assuming they are high-minded—is central to this selection, although the original Italian is not entirely clear in establishing such a clear-cut distinction. Nonetheless, it is worthwhile to probe the question with your students, asking them if there are conditions under which it is appropriate to say that the political means can justify a political end. The writing assignments in the text center on this question because it is both important and clearly essential to an understanding of Machiavelli.

Another interesting question to ask concerns the term *wise princes*, which Machiavelli uses near the end of the essay (para. 28). What would a wise prince be? Would that be a prince who has paid close attention to Machiavelli? Indeed, would a prince who paid very close attention to Machiavelli be a good prince? Or would that prince be merely a successful prince? You might ask your students if they think a distinction can be made between the two terms or if indeed a good prince must then be a successful prince.

Machiavelli's social structure assumes a noble class of citizens from which would arise the prince. But he also assumes the existence of "the masses," and he does not entirely write them off. It is worthwhile to examine the text with an eye toward what Machiavelli says about the people and their relation to the prince. He is concerned that they feel content and that they not hate the prince. It is useful to make some comparisons between Machiavelli's views and those of Lao-tzu and Rousseau.

Ultimately, the question is that of government. What kind of government does Machiavelli feel is most desirable? What does government seem to mean in the Renaissance Italy of his day? Is it relevant to our concepts of government today?

SUGGESTIONS FOR CLASS DISCUSSION

1. Can the desired qualities of the prince be taught, or are they inherent? Does genetics or the environment produce these qualities?
2. Is the prince really like our modern politicians? I last read over this material at a time when the newspapers were filled with statements from politicians that seemed to come right out of the passage. Ask your students to look through news magazines or newspapers—and do the same yourself if you can—for evidence that Machiavelli's ideas are still current.
3. One of the chief points I raise in discussing this piece is the question of ends and means. First-year college students can grasp this concept easily, and they are often direct enough and innocent enough (if you will) to make the discussion interesting. The phrase "one must consider the final result" in paragraph 24 hedges things a bit. You may want to point out that the original Italian is *si guarda al fine* and that it is often translated as "we must often look to the end." Translators using "result" are concerned that we not get too deeply into an ends-and-means tangle, but the fact is we have been doing just that for centuries. You will find that your students will warm to an examination of this issue. You also will find that later essays (Rousseau's concern for the social contract, Jefferson's declaration and break from England, Douglass's attitude toward slavery and his freedom, and King's explanation of his means and the desired ends) will richly reward a careful discussion of this concept here.

SUGGESTIONS FOR BRIEF ESSAYS

1. Define the terms *ends* and *means*, and explain why they are important.
2. Compare Machiavelli's advice with the behavior of a politician—past or present.
3. Under what political circumstances might the ends justify the means? (This could be seen as a trap, but it nonetheless is a stimulating topic.)

SUGGESTIONS FOR LONGER ESSAYS

1. Research Machiavelli's life, and compare his actions with the advice he gives here. Did he have the qualities of a prince?
2. Machiavelli advises the prince to study history and reflect on the actions of great men. Would you support such advice? Machiavelli mentions a number of great leaders in his essay. Which leaders would you recommend that a prince study? Do you think Machiavelli would agree?
3. Look up the term *Machiavellian* in an unabridged dictionary or encyclopedia. From reading this essay, do you feel that the definition is warranted? Do you feel it is a distortion of what Machiavelli really means?

4. In an essay titled "The Qualities of the Politician," give your own advice to the politician of your choice. Use Machiavelli's rhetorical technique of sharply focused, brief paragraphs on a single subject that usually contrast two kinds of behavior, as well as his technique of the aphorism. Be sure to use Machiavelli's categories so that you are sure to cover the full range of activities pertinent to political life.

5. What form of government would Machiavelli feel is most stable and desirable? Base your answer on an analysis of the recommendations Machiavelli gives his prince. Consider his views of individuals in society and their roles and responsibilities in regard to the prince. What governments of today might satisfy Machiavelli's demands for the way the state should operate?

SENTENCE OUTLINE: See p. 115 of this manual.

BIBLIOGRAPHY: See p. 184 of this manual.

JEAN-JACQUES ROUSSEAU
The Origin of Civil Society (pp. 237–257)

The fact that Rousseau influenced the Romantics may be of some use to you in beginning a discussion of this piece. He represents some of the innovative thinking that stimulated late eighteenth-century philosophers concerning alternatives to traditional forms of government. Beginning in the early seventeenth century in England, questions were raised about the ways in which the monarchy was to be served or was to serve. Rousseau was instrumental in producing an atmosphere in which ideals of democracy were at least tenable and in some circles fashionable. When he began writing *The Social Contract*, the Philosophes, dominant thinkers in France, held that the monarchy could behave despotically if the goal was to produce good behavior in its citizens. Rousseau seems to have believed that there is an essential goodness in people and that a despotic ruler is undesirable no matter what his or her goals. Thus, the problem of ends and means figures in Rousseau's thinking as it does in Machiavelli's.

Perhaps Rousseau's most romantic belief is in liberty as a value to be held above all. The question of what freedoms the individual forgoes in committing to a social contract is sometimes complex to consider, since it seems on the surface that the individual "alienates" his freedoms when he joins the civil polity. Maurice Cranston, in his introduction to *The Social Contract*, explains that what "Rousseau is saying is that instead of surrendering their liberty by the social contract, they convert their liberty from independence into political and moral freedom, and this is part of their transformation from creatures living brutishly according to impulse into men living humanly according to reason and conscience."

The abstract concepts of political and moral freedom are important to consider with your students. It is also important to ask what freedoms people give up—and which people give them up—when they accept a social polity such as the one we live in. Likewise, it is important to discuss what freedoms the individual gains in the social contract.

Discussing the relationship of equality and democracy might be useful, but before doing so, I usually try to give students some idea of the kind of government under which Rousseau lived. The reigns of Louis XV (1715–1774) and Louis XVI (1774–1792) were shabby imitations of that of the "Sun King," Louis XIV (reigned 1643–1715). The worst conservatism took hold, and the government avoided the reforms that might have forestalled the French Revolution, which Rousseau never lived to see. If some students have a background in the Revolution, you might give them a chance to say what they think about Rousseau's contribution. You might also point to Wordsworth and Shelley as democrats influenced by Rousseau.

Ultimately, I think, your energies will probably be devoted to helping your students define for themselves what Rousseau has in mind by the social contract. Further, your efforts will probably be largely involved with distinguishing between natural law and civil law or natural man and civil man. You also will find yourself examining the concept of liberty and the concept of government as Rousseau seems to be establishing it.

SUGGESTIONS FOR CLASS DISCUSSION

1. It would be good to discuss the use of analogy in this piece. Aristotle warned that analogy was useful only when the "fit" between the two elements compared was more or less exact. Discussing this analogy's appropriateness should help your students understand their responsibility in constructing their own analogies—something they all do anyway.
2. One of the most fruitful subjects of class discussion might prove to be Rousseau's comparison of the family to the state. You might go into the reasons why Rousseau makes this comparison—particularly why he considers the king to be a surrogate father and the country his family. The thought is comforting but unreal. Ask if anyone's family is run on the model of a government, using, for instance, democratic or autocratic methods.
3. It is important to raise the question of people voluntarily yielding their freedom in order to enter into a compact with leaders who will govern on their behalf. This is a complex and controversial concept that should stimulate discussion. How could people actually do what Rousseau postulates in the first compact? Ask your students if they think it reasonable that government could have begun this way. You might want to distinguish between a people's consciously entering into a contractual compact and their making a compact subconsciously or by implication. Ask your students what their relationship is to their government. What kind of compact exists?

SUGGESTIONS FOR BRIEF ESSAYS

1. What is a compact drawn between a people and their government? What are its qualities?
2. Compare the natural state with the civil state. Which is preferable?
3. Is the family a necessary antecedent to government, or is government a necessary antecedent to the generally accepted structure of the family?
4. Is it possible to have a natural state today? What would it be like, and what would make it possible (or impossible)?

SUGGESTIONS FOR LONGER ESSAYS

1. Choose the most significant idea Rousseau presents in his essay. Explain why it is significant and to whom. Further, defend your choice as if you were speaking to someone who disagreed with you.
2. Rousseau talks about primitive societies. What do you imagine is the governmental situation in most primitive societies? How does your view compare with Rousseau's?
3. What form of government would Rousseau approve of today? Describe briefly the kind of rulers, the kind of institution, and the behavior of the governed that would most please him. Does any such government exist? Could it exist?

SENTENCE OUTLINE: See p. 116 of this manual.

BIBLIOGRAPHY: See p. 191 of this manual.

THOMAS JEFFERSON

The Declaration of Independence (pp. 259–267)

Jefferson was specifically invited to write this Declaration because other members of the Continental Congress had been impressed by his style. John Adams and Benjamin Franklin worked and reworked the document until it was "scored and scratched like a school boy's exercise." In the original version Jefferson attacked the slave trade, but in the revision that attack was omitted. A number of other interesting items were removed or changed as well.

The question of style is important in analyzing this piece because most students are familiar with its content and can be persuaded to look closely at style. Jefferson said, "I did not consider it any part of my charge to invent new ideas, but to place before mankind the common sense of the subject, in terms so plain and firm as to command their assent." The introduction to the piece talks about some stylistic issues, and you may wish to raise others. The use of parallel structure can become wearing, especially in contemporary prose, but it is valuable to use this piece to show how it can work and be effective. Naturally, it is important to remind students that the style of this piece was designed to ensure it was memorable and effective in argument.

The content of the Declaration is important, too. The list of causes needs examination to see whether any one of them is so overwhelmingly important that individuals ought to be willing to fight and die for it even today. It may be that some students feel that none of these causes is worth dying for, either now or in Jefferson's time. If you get such a reaction, it would be worth pursuing it to see exactly what your students' views on the subject are.

In view of Jefferson's concerns for the law, it is also interesting to examine the list of causes to see which of them pertain to laws either rigged or ignored for the benefit of the monarch. Paragraph 22, "abolishing the free System of English Laws," is interesting on this account. The next paragraph concerns the abolishing of laws that the colonists established for themselves. The relationship between laws imposed from without and laws conceived from within is of special interest as well. Of course, as Jefferson reveals in paragraph 25, the monarch has also waged war against the colonies, and that fact colors some of what Jefferson says in the document.

SUGGESTIONS FOR CLASS DISCUSSION

1. Have your students define the range of the colonies' complaints against the crown.
2. Examine the document for seeds of democracy and republicanism. The members of the Congress were generally landed and patrician, and it is worthwhile to ask what made them different from their aristocratic overseers in England.
3. Stimulate a discussion of style. Mention Jefferson's concern for common sense, and see if your students agree that he achieved it.
4. If possible, have some students scan the opening sentences to determine their rhythms. If they can't, do it for them. Explain that some of the power of the document depends on the stately rhythms of the prose. This aspect of style is important to communicate to students.
5. Raise the question of Jefferson as a slaveholder and the value, in light of that, of his attitudes toward independence. Jefferson was a reluctant owner of slaves and opposed to its practice, but he did not free his slaves. Does his position as a slaveholder invalidate the Declaration? Does it invalidate the Revolutionary War?

SUGGESTIONS FOR BRIEF ESSAYS

1. How does the document seem to define *independence*? Use this definition as a basis for your own. To what extent does your definition of independence agree with or differ from Jefferson's?
2. By means of researching the background of the American Revolution, establish the political antecedents of the Declaration and what its consequences were thought to be.
3. What are the most important circumstances that brought the colonies to the point of rebellion?

SUGGESTIONS FOR LONGER ESSAYS

1. The Declaration was written after the first year of the American Revolution. What would be some of the reasons for writing such a document if the colonies were already in battle? To whom could it be useful? Consider its effect both in England and in the colonies.
2. Refer to Machiavelli's concerns for the way things turn out—the relationship between ends and means. What does the Declaration imply about the justification of rebellion to achieve the ends of independence? Do you feel confident that the means of rebellion—involving war, civil disorder, injustice, and death—can be justified by the end of independence? Do you feel that Jefferson thought these particular means were justified by the ends he had in mind? How would he have regarded Machiavelli's advice?

3. Analyze Jefferson's list of causes. Group them into three or four categories (economic, military, civil, religious, and so on), and discuss at least one in each category as a way of explaining what the category is. If you can compare one category with another, decide which of the categories Jefferson felt was most important and why.

SENTENCE OUTLINE: See p. 117 of this manual.

BIBLIOGRAPHY: See p. 181 of this manual.

ELIZABETH CADY STANTON
Declaration of Sentiments and Resolutions (pp. 269–277)

One of the interesting aspects of this declaration is the fact that it tended to polarize the then nascent women's movement. The radicals, of whom Elizabeth Cady Stanton was one, found themselves having to fight not only against men who wanted to defend things as they were but against women who feared that the radicals might be moving too swiftly, demanding too much, and acting unreasonably. It is always interesting to examine the demands Stanton makes here to see which might have been most frightening to those women who were brave enough to attend a conference such as the Seneca Falls Convention, but conservative enough to hold back.

It is also interesting to note that the women's movement split into two parties over the issue of securing the vote. Stanton and Susan B. Anthony organized the National Women's Suffrage Association in 1869, although the group had been loosely organized since 1851. Its members were so radical that an alternative organization, the American Woman Suffrage Association, existed in Boston. Eventually the two organizations were merged, but it is instructive to note that the Boston group feared that Stanton's organization would have a negative effect on the struggle to secure freedom for black slaves. The conservative group insisted that freeing the slaves was the first issue and that the ambitions of abolitionists would be undermined by the work of women who were angling to get the vote.

Women actually did have voting privileges in certain parts of the country in the eighteenth and nineteenth centuries, but they did not have the right to vote in national elections. After the end of slavery they still did not have the right to vote even though the freemen whom they had struggled for could actually vote (at least in theory).

One of the touchiest and possibly most interesting areas to discuss with students concerns religion. During the period of the Seneca Falls Convention, the American Northeast had undergone a fascinating period of religious revival. Evangelical preachers were traveling widely in New York State. Joseph Smith published his *Book of Mormon* in Palmyra, New York. The Adventist movement had begun in New York. The fervor for religious revival was intense, and even Elizabeth Cady Stanton fell under its spell, suffering an emotional collapse after hearing an evangelist preacher named Charles Grandison Finney. When she recovered, she felt somewhat cheated and began to examine religion critically. She began to see that the patriarchal structures of religion had systematically prejudiced society against women. The very choice of Eve as the sinner against mankind demonstrated that the Bible was not likely to be aligned with her cause. The position of apostles, making it impossible for women to take an active role in church government, also made it clear that religion was a hurdle that the women's movement had to leap. It may be too hot an item to touch, but you might also find it rewarding to explore the attitudes of the old Calvinist-based Presbyterianism, which Stanton professed, and the old revivalist religious teachings in relation to women's rights.

SUGGESTIONS FOR CLASS DISCUSSION

1. Ask your students if they think Elizabeth Cady Stanton proves her key claim: "The history of mankind is a history of repeated injuries and usurpations on the part of man toward woman, having in direct object the establishment of an absolute tyranny over her" (para. 3).
2. Have the class explore how effective the technique of parody is for demonstration of an injustice of the kind that Stanton puts forth in this essay. What are the virtues of parody, and what are its drawbacks?

3. What are Stanton's chief concerns regarding marriage as it exists in her community? She suggests that a wife may be "morally, an irresponsible being" (para. 10). Have students explain what she means by this.
4. To what extent are Stanton's issues tied in with economic opportunity? In this sense, does her indignation parallel that of Thomas Jefferson in the Declaration of Independence?
5. Which of Stanton's resolutions seem pertinent today? Have her concerns been satisfied in the century and a half since this declaration was issued?

SUGGESTIONS FOR BRIEF ESSAYS

1. In the beginning of the declaration, Stanton talks about a government that acts despotically against women. What does she mean by that? To what extent do you think the government she describes has actually been despotic?
2. By reading the declaration, try to establish exactly what Stanton's complaints are. What have women had to suffer? What has their lot been?
3. Compare the condition of women with the condition of the colonies as described in Jefferson's Declaration of Independence.
4. Would it be possible for women to write such a document today? What would be its effect?

SUGGESTIONS FOR LONGER ESSAYS

1. To what extent is it reasonable to assume that Stanton is correct in claiming that the direct object of man has been to establish a tyranny over woman? What elements in the declaration support such a view?
2. In a sense the declaration represents an agenda of things that must be done to help establish the equality of women. What do you see that remains to be done today? Is there enough progress being made in these areas? How do you think Stanton would feel about the condition of women today?
3. To what extent do you consider this document to be a statement of revolution? Does Stanton appear to you to be the radical that she very plainly was in 1848? What is radical about her thinking? Is there anything that would be shocking to a contemporary woman in what Stanton says here? How far do you feel she is ready to go in her fight for equality? Would she undertake disobedience to the law as Thoreau recommends in his essay?

SENTENCE OUTLINE: See p. 118 of this manual.

BIBLIOGRAPHY: See p. 192 of this manual.

HANNAH ARENDT
Total Domination (pp. 279–292)

Hannah Arendt is one of the most important modern thinkers on government. She understood the nature of totalitarianism better than most contemporary philosophers, in part because she saw the way Hitler radicalized Germany and transformed it into a frightening totalitarian state. One of the first things you will probably want to do is discuss the subject with your students in order to help them begin to understand the implications of totalitarianism. You may have students who know a great deal about Hitler, the Nazis, the nature of their government, and the concentration camps. Some may even know about the Russian gulags or pogroms. But many of your students will know very little about them. Therefore, you will need to help bring them up to speed, either by telling them about the concentration camps or—if enough of your students can contribute information—by listening to their informed discussion.

You may need to spend some time explaining that the governments of Germany and Russia exercised power in such a way as to maintain a constant reign of terror. They founded their regimes on rigid ideas about race, class, and history and used those ideas to rationalize the mass killings of members of racial and other groups they deemed to be inferior, such as Jews, Gypsies, homosexuals, and other "undesirables."

Arendt's primary point is that terror is essential to the totalitarian state. One way to produce terror is through the concentration camp, in which all human dignity is destroyed, in which all the pluralities of behavior and response are reduced to the single response of terror.

Naturally, you may wish to extend the discussion to include references to contemporary circumstances. For example, you may wish to explore the ethical issues involved in responding to the existence of concentration camps. Should totalitarian governments be destroyed when they are identified and when they behave as Hitler's Germany behaved? One reason for ousting Iraq's Saddam Hussein was to remove a tyrant from office and to end a decades-long reign of terror. Is such a move an ethical imperative? What about the West's lack of response to the genocides in Rwanda and the Sudan? Is such inaction an ethical failure? These are important issues and may be matched by more recent global political developments by the time you use this selection.

SUGGESTIONS FOR CLASS DISCUSSION

1. Begin by asking students to define or examine their ideas of the kind of terror imagined in concentration camps.
2. Of what use is terror to a totalitarian government?
3. Students should be asked to discuss the fourth paragraph's assertion that "unlikely as it may sound, these camps are the true central institution of totalitarian organizational power."
4. Why is it important for a totalitarian government to commit crimes on the vastest scale possible? How does this solidify totalitarian domination?

SUGGESTIONS FOR BRIEF ESSAYS

1. What is the United States' attitude toward totalitarian governments? Are there conditions under which the United States will tolerate such governments? What safeguards does the United States have in place to prevent it from becoming a totalitarian state?
2. In paragraph 8 Arendt states; "What common sense and 'normal people' refuse to believe is that everything is possible." For that reason, they tend not to believe that concentration camps could exist or that total domination is possible. Explain why "normal people" have difficulty with the concept that "everything is possible."
3. What seems to happen to people who are subjected to the terror of the concentration camp? Describe the changes in their psychology. Arendt describes it as something like a living death. Why would a totalitarian government want to produce such an effect on its own people?
4. Some people today do not believe the Nazi concentration camps existed. Why would it be easy for someone today to disbelieve the documented horrors of Buchenwald, Auschwitz, Bergen-Belsen, and others? Would it shock Arendt to know that some today do not believe the Nazi concentration camps existed? Why or why not?

SUGGESTIONS FOR LONGER ESSAYS

1. In paragraph 7 Arendt tells us: "The road to totalitarian domination leads through many intermediate stages for which we can find numerous analogies and precedents." She tells us that at first terror is used to defeat the opposition. But once the opposition is defeated, the goal of total domination defines the next stage. Examine her description of the stages of totalitarian development, and try to clarify her views for someone who has not yet read this selection. Add your own views on how you imagine a totalitarian government would progress from defeating the political opposition to the creation of concentration camps designed to exterminate certain segments of a population.
2. Examine the current political situation in any sector of the world, and decide whether or not there are true totalitarian governments in operation. Are there signs of the development of totalitarianism in the behavior of any current governments? Establish the nature of such governments in their progress toward creating a totalitarian state.
3. Arendt states that "the politically most important yardstick for judging events in our time" is "whether they serve totalitarian domination or not" (para. 10). Examine the events in your time that

you think may be tending toward serving totalitarian domination. Describe those events, clarify their tendency toward producing totalitarianism, and suggest how the world should react to those events in order to prevent the development of totalitarianism.

4. Near the end of the selection, Arendt tells us that inmates in concentration camps are "more effectively cut off from the world of the living than if they had died" (para. 13). Explain what she means, and consider how being cut off from the rest of the world would affect the behavior and emotional life of an individual in a camp. In what modern contexts can you imagine people being effectively cut off from the rest of society? Examine as best you can the responses likely from people who are cut off in that fashion. What might happen to them when they "return to life"?

SENTENCE OUTLINE: See p. 119 of this manual.

BIBLIOGRAPHY: See p. 169 of this manual.

MARCUS TULLIUS CICERO
The Defense of Injustice
(bedfordstmartins.com/worldofideas/epages)

I have wanted to include something of Cicero's for some time in an edition of *A World of Ideas,* and this one seemed just right for a number of reasons. For one thing, the argument Philus works up from the words of Carneades is so compelling that it is virtually certain that most of your students will agree with him. The options Philus offers people are not, of course, the only options available, but the way he sets up the argument makes it seem as if they are. Hence, the only reasonable position will be to accept the position he outlines. It is a clever argument you will want to examine and possibly refute. In any event, because your students are likely to concede to it, you should have plenty to work with in the classroom.

Moreover, because your students may indeed find it an appealing argument, they will be well set up for the selections by Thoreau and King, whose views are quite different and whose positions are extremely appealing. When students read Rawls's essay, they will have a hard time maintaining the defense of Philus's position unless they are willing to declare themselves opposed to justice in society.

The technique of arguing against a position in which one believes is in itself remarkable and in many ways contrary to any expectation of the average student. Samuel Johnson is recorded by James Boswell as sitting and observing an argument for some time before entering into it. Boswell asked Johnson why he hesitated so long, and Johnson said that he was simply waiting to see which side of the argument was losing ground so that he could go in and shore it up.

Another important benefit of the technique Cicero uses is that Philus makes us face the truth about our own views of justice, helping us to see our own limitations and fears. Most of us want justice that benefits us with freedom but does not deprive us of privileges. In other words, we approve of justice when it does not cost us anything.

The argument itself has the further benefit of helping us see very clearly the positive qualities of justice, because injustice is so clearly its opposite. Cicero was very clear in his own life about the need for justice, but like most people he was also aware that in order to provide justice a nation must be stable and must be certain of its deepest values. He was a practical politician as well as a philosopher. His personal philosophy was close to that of the Stoics, who felt that their commitment was to social good and political action to achieve social good. Cicero himself was never thought of as a hero, but in his last years he wrote some of his most lasting pieces, and he took immense risks in his *Philippics* (so named because he addressed Philip of Macedon), which harshly criticized those who struggled after the death of Caesar to reconstruct the government. Cicero constantly held up to them the basic values of Rome and showed them how far they fell short of these values.

SUGGESTIONS FOR CLASS DISCUSSION

1. What concrete evidence is there to support the argument that Cicero did not accept the views that Philus promotes in his speech?
2. What are the principal values that Laelius upholds in the last paragraphs of the selection?
3. Why does Philus compare the different ways in which justice is observed in other nations?
4. Compare the ideas of wisdom and virtue in Philus's argument. Is wisdom true wisdom, and is virtue true virtue?
5. Why does Philus begin his dialogue by complaining when Laelius invites him to defend injustice that he is asked "to speak in favor of evil!"? Does he seem to be speaking in favor of evil?

SUGGESTIONS FOR BRIEF ESSAYS

1. Write a brief essay that attacks Philus's position in defense of injustice. Try to respond to each of his important points and use some of his own techniques, such as offering a historical survey and using argument by analogy.
2. If you have access to a copy of Shakespeare's *Julius Caesar,* read the play and write a brief statement on how you think Shakespeare regards Cicero, and how other characters regard him. In real life, Cicero was very important to both sides of the controversy over the assassination of Caesar. It was said in ancient times that Cicero was not included in the conspiracy because he was likely to have talked too much. Is that characteristic evident in the selection?
3. In paragraph 5 Philus says of Carneades that he "uses his own peculiar method of argument, analyzing everything from a purely verbal rather than a factual point of view." Does Philus, in imitating Carneades, do the same? Explain by analyzing his argument.

SUGGESTIONS FOR LONGER ESSAYS

1. Philus begins his argument by saying he will use the techniques of Carneades, who proposed an argument against justice. Carneades was a skeptic philosopher famous for arguing against many worthy positions and beliefs. He made a point of undermining positions that were thought to be obvious and secure—such as the position that supports justice as a positive virtue. Try his method by arguing against an obviously desirable position. For example, construct an argument that condemns one or more of the virtues Jefferson recommends in "The Declaration of Independence."
2. Laelius's paragraphs at the end of this selection are among the best known in this work by Cicero. They are not well developed as arguments, but it may be argued, on the basis of the way Cicero lived his life, that these represent his own personal views on justice. For the reader, they represent a strong alternative to Philus's case. Write an essay that establishes whether Philus's argument against justice or Laelius's argument for justice is the argument that we, as rational citizens, must accept.
3. To what extent do you observe the United States, either recently or in the far past, responding to the ideas that are represented as wisdom by Philus? Does the United States seem to behave in a manner similar to that described in paragraph 17? How does justice figure in the example that Philus offers us in this segment of the essay?
4. In paragraph 15 Philus echoes Cicero's personal view (and the view of many ancients) that government by the people would result in chaos and disaster. None of them was thinking in terms of the governmental structure of modern democracies, which balance executive, legislative, and judicial powers and which base themselves on patterns of public voting. What they were thinking of was a direct democracy in which the people would rule without leaders or "strongmen" (whether male or female) to tell them what to do. Do you agree that such a rule by the people would result in turmoil and disaster in a state? Construct an argument that either attacks or defends Philus's view.

SENTENCE OUTLINE: See p. 120 of this manual.

BIBLIOGRAPHY: See p. 174 of this manual.

ETHICS AND MORALITY

The eight essays in Part Three approach the issues of ethics and morality in diverse ways. Henry David Thoreau offers the view of a citizen who cannot abide laws that he feels are immoral because they support slavery. Frederick Douglass, a former slave, gives us a view of a society that thought of itself as moral while at the same time owning slaves. Friedrich Nietzsche attacks contemporary morality as being against the demands of nature. Iris Murdoch considers the relationship between religion and morality. Rev. Martin Luther King Jr. sits in jail while protesting in much the same fashion as Thoreau had before him. Kwame Appiah examines the case for a virtue ethics, a theory that connects virtue with character. Michael Gazzaniga consults the findings of evolutionary biologists to consider whether there is some form of moral hard-wiring in the brain. Aristotle seems to take a personal view because his primary audience is his son, but his advice is meaningful to everyone who reads his thoughts on ethics.

HENRY DAVID THOREAU

Civil Disobedience (pp. 301–325)

One of the most important concepts to emphasize in discussing this essay is the question of *conscience*. It is often said that Thoreau is the conscience of the nation, and it is worthwhile to have students hash out just what that might mean. It helps to give some background for the term, including the etymological implications of knowing what is within us, within our hearts. The religious tradition Thoreau draws upon is avowedly Puritan, figuring prominently in the works of Calvin and especially in the prose and poetry of Milton, which Thoreau surely knew well. The implication of such a consideration is that the individual is sovereign and must always act according to what he or she knows is right. This was Milton's view; he was a champion in the eyes of later revolutionaries of conscience. Translating this concept into contemporary terms is not difficult. Consider the Nazi trials at Nuremberg, where individuals were held accountable for following Hitler's orders, or the atrocities in Vietnam, or the stockpiling of nuclear weapons. The contemporary examples proliferate.

It is also helpful to mention something about the Fugitive Slave Act of 1850, which was intended to enforce the already existing Fugitive Slave Law of 1793. The act was designed to tame those Northerners who expressed open hostility to slavery and who had been operating the highly efficient Underground Railway, which spirited slaves away from the South and into safety in Canada. Anyone who helped or harbored a slave anywhere in the nation was subject to a $2,000 fine. This amount was a small fortune in 1850. The fact is that northern states resented the law and passed counterlaws—the Personal Liberty Laws, which had the effect of nullifying the act. However, it ought to be mentioned that in border states the act was enforced even during the early years of the Civil War.

Students might be led to see the significance of having to capitulate to laws that are clearly unjust, immoral, and inhuman by reflecting on how they themselves would act if they had to deal with a law such as the Fugitive Slave Act.

SUGGESTIONS FOR CLASS DISCUSSION

1. Ask your students what it means to say, "That government is best which governs least" (para. 1).
2. Thoreau says, "That government is best which governs not at all" (para. 1). What do your students think he means by this? Ask if they agree. Would such a government be ethical, or not?

3. In paragraph 2 Thoreau says about the government, "*It* does not keep the country free. *It* does not settle the West. *It* does not educate." Is this still true? Is Thoreau's view of government accurate? What exactly does government do?

SUGGESTIONS FOR BRIEF ESSAYS

1. In paragraph 11 Thoreau says, "All voting is a sort of gaming." What does he mean by this? Is this true? What is the gaming aspect of voting? Why is Thoreau so harsh about voting? (Remember that in his time only men had the right to vote.) Does one have a moral responsibility to vote?
2. Thoreau mentions a "wise minority" in paragraph 16. What does he mean by this? Is it possible to have a wise minority in the sense that he describes? If there is such a minority, what should government do? What should the wise minority do? How would a wise minority be likely to behave? To what extent does "wise" mean ethical and moral?

SUGGESTIONS FOR LONGER ESSAYS

1. Compare the government of Thoreau's day with that of our own. How much are they alike? What specific qualities do the governments have in common? How do they differ? Do you believe that the U.S. government has improved since Thoreau's time? Do you think Thoreau would retract some of the things he says if he were alive today? Is our age more concerned with ethics?
2. What do you think Thoreau means by "conscience"? According to Thoreau, what should the role of conscience be in government? Is it possible for a government to act out of conscience? If a government did act out of conscience, how would it act? Does our current government act out of conscience? Does any government that you know of act out of conscience?
3. What do you think Thoreau's attitude toward school segregation would be, whether it were voluntary or forced by circumstances? Would the difference be important to him in his analysis? Do you think Thoreau would approve of affirmative action laws that grant preferential treatment to minorities in matters of college admission and job appointments? Would he think such programs are just or unjust?

SENTENCE OUTLINE: See p. 121 of this manual.

BIBLIOGRAPHY: See p. 193 of this manual.

FREDERICK DOUGLASS

From *Narrative of the Life of Frederick Douglass, an American Slave* (pp. 327–341)

Douglass's narrative is an accessible document that needs little preparation or background. Among the fascinating aspects of the excerpt presented here are the portraits of people, slave and free, who are part of Douglass's life. He records very carefully their views and attitudes and reveals his own as he writes. His new mistress, Mrs. Auld, was a Northerner who married and moved to Maryland to take up the life of the slaveholder. Her original occupation, weaving, is a coincidental metaphor for creating a life, weaving a fate. Douglass constantly reminds us of the tenderheartedness of this woman but also shows that slavery makes her as sinister as those who were born into slave-holding families. Douglass was an especially fair-minded man, active in movements toward freedom and justice for many people. He died just after attending a meeting on women's suffrage on February 20, 1895. During his life he was sometimes criticized for marrying a white woman in 1884, after his first wife died. When he was confronted by his critics, he said simply that his first wife was the color of his mother and his second wife was the color of his father.

SUGGESTIONS FOR CLASS DISCUSSION

1. Direct a discussion of the following questions: What were Douglass's expectations of his new mistress? What surprised him, and why? Did his mistress seem to have a clear idea of what it meant to be the mistress of a slave? How was her sense of ethics affected by learning to be a slaveholder?
2. Ask if your students think Douglass's views about the power of learning are still persuasive today. Can it still be advantageous for people to deny others the right to an education? Do all oppressed people feel that education is a key to freedom? Why is it immoral to deny someone an education?

SUGGESTIONS FOR BRIEF ESSAYS

1. Douglass learned his letters by observing the markings on pieces of timber used in building a boat (para. 12). Explain the symbolism in his observations. To what extent was literacy like a boat to him?
2. Reading becomes the pathway to freedom for Douglass, and he is determined to learn to read despite his master's efforts to stop him. To what extent is Douglass right about finding the pathway to freedom? Is his insight still useful to us today? Does the experience of discontentment that Douglass felt contribute positively to improving the lot of those enslaved? Does he offer us a model for behaving ethically?
3. Why is Douglass so disturbed over the fate of his grandmother after the death of Master Andrew? What had his grandmother meant to the slave owners? How did they treat her in her old age? What would Douglass have rather had her fate be?

SUGGESTIONS FOR LONGER ESSAYS

1. Douglass tells us about a period in his life marked by change and growth. How did the changes contribute to his determination to secure his freedom? What political lessons does Douglass learn about the nature of morality, and how does he impart them to us?
2. To a large extent Douglass tells us about the degrading effects that slavery had on white slaveholders. What evidence does Douglass give us for the changes that take place in slaveholders? Consider the evidence of the proper behavior of a slave as implied in the opening of the essay. What political realities does Douglass reveal that would affect the behavior of those in power? What effect does power have on those who hold it? How does a sense of power relate to a sense of morality in the hands of the powerful?
3. Tell a story in the first person of your relationship with people who hold power over you legally. Tell your story in such a way as to reveal the political realities that affect both you and those with power. To what extent is your situation similar to Douglass's? Is there an ethics of power?

SENTENCE OUTLINE: See p. 122 of this manual.

BIBLIOGRAPHY: See p. 176 of this manual.

FRIEDRICH NIETZSCHE

Morality as Anti-Nature (pp. 343–357)

This is a sprightly selection that ought to stimulate plenty of discussion. It should be completely unexpected on the part of your students, who will not know the reputation of Nietzsche as a critic of his culture (and ours). They will also not know that Nietzsche was a hero of Hitler and the Third Reich because of his critique of morality and his view of the superman and the will to power. Of course, Nietzsche would have had nothing to do with the Nazis—he even broke with Wagner eventually. But the tradition of Nazi hero worship of Nietzsche really stems from Elizabeth, his sister, and her longstanding anti-Semitism, which drew her into Hitler's circle. Nietzsche himself seems never to have shared her views.

For some classrooms, this selection might be incendiary. For others it might be a breath of fresh air. The point of it all is that it calls into question the nature of morality and ethical behavior. It is clear that Aristotle's piece is a product of a culture whose concerns are stability and good behavior. When Nietzsche takes issue with them he speaks from an isolated position, even though he pluralizes himself when he says, "we immoralists."

My view is that it is good to stimulate students to think, even if that process is complex and uncomfortable. Nonetheless, Nietzsche is one of the most important of modern thinkers, and it is valuable to have students confront his thinking head on. This particular selection is "in your face" in a way that I hope will produce some good reactions and good analyses.

SUGGESTIONS FOR CLASS DISCUSSION

1. Which moral precepts seem most to involve sensuality?
2. In what sense does Nietzsche think he is an affirmer rather than a negator of morality?
3. Which of the Ten Commandments is Nietzsche most likely to break?
4. Why is confusing cause and effect a problem? Why would it cause misunderstanding?
5. What is an imaginary cause? Why is it important?

SUGGESTIONS FOR BRIEF ESSAYS

1. Explain what Nietzsche means by "Cornarism" (paras. 13–15). Why is his discussion important for anyone who wishes to understand truth?
2. In paragraph 27 Nietzsche says, "Men were considered 'free' so that they might be judged and punished—so that they might become *guilty*." How do you react to this statement? Does it respect your views of the purposes of assuming that people are free to behave as they wish? Does it make sense to you that free will is a necessary ingredient for determining guilt?
3. Why would Nietzsche say, "Christianity is a metaphysics of the hangman" (para. 28)? What does he mean by this statement, and how would you argue with him concerning it? What is a valid counterargument?

SUGGESTIONS FOR LONGER ESSAYS

1. If Nietzsche is right in saying, "Radical means are indispensable only for the degenerate" (para. 3), what form of morality would be appropriate for those of us who are not degenerate? Nietzsche's view is that we are all being punished for the behavior of the weak and degenerate and that the rest of us could do without the moral precepts in most of the Ten Commandments. Is he correct?
2. What is Nietzsche's ultimate definition of "peace of soul" as developed in paragraph 7? What do you define as peace of soul? Is it a desirable quality? How can it be attained? Write an essay that clarifies the concept and offers hope to someone who ardently desires peace of soul.
3. In paragraph 26 Nietzsche talks about "the error of free will." Explain what he means by this phrase and how free will operates to achieve what he describes. Is he correct when he says "the doctrine of the will has been invented essentially for the purpose of punishment" (para. 27)?
4. How reasonable is Nietzsche's condemnation of the concept that "man *ought* to be such and such" (para. 10)? What is wrong with the command "Change yourself!"? Write an essay that analyzes Nietzsche's complaints. Is he all wrong? Is he partly right? What should be the view of a reasonable person in regard to the moral issues at stake here?
5. One of the most inflammatory aphorisms in this selection is "One has renounced the *great* life when one renounces war" (para. 6). What could he mean by this statement? What has it to do with living a moral life or with the prohibitions of the moral precepts Nietzsche argues against?

Nietzsche had seen the horrors of war up close in a military hospital. How could he say something like this in an essay of this sort?

SENTENCE OUTLINE: See p. 123 of this manual.

BIBLIOGRAPHY: See p. 188 of this manual.

IRIS MURDOCH
Morality and Religion (pp. 359–373)

Because this is a challenging piece concerned with a major human issue, you should advise your students to read my introduction carefully. I try to enumerate each paragraph and discuss its content and the essence of its argument. I deemphasize, to some extent, my usual comments on rhetoric in order to help clarify a dense argument that has no essential resolution.

It is characteristic of Murdoch in all her writing to be able to balance contradictions and not let them worry her, so it's no surprise that she explores this interesting issue without ultimately establishing a firm position. On the one hand, she says that morality is more naturally supported by religion and religion's need for unity. But on the other hand, she implies that the institution of religion is corrupt in some ways—or has been corrupt—and that certain ages, such as the Enlightenment, felt that it militated against a serious moral position.

Interestingly, Murdoch in her own life was what some people might call immoral in her behavior. She took lovers when it pleased her and engaged in certain kinds of sexual behavior that might be thought of as sadistic or masochistic. Even after she married John Bayley—a man who lost his virginity at the age of twenty-nine—she had occasional affairs, with his full knowledge. He wrote about some of his feelings in his *Elegy for Iris,* an elegant and touching book. But when she was asked by an interviewer about her views on sexual promiscuity, she condemned it outright, apparently without much sense that her reply suggested a contradictory attitude.

She herself was not very religious. She loved religious art, however, and she reveals as much when she talks about the images of Christ and the impulse of the Christian religion to invite imagery. She has been described as an atheist, but most commentators take issue with that view, although they cannot substitute a clear religious view that resembles conventional religious practice.

These lectures were enormously prestigious. The Gifford Lectures have attracted some of the finest minds of the day, going back to the early 1800s. When she was writing them she was at the height of her intellectual prowess. Her Alzheimer's set in about five years before she died, although she was writing her last novel in the early stages of the disease. She was criticized at the time for considerable redundancy in her writing—a somewhat cruel criticism in view of her condition.

SUGGESTIONS FOR CLASS DISCUSSION

1. Why is it important to clarify the relationship of morality to religion?
2. Why might anyone doubt that religion and morality are intimately connected?
3. Can there be a moral code without a religious underpinning?
4. What is duty, and what is its relation to morality?
5. In what sense can it be said that people can be virtuous without thinking about it?

SUGGESTIONS FOR BRIEF ESSAYS

1. Murdoch discusses duty in this essay. What is your concept of duty? What duties do you fulfill that might also be considered a part of moral behavior? Explore Murdoch's views on duty and its relation to morality in paragraph 3 of her essay.

2. As an experiment, try to keep a diary in the fashion of Francis Kilvert. Observe your world carefully. Be specific in your observations, and see how close you come to Kilvert's sense of the presence of God. In a way Kilvert was observing what he thought of as God's creation—and therefore an aspect of God himself. How close can you come to this kind of observation?

3. What is the best form of moral education for children? Outline a program of moral education you think parents of young children should follow. Must they include religion in their teachings to children?

SUGGESTIONS FOR LONGER ESSAYS

1. Murdoch suggests that humankind may be so sinful that only a strict set of moral rules can keep us from killing and destroying one another. Is she correct in this view? Is it true that only a strict set of rules can maintain a moral population? What rules might work to keep us from destroying humanity?

2. Murdoch says that religion, "being a soothing drug, is less easy to give up in later life" (para. 1). Marx called religion "the opium of the people." To what extent do you agree with this view? Take one side of the argument and try to convince someone who holds the opposite view.

3. If parents believe that "religion just *isn't true*" (para. 4), should they hold to what they feel is the truth and tell their children what they feel is the truth about religion? If their children grow up without religion, would it be possible for them to be moral people? What is the parents' ethical obligation to their children if they wish them to be moral citizens?

4. Murdoch mentions and defines high morality in paragraph 4. What do you define as high morality? What are the standards that a serious person should aim for in order to live a moral life that holds to the highest ethical standards? And if there is a high morality, what might a low morality consist of? Why would a high morality be more desirable than a low morality?

5. Murdoch discusses guilt extensively in paragraph 6. Why do you think guilt is important in any discussion of morality or ethics? How does guilt function to promote morality? Does the sense of guilt always imply a religious base, or is it normal to have a sense of guilt even if one is not religious or belongs to no religion? Does a code of morality actually promote guilt, and is this guilt productive for humankind?

SENTENCE OUTLINE: See p. 124 of this manual.

BIBLIOGRAPHY: See p. 187 of this manual.

MARTIN LUTHER KING JR.
Letter from Birmingham Jail (pp. 375–395)

One of the intriguing qualities of this piece stems from its being a letter. I like to talk about the letter as a form—however vague that concept is. I usually bring in some other letters, such as passages from the letters of Paul in the Bible and letters from a collection called *The World's Great Letters*, edited by M. Lincoln Schuster (Simon and Schuster, 1940). I read letters by Beethoven, Leonardo da Vinci, and others. I try to point out to my students that letter writing is important, that it is one of the forms that they will continue to use long after they've left the classroom, and that it is not just a catch-as-catch-can enterprise.

Beyond this, I try to emphasize King's concern with the issues of ends and means. He felt that the means could taint the desired ends. He emulated Mahatma Gandhi—a figure we must introduce to our students—who insisted on passive resistance and whose methods freed an entire nation. I also emphasize that King remained nonviolent despite repeated acts and threats of violence against him. Finally, there is the question of law again. King's views on how we should react to unjust laws are worthy of careful examination.

SUGGESTIONS FOR CLASS DISCUSSION

1. Discuss the question of what one does when one must face an unjust law. What are the real choices? What are the moral imperatives?
2. If you want to talk about this piece of writing as a model of the letter, ask your students what they have learned about how to write a letter. What could they actually do better now that they have looked closely at this model?
3. King worked very hard on behalf of African American people in the South. It is useful to see in the letter the extent to which he expressed concern for one race over another. To what extent is this a "nonracial" document?

SUGGESTIONS FOR BRIEF ESSAYS

1. Examine the letter for details that permit you to define the nature of "Birmingham society" during King's lifetime.
2. Examine one of St. Paul's letters in the Bible (see the suggestions in Writing Assignment 5 in the text, p. 394), and analyze the effectiveness of King's use of the topic of testimony.
3. Which method of development is dominant in King's letter? Choose one, and then defend your choice by showing how often it is used.

SUGGESTIONS FOR LONGER ESSAYS

1. Write a letter of response from the clergymen addressed by Martin Luther King Jr. How would they respond to his letter, given the positions they have already held? How could they counter the reasoned argument King presents? What references from the Bible could they use? As a hint, you can rely on a concordance to locate uses of the concept of the law in the Bible.
2. King's letter is profoundly rational, reasonable, and logical. However, the letters in the Bible are often passionate and emotional as well as rational. Which sections of King's letter are emotional? What is the difference in style between the emotional and rational passages? Which is more impressive? Which is easier to emulate?
3. King says that to defy or evade the law is to invite anarchy (para. 20). Look up *anarchy* in a good dictionary or an encyclopedia. Would anarchy be less or more desirable than the conditions that existed in Birmingham in the 1960s?

SENTENCE OUTLINE: See p. 125 of this manual.

BIBLIOGRAPHY: See p. 183 of this manual.

KWAME ANTHONY APPIAH

The Case against Character (pp. 397–413)

As I mention in the introduction to Appiah's selection, he has been strongly criticized for his criticism of Afrocentrism. Yet he has taught African studies and African literature in recent years and maintains a vision of cosmopolitanism that centers on understanding other cultures, while at the same time maintaining a strong sense of the value of life. He does not see the need to abandon one's cultural values while admiring the values of other cultures. His ethics is based on the value of the individual life, and he has problems with cultures that may not respect the individual as much as he feels is reasonable.

When you work with this essay you will find it useful to examine Rosalind Hursthouse's three claims in paragraph 7 and ask your students to work through them and either validate or invalidate each of them. Your students will also probably find the concepts of situationist ethics easy to understand and probably very meaningful to them. We all can think of situations in which we might have acted virtuously, but did not. Consider our behavior when a friend is mocked or threatened but we did not come to our friend's aid. Even listening to someone trash an absent friend might give us an opportunity to come to that friend's aid—but the situation might cause us not to. It is worth examining the situations that your students will come up with that might help illuminate Appiah's concepts.

Then, the word *eudaimonia* is worth spending some time discussing. It is sometimes translated simply as happiness, but you might note that "eu-" is a prefix meaning "good," while the root, "daimon," means spirit. So happiness in this sense implies a goodness of spirit in the individual, and that translates into a happy spirit. However, you will probably have a number of students who will argue that practicing certain vices can make a person happy. Let your students examine that conundrum.

You can also find it valuable to have your students enumerate the virtues that they think are indispensable to a good person, then enumerate the vices that they see in action among their peers. What are the basic virtues? What are the basic vices? You might refer to the seven deadly vices and the seven virtues.

Then the question of whether virtue is in the act or in the agent is very interesting and will certainly create a bit of discussion in your classroom.

SUGGESTIONS FOR CLASS DISCUSSION

1. Is virtue in the act or in the agent?
2. Aristotle sees eudaimonia as the highest good. Why would he think so? Do you agree?
3. How does the trait of honesty express itself? Is it a virtue?

SUGGESTIONS FOR BRIEF ESSAYS

1. Describe the most virtuous person you know, and validate your judgment with examples of that person's acts. Try to analyze that person's character. What evidence do you have to show that this person has possibly achieved the eudaimonia that Aristotle talks about? Does this person fit the model of virtue ethics or situational ethics?
2. Aristotle links virtue and happiness. To what extent do you think that a virtuous person can be unhappy rather than living a happy life? Would a life of vice result in unhappiness? Could a vicious person be happy and feel in possession of the highest good?
3. Cheating is common in schools and colleges. Does cheating seem to be an act of character, or is it rooted in the situation that the cheater is in? What has been your experience with cheating in school or college? Do you consider it a vice? What is its relation to virtue? Do you find yourself respecting those who cheat? Do you know people who, no matter what the circumstances, definitely would not cheat?

SUGGESTIONS FOR LONGER ESSAYS

1. Summarize Hursthouse's argument in favor of virtue ethics, and specifically her view that virtue is a part of the character of the agent. Then summarize Appiah's description of situationist ethics. First, decide whether these are the only two arguments to consider regarding the nature of virtuous behavior. Then, argue in favor of one point of view or the other. As much as possible, use examples, real or hypothetical, that would argue your case strongly enough to demand agreement from your reader.
2. The ancient Greeks felt that if you truly possessed one of the virtues—temperance, wisdom, justice, and courage—then you possessed them all. What do you think they meant by this observation? Do you feel that if you truly possess one of these virtues, then you possess them all? If you could truly possess only one of these virtues, which would you choose? Which one is most likely to lead you to possess all the rest?
3. The question of being in a good mood is raised in paragraphs 23–25. Why is one's mood involved in the question of virtue? Clarify Appiah's argument regarding mood and behavior, and in your analysis of his findings, decide whether he is right or wrong. What have you observed about your

own mood and your behavior? Does your sense of virtue alter with your mood? Do you observe that others' sense of virtue is altered by their mood? What does it tell you about one's character if one's emotion can alter it?

4. In paragraph 23 Appiah says, "We can all agree that the more evidence there is that a person's conduct is responsive to a morally irrelevant feature of the situation, the less praiseworthy it is." What does he mean by that statement? Do we all agree with that statement? Does Appiah give us any morally irrelevant features of a virtuous act to help us understand his view? What would such a feature be? What would we consider morally relevant in a virtuous act? Consider some virtuous acts that you have heard of or that you have witnessed, and decide whether there can be reasons for not praising such acts. What could be a morally irrelevant detail that would make judging the act difficult?

5. The act of compassion seems to be an important virtue for Appiah. It is not specifically referred to as a virtue by the ancient Greeks, nor is it one of the seven heavenly virtues. What other virtuous qualities does Appiah mention in his discussion? What constitute Appiah's virtues? How universal do you think they are? How do they contrast with the seven deadly vices: lust, gluttony, greed, sloth, wrath, envy, and pride? How universal are these vices? Which four of these vices are the worst?

SENTENCE OUTLINE: See p. 126 of this manual.

BIBLIOGRAPHY: See p. 169 of this manual.

MICHAEL GAZZANIGA
Toward a Universal Ethics (pp. 415–432)

The beginning of this selection may be very controversial for some students. Gazzaniga has been criticized in reviews for his giving short shrift to philosophers such as Kant and Hobbes in this particular chapter (Chapter Ten) of his book. It is true that he reduces the work of several millenia's worth of philosophical and religious consideration of human nature to mere "stories." He puts this in such a severe way so as to distinguish supposition and guesses from scientific research, much of which is also guesses (but he doesn't mention that). The basic point is that science is beginning to be ready to take up the issues of ethical behavior and moral reasoning from an evolutionary point of view and perhaps overthrow some of the moral wisdom that is central to established religions. All of this may be upsetting to some of your students, but that should help stimulate class discussion.

I have suggested questions for class discussion that should open up the central issues and give students a chance to work out their thinking on whether a unversal ethics could be derived from what is known of how the systems of the brain function and how a social animal such as humans must behave if the species is to survive. Some of this will be a novelty to most of your students, so you may find the interplay of student opinions very stimulating.

One important issue in the passage has to do with the so-called hard-wiring of the brain. This computer metaphor may be distracting both to you and to some students, so it would not hurt to mention that it is only a metaphor and that its force may distort the idea. The point is that there seem to be predispositions of certain brains—something we all know about when we look at our talented neighbors or when we are told that we get one trait or another from "uncle Louie" or some other forebear. If it is true, as language experts now tell us, that the brain is hard-wired to develop language, then is it also possible that Gazzaniga's idea that it is hard-wired to respond to moral and ethical issues is realistic?

However, you'll see that the selection mainly aims at pointing to the beneficial effects of good moral judgment. What about bad moral judgment? If Gazzaniga is right about good social behavior, would it not also be reasonable to consider that antisocial behavior can be hard-wired too? And if so, what does that say about the role of evolution and the survival of the species?

SUGGESTIONS FOR CLASS DISCUSSION

1. Why does Gazzaniga call the wisdom of the ancients "stories"?
2. What is the difference between close-up and long-distance altruism?
3. Are human beings big animals? What is the point of Gazzaniga's suggesting so?

SUGGESTIONS FOR BRIEF ESSAYS

1. Review what Gazzaniga has to say about theory of mind, beginning with paragraph 15. Test his ideas by keeping track of your own encounters with people and your sense of whether or not his theory of mind is at work in you. Review his ideas on mirroring, and again explain either how your mind works in parallel with what he points out or how it does not mirror others.
2. Test the trolley problem by interviewing a good number of people, both young and old. See how they respond to the problem, and see if you can find a trend in the responses in terms of age, gender, or other distinctions. If you like, you can embellish the problem in such a way that it is more interesting for you. What ultimately are your conclusions about the ethical issues at stake and the attitudes of the people you interview?
3. Do you feel we all possess personal survival instincts? Are they inherited, or are they just socialized in us? Are you aware of your own survival instincts? Do you feel they have been developed by general social experience, or do you think they are genetic and thus evolutionary? How do your conclusions affect Gazzaniga's theories and his conclusions? How aware have you been of your survival instincts, and how have you dealt with them? If possible, cite specific instances of your instincts having helped you.
4. Examine James Q. Wilson's suggestions for universal ethics. Decide whether you agree with the items that he has chosen, and then examine each to see if it is universal. See paragraph 7, especially the last sentences. Wilson says, "All societies believe that murder and incest are wrong, that children are to be cared for and not abandoned, that we should not tell lies or break promises, and that we should be loyal to family." What else might you add to this list? Would Kwame Anthony Appiah see these as sufficient as universal ethics?

SUGGESTIONS FOR LONGER ESSAYS

1. Consider the problems raised by Joshua Greene in paragraphs 18 and 19. What are your ethical obligations to people who request funds that they assure you will save lives? When is it reasonable and ethical to refuse them? When must you satisfy them with your donations of money? If you do not provide funds for humanitarian purposes, are you acting unethically? Do you have a moral obligation to save other people's lives, including those of total strangers? Argue the case using examples wherever possible.
2. Write an essay explaining simulation theory (paras. 24–30) to an audience that has not read this selection. Explain what the theory says, including careful definitions as necessary. Then consider alternative theories and their difficulties. Research the theory, first by practicing it yourself and then by consulting others and asking them to practice it as well. How reasonable is the theory? Argue that it is important, or argue that it is not. What evidence can you bring to bear on the issues Gazzaniga explores in his essay?
3. Marc Hauser in paragraph 21 is quoted as saying that "if moral judgments were derived from rational processes, one would predict that people from different cultures, of different ages and sexes, would respond differently to a common challenge." He says that when different people are presented with a common problem they seem to react more or less similarly. That suggests a basic moral instinct. Set up a simple experiment presenting various people with a moral problem, and ask for an instant response. To what extent are people's responses similar, and to what extent are they different? See if you can either validate or invalidate what Marc Hauser suggests is true.
4. After having read this selection, write an essay that tries to convince an audience that ethics is the key to our survival as a species. Assume a doubting audience, but also an audience that is responsive to careful analysis and evidence. If possible, read some of the authors Gazzaniga cites

and include their testimony in your essay. In the process of writing the essay, include some of the brain research that implies a moral center or a moral function in the brain.

5. If there is a "moral reasoning center" in the brain, is it obvious that the brain will always indicate an ethical solution to any moral problem? Is it possible that there may be people whose brains either do not have a "moral reasoning center" or have a center that that may impel them to do awful things? If that is possible, then what are the legal responsibilities of the society and the legal consequences for the individual whose moral center malfunctions? Should people be held responsible whose brains are developed in such a way as to make them do antisocial and dangerous things?

SENTENCE OUTLINE: See p. 127 of this manual.

BIBLIOGRAPHY: See p. 180 of this manual.

ARISTOTLE

The Aim of Man

(bedfordstmartins.com/worldofideas/epages)

This has been a very popular piece, despite the fact that it is somewhat abstract and difficult. Students can see into the piece enough to translate the abstractions into practical ethical issues. Class discussion of ethical issues is always lively, in part because there always seems to be some significant piece of news that brings the question of ethics to our attention. Of course, there are many differences in the social circumstances of our time and that of Aristotle, and it bears some discussion in order to help students come to a better understanding of Aristotle's concerns. Some of the suggestions for class discussion reflect my interest in following up on historical distinctions. The entire character of the discourse—the pursuit of the good—is a novelty that attracts many students and stimulates class discussion. The question of personal happiness is very important to contemporary students, but so is the question of the good of the community. Seeing that there may be a connection between the two is very useful.

Students bring up the question of the passage's abstract nature, and I try to use those questions to help explore the rhetorical problems inherent in discussing the kind of subject Aristotle chooses. I also try to point out that moving toward the concrete is a modern—and probably necessary—strategy that ought to guide both my students's thinking and their writing. Certainly, they can see the value of the concrete in relation to the abstract when they work their way through the piece. I have been very pleasantly surprised at the eagerness of some students to come to terms with this piece.

SUGGESTIONS FOR CLASS DISCUSSION

1. Could Aristotle's views on the nature of goodness, happiness, and virtue be used as part of a religious document, the way the Ten Commandments are used? What would be the problems in discussing Aristotle in terms of religion?
2. Do Aristotle's views on happiness apply to you? What parts of it are most interesting to you and most relevant to your own life or your ambitions in life?
3. What qualifications would you have regarding Aristotle's definition of the most important good in human life?
4. How do you understand the nature of virtue after reading Aristotle?

SUGGESTIONS FOR BRIEF ESSAYS

1. Define the "highest good" twice: once as Aristotle seems to have seen it, and once as you see it.
2. How do Aristotle's recommendations for establishing the "aim of man" seem to compare with the advice we "absorb" from our own culture?
3. Aristotle proposes happiness as the highest good. If we did not choose happiness, what are some other possibilities? Is it possible that there really is another highest good?

SUGGESTIONS FOR LONGER ESSAYS

1. Imagine a name for your son or daughter (or both), and address an essay that constitutes an ethics to him or her. Try to include most of the major areas of concern that interest Aristotle, but avoid duplicating the things he has said.

2. Inventory Aristotle's essay for all the definitions he offers of "happiness." Offer your interpretation of what he means by the term. Try to clarify the meaning of the soul and its relationship to virtue and to the individual's quest for happiness. Is it true that happiness is the greatest good? Would it ever be necessary to give something up, to refrain from some pleasurable action, to be happy? What is Aristotle's view of the relationship of pleasure to happiness?

3. Relying on personal experience, on research on important figures, or on information you have regarding other people, attack or defend the proposition Aristotle makes in paragraph 30: "[W]e hold that the truly good and wise man will bear with dignity whatever fortune sends, and will always make the best of his circumstances, as a good general makes the most effective use of the forces at his command, and a good shoemaker makes the best shoes out of the leather that is available, and so in the case of the other crafts." Remember that it is important to offer definitions of key terms Aristotle uses as well as of key terms you introduce.

SENTENCE OUTLINE: See p. 128 of this manual.

BIBLIOGRAPHY: See p. 170 of this manual.

PART FOUR

WEALTH AND POVERTY

The six essays in this section consider the power and the responsibility of wealth as well as the nature of wealth itself. Alternative economic systems represent one point of focus in this section, while the entire issue of poverty and the responsibility of any economic system to address it either directly or indirectly are central to most of what is written here.

ADAM SMITH

Of the Natural Progress of Opulence
(pp. 441–451)

The Wealth of Nations is a complex and difficult book. Economists still hold it in high regard, as do historians of ideas. Indeed, much of its theorizing remains valid today, and in many ways it is the central text of modern capitalism. When it was first published, David Hume, a close friend of Smith, read it with interest and told him that it deserved a wide audience but that because it was reasoned so closely, it was not likely to get much readership at all. Smith's publisher, Strahan, was surprised that the sales were larger "than I could have expected from a work that requires much thought and reflection (qualities that do not abound among modern readers)." Therefore, it is clear that some time needs to be spent explaining some key ideas.

One of the more interesting aspects of this essay concerns Smith's assurance that he is describing a "natural" progression of "every civilized society" toward wealth. He almost seems to be taking a pre-Darwinian attitude toward the concept of developing systems. The natural progression, he claims, derives from the simple fact that agriculture produces more than the producers can consume. With the surplus, agricultural workers create a market in the town. Those in the town use the raw materials to manufacture goods that people in the country, as well as in the town, can consume; the town can then pursue foreign trade.

Because foreign trade is such an important issue in today's economy, it may be interesting for you to devote some attention to Smith's deep confidence in the value of land. In the eighteenth century, land owners were often landlords. Extremely wealthy land owners were always landlords. They rented portions of their holdings to small farmers, who raised livestock, grew wheat and other grains, and ultimately sold them at market and paid a handsome fee to the landlord. One problem in the system was that the people doing the actual work would virtually never be able to build up enough surplus to buy land on their own. That may explain, for example, why colonists in North America placed so much importance on their ownership and cultivation of land. Possessing land meant a continued stream of income as long as labor was available.

One important avenue of discussion might center on Smith's attitude toward capital. He sees ownership of land as a means of guaranteeing opulence. However, he does not talk about how one acquires land for cultivation except to say that in some countries land would not be available at a reasonable price. In this sense, Smith seems interested in the general system rather than in the individual members of that system. A comparison with the attitudes of Karl Marx only seventy-five years later might be very interesting. Marx reacted to the industrial revolution, which Smith was only just beginning to observe. Therefore, their viewpoints are quite different—but instructive.

SUGGESTIONS FOR CLASS DISCUSSION

1.   Have your students discuss what land represents for Adam Smith. Why does he emphasize it so heavily?
2.   What is the relationship today between the country and the town? How have things changed?
3.   Smith mentions nothing about poverty in this essay (and he says little or nothing about it in the rest of his book). Explore with your class the possible reasons he ignores the question of poverty.
4.   In paragraph 4 Smith says, "The inhabitants of the town and those of the country are mutually the servants of one another." How true does that seem to have been in his time? How true is it today?

SUGGESTIONS FOR BRIEF ESSAYS

1.   How would you defend Smith's views as expressed in this essay? In what sense is he right in establishing the "natural progress of opulence" as you observe it yourself? He describes the world as he knows it in his own time and then imagines how it might have become that way. How well does he satisfy your curiosity about the way in which nations grow rich?
2.   Smith places a great deal of faith in the value of land for maintaining wealth. Since most people today, including wealthy people, do not necessarily see their wealth in terms of land, what in our time might substitute for land? What would a wealthy person interpret as a secure or conservative capital investment?
3.   Argue in favor of or in opposition to Smith's statement in paragraph 8: "According to the natural course of things, therefore, the greater part of the capital of every growing society is, first, directed to agriculture, afterwards to manufactures, and last of all to foreign commerce." Because in the early 2000s the United States is in the midst of a "new economy," this statement will need to be examined closely and augmented. How would you continue the "evolution" that Smith observed?

SUGGESTIONS FOR LONGER ESSAYS

1.   In paragraph 3 Smith says, "If human institutions had never thwarted those natural inclinations, the towns could nowhere have increased beyond what the improvement and cultivation of the territory in which they were situated could support." What natural inclinations does he refer to, and how did human institutions thwart them?
2.   Write an essay that examines the accumulation of wealth in our time. How would you describe the natural progress of opulence in the twenty-first century? How do nations get rich and stay rich? What role would land play in the modern scenario for accumulating wealth? Is the question of surplus still important in the commerce between individuals or between nations?
3.   Smith makes a great deal out of the relationship of the country to the town. In 1776 and earlier, it was certainly true that the town subsisted on the produce of the country. It is also true that the economic intercourse of country and town produced wealth. Assuming that things have changed in the twenty-first century, what two groups today profit in a similar fashion and help each other produce wealth? What might be a modern equivalent for country and town?
4.   Examine Reich's discussion of labor in "Why the Rich Are Getting Richer and the Poor, Poorer." How does his analysis of the various segments of the economy affect your understanding of Smith's argument about "the natural progress of opulence"? What new "natural progress" is Reich talking about, and how will it affect you? How does it cause you to re-evaluate Smith's argument?

SENTENCE OUTLINE: See p. 129 of this manual.

BIBLIOGRAPHY: See p. 192 of this manual.

KARL MARX

The Communist Manifesto (pp. 453–479)

Most students are familiar enough with the author and title of this work that little preparation is needed before discussing what Marx has to say. You might point out by way of background that Marx is redefining communism for his time (and ours). The ideal of communism had been well accepted in his time as rooted in certain religious teachings stressing equal sharing of property and equal work. Robert Owen's 1825 experiment in New Harmony, Indiana, was based on his visionary socioeconomic theories developed in England, but it was also typical of many such experiments in the United States. Most famous in literary history was Brook Farm in West Roxbury, Massachusetts (1841–1847), started by the Rev. George Ripley. Most experiments of this sort were devised for religious or spiritual purposes, and all were severely limited in size. Some screened those who wanted to be admitted.

Marx is notable for his materialism—which is to say his lack of concern for religious or other special spiritual values. For him communism is not a spiritual adventure; it is an economic necessity. The inevitability of communism is one of the key points to be raised in discussing the *Manifesto*. Marx developed the view that in the sweep of history, communism in his time was as inevitable as was the end of feudalism. He regarded his social science concepts as scientific in their certainty. If your students have read Hannah Arendt, you will want to focus on this point and see how your students react to Marx's ideas in light of how they later were put to use.

SUGGESTIONS FOR CLASS DISCUSSION

1. Marx attempts to clarify communism for his audience. You might ask your students what they think his audience's views were. What did people living in the mid-nineteenth century think about communism? What do your students think of it today?
2. You should be able to develop a useful discussion based on the impressions your students have of communism after reading the *Manifesto*. You might consider how contemporary Chinese communism compares with what Marx proposes.
3. I think it useful to talk about the question of spiritual values. What is the role of religion in Marx's view? You might bring up his famous observation, "Religion is the opium of the people" (from the introduction to *Critique of the Hegelian Philosophy of Right*, 1844). See if the class can take a stand on Marx's communism as being devoid of religious values.
4. One important line of discussion should concern the recent failure of communism in the Soviet bloc. Some of your students will know something about the pains that have been suffered by communist nations in trying to convert to a market economy.

SUGGESTIONS FOR BRIEF ESSAYS

1. Define *proletarian* for our time. Begin with Marx's definition (footnote 4), and move on to your own.
2. Speculate on what antecedent social and economic conditions of Europe made *The Communist Manifesto* an important and influential document. Why was it written?

SUGGESTIONS FOR LONGER ESSAYS

1. Comment on Marx's rhetorical strategies in the second section. Does he deal fairly with all the objections against communism? What audience does he assume for his writing? When you have finished reading this section, are you sympathetic or antagonistic toward him? Since he feels communism is historically inevitable, why would he want to convince us of anything in regard to it?
2. Establish Marx's views of the family (refer to paras. 98–104). What does he recommend as its proper structure? Do you feel today's family is structured in more or less the same way as the family was structured in Marx's time? Do you approve of his suggestions for change?

3. Do you think Marx would agree with Machiavelli's views on the degree to which desired ends justify undesirable means? How far will Marx go to achieve communism? Does he seem to sympathize with Machiavelli's general advice?
4. What might Marx have said in response to Adam Smith's essay? How would he have attacked it? Write an essay from Marx's point of view dealing with the principal ideas in Smith's essay.

SENTENCE OUTLINE: See p. 130 of this manual.

BIBLIOGRAPHY: See p. 185 of this manual.

ANDREW CARNEGIE

The Gospel of Wealth (pp. 481–497)

The most powerful thing about this selection is that your students may have widely varying opinions on whether Carnegie is right in his contention that the natural order of things will produce vast wealth in the hands of the few. You may also find many different views on the question of whether or not such economic inequities as Carnegie praises are good or bad for the nation or the individual. Arguing against Carnegie is an interesting challenge because many students will find some of his basic points very congenial. The law of competition and the law of accumulation (remember what Ruth Benedict said about our society's urge to accumulate) may seem very reasonable to many students who are already living by those "laws."

Of course, the regulations and legislation of Carnegie's time were almost nonexistent for a long while. The *laissez-faire* economy produced many abuses that hurt labor directly, and it also produced many economic crashes that hurt everybody. The government's relaxation of many regulations in our own time have also contributed to the accumulation of great wealth in the hands of the few and also the periodic recessions that usually result from a mess that might have been avoided by regulation. But regulation, to Carnegie, would have simply impeded the improvement of civilization. Exploring this issue with your students should give you plenty to discuss and examine in class.

One of the most controversial aspects of this essay, which is complete, is that Carnegie is absolutely certain he is the best judge of how to spend money on behalf of the community. He constantly says that his spending large sums will do much more good for the community and the improvement of the race than if he gave small amounts of money to a large number of people. He is clear in his view that the mass of people will not use money wisely and will not provide for themselves the institutions that will lead to self-improvement. This is one of the familiar examples of patriarchal thinking that dominates the "robber barons" of the age. However, you may find that the majority of your students will agree with Carnegie on this point. You should have an interesting time discussing this issue alone.

I also point to the question of social Darwinism and would suggest that you describe the movement briefly and see to what extent your students understand it and agree with Carnegie's views on "improving the race." It's important to point out that the social Darwinists generally praised what seemed the natural way to develop society, but they did not always take into account the questions of morality that should enter into any discussion of social organization. You might find that raising moral issues—such as Carnegie's reputation for working his laborers hard and giving them as small wages as possible—will produce some powerful reactions from students.

SUGGESTIONS FOR CLASS DISCUSSION

1. What are the three possible solutions for what to do with a fortune?
2. Carnegie says that the inequality in the distribution of wealth is temporary. What does he mean, and why should that idea help satisfy us that his ideas are correct?
3. Carnegie says that "one of the serious obstacles to the improvement of our race is indiscriminate charity" (para. 20). Do you agree? Why?

4. In paragraph 23 Carnegie says that "the millionaire will be but a trustee for the poor." Do you think Carnegie is correct and that the millionaire is now a trustee for the poor?

SUGGESTIONS FOR BRIEF ESSAYS

1. To what extent is Carnegie in agreement with Ralph Waldo Emerson's views on charity and philanthropy in *Self-Reliance*? To what extent is it likely that Carnegie read and agreed with Emerson on basic issues that Emerson raises in his essay? Are you convinced by their views? Is indiscriminate charity a serious threat to our society? Is our welfare program what Carnegie might call indiscriminate charity? Would he approve of our welfare programs?
2. Carnegie ends his essay by saying that he thought that obeying the dictates of his *Gospel of Wealth* would someday solve the problem of the rich and the poor and bring "Peace on earth, among men Good-Will" (para. 24). Do you think that wealthy people should follow Carnegie's example? Bill Gates, who recently quoted from Carnegie's essay, has left his post at Microsoft and is devoting himself to giving away his wealth through his foundation. Do you feel such activity will "solve the problem of the Rich and the Poor" (para. 24)?
3. It's interesting that Carnegie approves of the estate tax that hits millionaires heavily. Considering that the estate tax affects a relatively small number of families in any given year, do you feel he is correct in his views? Why is he so rigidly in favor of this tax? Where do you stand on the issue? If your parents were enormously wealthy, would you want their estate to be heavily taxed? Would it be good for the nation if it were heavily taxed?

SUGGESTIONS FOR LONGER ESSAYS

1. What are the dangers of leaving great fortunes to the children of those who accumulated those fortunes? Carnegie talks in detail about how individual children are spoiled by wealth, but he also talks about the danger of creating a hereditary class. He was speaking in 1889 when such classes were evident in Great Britain and becoming evident in the United States and Canada in the form of "old money." What are the dangers to society of encouraging a hereditary class? To what extent has such a class already been in evidence in this country? What examples do you know of great wealth harming the children who inherit it?
2. Carnegie was able to accumulate such wealth in part by being energetic and clever, in part by taking advantage of opportunities made available to him by friends, and in part by the fact that there were very few governmental regulations that would have made accumulation more difficult. Also, there was no income tax to take a slice of his profits. Today regulations are an important issue. Defend or attack the concept of imposing regulations on industries for the purposes of controlling unfair competition.
3. Carnegie talks about how his views will help "bind together the rich and poor in harmonious relationship" (para. 1). What do you feel are the chances that his program would achieve such a result? To what extent are the rich and the poor in a "harmonious relationship" in your experience today? Do you think the current conditions with which you are familiar lead in the direction of producing such a harmonious relationship? Is it essential that such a relationship be obtained? How could it happen? Will it happen?

SENTENCE OUTLINE: See p. 132 of this manual.

BIBLIOGRAPHY: See p. 173 of this manual.

JOHN KENNETH GALBRAITH

The Position of Poverty (pp. 499–511)

This essay is important because it is the only essay in Part Four to focus on the condition of the poor. Galbraith exhibits a social conscience combined with a good understanding of economics. One of the things that I try to focus on is the general attitude students have toward poverty in America and the feelings they have toward the poor. Welfare reform in the last years of the twentieth century implied that the public's attitude was very different from what it was in mid century, and it is worth discussing your students' sense of how the nation feels about the poor today. Galbraith points out that the poor are degraded and that the result is that those who are well off hold the poor in contempt. This may be an unconscious feeling, and it helps to explore the issue with your students. Sometimes students are surprised by their own feelings.

The students' status as college students inevitably colors the discussion. And the student from the affluent suburbs will hold different views from the student from the city projects. Such differences of opinion and feeling should be a source of excitement in your classes while these issues are discussed.

An interesting point raised by Galbraith is that the poverty-stricken constitute a minority in the population today. It is a large minority but nonetheless a minority. In times past, the minority was the rich. Such a condition definitely makes the problem of dealing with poverty very difficult, simply because the wealthy majority holds the impoverished minority in contempt. The old question, "I made it, why can't they?" is all too commonly heard. Galbraith's observation regarding this change should be stressed.

You might watch for editorials or other current commentary on the plight of the poor in order to reveal the current attitudes of the press or government. The whole question of what the government is currently doing about poverty ought to be of immense interest to all students.

The question of cause and effect is important in the context of this essay, too, because the effects of poverty are felt by everyone. On the one hand, there is the rising toll in taxes required by poverty programs. On the other hand, there is the rising prison population, making the construction of new prisons a necessity for the first time in generations. Much crime is rooted in poverty, if not caused by it, and thus all members of society are affected by poverty.

Finally, one subject for class discussion probably should be the question of what our society ought to do about poverty. The fight against poverty is conducted by amateurs without power; however, all citizens are amateurs, and most of us feel as if we have relatively little power. But we all have the power of the vote, and such a discussion might help your students decide how they wish to use that power when they have the chance. An exploration of these issues is a good contribution toward an important social cause. The question of whether private resources or government resources ought to be used to rid the country of poverty is central and should be addressed.

SUGGESTIONS FOR CLASS DISCUSSION

1. Have your students define "insular poverty" (para. 8) by referring to specific islands of poverty that they either know firsthand or have heard about.
2. Open a discussion of the following question: What are the characteristics of insular poverty?
3. Ask if your students agree with what Galbraith says in paragraph 17: "The corrupting effect on the human spirit of unearned revenue has unquestionably been exaggerated as, indeed, have the character-building values of hunger and privation."
4. Explore with the class what they think Galbraith means when he says, "The concern for inequality and deprivation had vitality only so long as the many suffered while a few had much" (para. 16).
5. Ask students to clarify what they regard as the effects of poverty on our society. What effects has poverty had on them personally?

SUGGESTIONS FOR BRIEF ESSAYS

1. Galbraith admits that increased output cured the general condition of poverty when most of the population was poor. Explain why increased output cannot cure the poverty of those who remain poor.
2. Examine Galbraith's suggestions for how to cure case poverty and insular poverty. Do you feel that his suggestions will work if they are carried out as he recommends? His discussion of the cures for poverty begins in paragraph 17.
3. Galbraith blames our poverty on the nation's "insufficient investment in the public sector" (para. 22). Is he correct? What evidence have you to support your view? How could America invest more in people? Why should it do so?

SUGGESTIONS FOR LONGER ESSAYS

1. One of Galbraith's most basic premises is that America is now an affluent society. Examine in detail the society that you know for the purposes of validating or contradicting that assertion. Is America an affluent society? What are the signs of affluence? What qualifies as affluence? What are the results of affluence?

2. In paragraph 17 Galbraith admits that it may be possible to prevent self-perpetuating poverty by giving those who need it the basic income that would support a decent lifestyle. Do you agree with him? If you do not agree, how do you propose to ensure that those who need it will get the basic income they need? If you agree, how then should we proceed? What should we do to guarantee a minimum level of income for the poor? Is it possible to achieve that goal?

3. One important issue that Galbraith never mentions is the obligation that the affluent have toward the poor. Do you feel that those with affluence should make special efforts to help those who remain in poverty? What kinds of efforts should they make? Why should anyone think that the affluent are obligated to help the poor? Is it reasonable for the affluent to feel that other people's poverty is their own fault?

4. In discussing the causes of insular poverty, Galbraith cites the "homing instinct" (para. 10) as a possible factor. Examine the concept of the "homing instinct," and, relying on your own experiences and observations, qualify it as a possible cause of insular poverty. Why would it be a cause of poverty rather than a cause of wealth? Do the wealthy exhibit a similar "homing instinct"? Do people you know exhibit it? What seem to be its causes and its consequences?

SENTENCE OUTLINE: See p. 133 of this manual.

BIBLIOGRAPHY: See p. 179 of this manual.

ROBERT B. REICH

Why the Rich Are Getting Richer and the Poor, Poorer (pp. 513–531)

I did not choose this piece because Reich was an economic guru for the Clinton administration, but because I found the arguments and analyses in *The Work of Nations* to be compelling and worth examining. One thing I try to explain to students is that their training in language, writing, rhetoric, and explication of texts prepares them to think in ways that will eventually be valuable to them in the marketplace. Many students insist on graduating as pharmacists, electrical engineers, accountants, or some other such calling. They gain a greater sense of security when they enter the job market. However, English majors or history majors (and physics majors, too) enter a job market with no clear sense of their worth. Reich's discussion of the symbolic analysts provokes students into revaluing their education. I find it useful to get them thinking in terms of the future job market and its relation to their college preparation.

Reich is, however, a controversial figure. Despite his conciliatory skills, he sometimes sparks criticism. He has been attacked for being cavalier with figures and facts. Some commentators have pointed out his looseness with detail and his ability to overstate a position based on relatively little information. Such complaints began more than twenty years ago, and they may have prompted Reich to exert the kind of care he displays in this essay. Students may wonder why he footnotes so many details, when other economists rarely do. The answer is almost certainly that he wishes to defend himself against attackers.

It also has been said that Reich has changed his views on a number of important issues. For example, in earlier books, he has been less than kind toward Japanese corporations, reminding people that no matter how much money these corporations may bring in locally, they still owe little to the community and ultimately send their wealth home to Japan. In this book, however, he insists that the nationality of the corporation is essentially less important than its contribution to the local economy. Several of his positions have changed since he began writing, but rather than seeing that as a problem, I regard it as a symptom of his willingness to rethink his views. In any event, it is evidence of either inconsistency or growth, and we may decide on our own terms.

One amusing detail regarding Reich's use of the metaphor of the boats and the tide is the fact that at Dartmouth he was the outstanding cox in crew. It was the sport that ultimately qualified him for the Rhodes fellowship. He was probably thinking less of that, however, than of the stock market cliché that says that when the tide comes in all the boats rise—a description of an expanding economy.

Underlying all the careful analysis of routine, in-person workers, and the symbolic analysts, however, is the fear that Reich may be totally correct. If so, the implications for a stratified society are rather depressing. If the educational system remains as it is, the inevitability of the breach between the poor and the rich is potentially disastrous. One of the questions I like to pose to students is how we may avoid such extreme polarization.

SUGGESTIONS FOR CLASS DISCUSSION

1. Ask students to explore in what ways the potential for a split between the very rich and the very poor has serious social consequences in the United States.
2. What changes in education will be needed in order to avoid a society in which workers are rigidly stratified?
3. Have the class discuss the following question: To what extent is it true that "your real competitive position in the world economy is coming to depend on the function you perform in it" (para. 1)? Do your students feel this will be true for the foreseeable future? Or are things about to change?
4. With which economic group does Reich show sympathy?
5. What role will labor unions take in the economy of the future?

SUGGESTIONS FOR BRIEF ESSAYS

1. If you have personal experience of companies moving because they sought cheaper labor, describe what you feel the most important effects of such a move are.
2. What do you feel is the best educational preparation for doing well in a global economy such as the one we now enjoy? Describe that education beginning with preschool experience.
3. Reich defines three kinds of workers—routine producers, in-person workers, symbolic analysts. Are there any more kinds of workers? If so, describe them and their economic fate in terms similar to those Reich uses. Is their "boat" rising or sinking?

SUGGESTIONS FOR LONGER ESSAYS

1. If Reich is correct, there will be very few genuine opportunities in the new economy for people who drop out of secondary school. It seems clear that unless education is radically overhauled immediately, there will be many more dropouts than there are jobs for dropouts. What will be the long-range effects of such a condition?
2. To what extent is it the government's responsibility to provide jobs to people who would otherwise not be able to get them? For example, should the government provide jobs for routine workers if their opportunities dry up? What arguments favor or oppose such a proposal?
3. Should successful symbolic analysts be taxed disproportionately in order to provide Social Security and services to routine and in-person workers who earn much less? What impact would increased taxes have on symbolic analysts? Reich says they would probably want to work even if they did not make huge sums of money. If that were true, would they not be willing to pay extra taxes in order to secure social stability?
4. Are the distinctions that Reich describes similar to the class differences that Karl Marx focuses on in *The Communist Manifesto*? If they are, would any of Marx's suggestions be effective in providing an equitable distribution of wealth among the groups Reich defines?

SENTENCE OUTLINE: See p. 134 of this manual.

BIBLIOGRAPHY: See p. 191 of this manual.

MILTON AND ROSE FRIEDMAN

Created Equal

(bedfordstmartins.com/worldofideas/epages)

This essay does not appear on the surface to concern itself with wealth or poverty, but once you begin to analyze its messages, you should be able to convince students that it concerns both at a very important level. The Friedmans have been an important voice for conservative economics since the 1960s. Milton Friedman is the author of a very successful textbook in economics and has influenced the thinking of thousands of students and teachers over the years. He and his wife have made their voices heard in national politics, and now, in their "retirement," they use their foundation as a way of influencing parents and children.

The child of immigrants who worked and scraped in order to succeed in America, Milton Friedman is a good representative of the tough-minded and rugged individualist who respects the essential opportunities only the United States can offer. In that light it is easy to see that the thrust of the Friedmans' essay is to preserve opportunity and to guarantee the chances of entrepreneurs and hard-working people to succeed without artificial barriers being placed in their way.

The concept of laissez-faire capitalism is not especially foregrounded in the essay, but it is clear that the Friedmans believe in a free trade atmosphere and that they feel that the less government interferes with business, the better. Their essential argument is that equality as understood in the Constitution does not guarantee all people economic success. The entire argument regarding "equality of outcome" is devoted to establishing that the basic nature of life is unfairness and inequality in terms of intelligence, talent, and skill. Therefore, it is ridiculous to guarantee that all business people will succeed, that all working people will become well off, or that everyone, regardless of skills, will be more or less equal economically.

The Friedmans use a number of examples and arguments to make their case, and you may wish to go over the arguments point by point and decide which are most convincing. You may also wish to poll your class after they have read the piece to see how many of your students agree with the essay. If you find that a great many students agree with the essay, you may take that opportunity to compliment the argumentative skills of the Friedmans. Should most of your class not agree with them, you may wish to ask where the weaknesses in their arguments show up.

One point you may want to examine appears in paragraph 5: "A very different meaning of equality has emerged in the United States in recent decades—equality of outcome." You may wish to ask your students (a question appears below) whether or not it is true that the United States has decided that *equality of outcome* is what is meant by *equality* in the Constitution. Are current or past practices concerning welfare tantamount to guaranteeing equality of outcome? Why are taxes being collected for welfare families if that is not the case?

Milton Friedman is a monetarist, one who carefully manages the amount of money in circulation so as to control (not eliminate) unemployment and inflation. For Friedman, inflation is the most serious threat to the economy. Clearly, his theories have been adopted in part by both major political parties. Controlling inflation definitely helps preserve the wealth of the wealthy, and it also helps reduce the pain of poverty. But you may find that the theories concerning employment are more important for the poor than for the wealthy, because far more of the poor will be unemployed than the wealthy.

Free market economics has been in the ascendance since the late 1970s and looks as if it will continue and grow worldwide. Some of the problems that Karl Marx talks about in his concerns for globalism are evident now in the global economy. Most of your students will probably not be aware of the disturbances caused at meetings of the International Monetary Fund and the World Bank, but those who are should be encouraged to discuss their views about free market economies and globalization, both of which the Friedmans support.

During the discussion of this piece you might ask your students what consolation the Friedmans offer to the poor. Milton Friedman certainly knew what it means to be poor from his own experience. Do your students feel he is sympathetic to the conditions of the poor? Do your students think he is indifferent? What is his recommendation to the poor, apart from assuring them that life is not fair?

SUGGESTIONS FOR CLASS DISCUSSION

1. Have your students define some of the terms the Friedmans use: *equality, liberty, fairness.*
2. The Friedmans ask whether the ideals of equality and liberty expressed in the Declaration of Independence can be realized. Open a discussion of this issue by asking your students if they think such an outcome is possible.
3. Which current politicians seem most influenced by the Friedmans' attitude toward equality?
4. Does the term *equality,* as understood today in the United States, mean "Everyone should have the same level of living or of income"? What do your students think it means?
5. Have the class discuss what it would have meant for Jefferson to think that "some men were superior to others."

SUGGESTIONS FOR BRIEF ESSAYS

1. Personal equality, the Friedmans say, is important because it preserves individuality. Explain why this is such an important value in this essay.
2. Who are the "elite" that the Friedmans refer to? In our society today, who would such an elite be?
3. If the "elite" are the successful people in a society, those who know how to succeed and who hold the values that would guarantee success of the society, why would it not be a good idea for us to give them the right to rule over us? (See paras. 8–9.)
4. Explain the Friedmans' attitude toward slavery, both morally and economically.
5. If equality of opportunity is actually impossible to achieve, why do the Friedmans—and we—make such a point of emphasizing it?

SUGGESTIONS FOR LONGER ESSAYS

1. One of the Friedmans' basic views is that there should be very few restrictions on the operations of businesses in the United States. Likewise, individuals should not be encumbered by excessive taxes or obligations that would slow them down from making their fortunes. What aspect of the Friedmans' argument convinces you that their position is essentially correct and good for the nation? What aspect convinces you that their views would actually damage the economy of the nation?
2. How should a government that is striving to achieve equality of opportunity in the literal sense address itself toward the economy so as to support as much equality of opportunity as possible? If a child is born disabled, or born into a family that does not care for it, or into a family with dissolute parents who make it impossible for the child to get an education, what would a government's obligation be to that child? Does the government have any obligation? Consider some of the arguments of John Kenneth Galbraith in answering this point.
3. The Friedmans talk a good deal about liberty and its relation to equality of opportunity. Examine their argument and attempt to define what they see in the connection between the two. They emphasize that liberty is affected if opportunity is denied to individuals for any reason, such as prejudice of all varieties. In what ways are the Friedmans most anxious to promote liberty, and what would be the result of that liberty for the individual?
4. The Friedmans are seriously interested in education. They regard it as important in terms of promoting liberty and equality of opportunity. What problems do you see in your community that might call some of their thinking into question? Are all schools providing equal opportunity for all students? What kinds of inequities do you see or have you experienced that might affect the Friedmans' views about the role of education in providing equal opportunities for individuals?

5. Compare what the Friedmans say about equality with what Alexis de Tocqueville says about it. Do the Friedmans, two centuries later, interpret the concept of equality very differently from the way it was interpreted by Tocqueville? In what ways do they all interpret the term similarly? In discussing this point, establish the extent to which Tocqueville was concerned with economic equality. Examine, too, the evaluations that the Friedmans provide of Tocqueville's position, and see how much you agree with the Friedmans.

SENTENCE OUTLINE: See p. 136 of this manual.

BIBLIOGRAPHY: See p. 179 of this manual.

EDUCATION

The seven essays in Part Five cover a considerable range, demonstrating impressive changes in educational style and technique over a period of centuries. One constant among these essays is the need to respect the student and to humanize the process of education. The point of including these selections is to help students become more conscious of the fact that they are participating in a process that has been given very close examination. My feeling is that these essays will help students evaluate their own education as well as their attitude toward education in general. The selections should produce many opportunities for writing, if only because all our students have experienced the process of education and will have something to say about it.

HSÜN TZU
Encouraging Learning (pp. 543–553)

One of the advantages of beginning with an essay like Hsün Tzu's is that you have a chance to talk about principles of education that do not involve worrying about the job market, the earnings of college graduates, or the question of training for a profession. Of course, you will probably get plenty of resistance from students who have been convinced that the only real purpose of a college education is to get a job and rise in the economic ranks. Their resistance to Hsün Tzu should prove useful to you in the classroom. I expect a great deal of debate among students, and I think that you will enjoy coping with one of the bedrock issues of education: the development of the individual. Education for its own sake will probably not appeal to most of your students—it may not appeal to you—but it's an interesting antidote to the anxiety that prevails in modern colleges.

It will also be interesting to discuss the relationship of education to the moral improvement of the individual. The likelihood is that such a relationship would not have occurred to most students, except perhaps to some who may have gone to a religious school. One important point of discussion would be simply to ask whether your students think there is a connection between education and moral behavior—or whether there should be one. That may lead you to a discussion of whether or not your students think we are born with a moral predilection, which in turn should help you connect this essay to Kwame Anthony Appiah's "The Case against Character" or to Michael Gazzaniga's "Toward a Universal Ethics." In some of the critical discussions of Hsün Tzu he is connected to virtue ethics because of his feeling that education imparts ethics to one's character. You might have a profitable discussion about these issues.

SUGGESTIONS FOR CLASS DISCUSSION

1. Are Hsün Tzu's theories of education irrelevant in our modern technological age?
2. To what extent can one's moral nature be affected by education?
3. If Hsün Tzu were a student in your college, what would his major be?

SUGGESTIONS FOR BRIEF ESSAYS

1. Comment on Hsün Tzu's style—his use of analogies, comparisons, and examples that help him make his points. Which ones are most interesting to you, and which are most effective? Which ones would you expect to be most convincing for the reader? Which of his stylistic techniques can you most easily appropriate? Try writing a short essay that uses some of his rhetorical techniques.
2. In paragraph 5, Hsün Tzu says, "Pile up good deeds to create virtue and godlike understanding will come of itself; there the mind of the sage will find completion." How does this relate to the

process of education as you have experienced it in your classes? What is it that you are piling up as you move from class to class, from book to book, and from lecture to lecture? How does this piling up help you "create virtue and godlike understanding"?

3. Hsün Tzu gives examples of natural things that have been affected by alteration—for example, he points to a piece of wood that has been steamed into a circle and remains a circle even after it dries. How has your education changed you? What are you aware of that implies you are different now from when you began your higher education? Can you see changes in your friends? Do your friends back home see changes in you? How does education change people? Would the changes you observe please Hsün Tzu?

SUGGESTIONS FOR LONGER ESSAYS

1. If you play a musical instrument, comment on the principles that Hsün Tzu elaborates in his essay by relating the path or Way of mastering a musical instrument to the rituals that are involved in the lifelong process of learning and playing. Hsün Tzu had enormous respect for music because he saw in it the principles that he discusses as central to one's education. He also saw a moral purpose in the regularity and harmony of music itself. Comment on your own experiences in learning to play music and on relating that learning to this essay.

2. In paragraph 4, Hsün Tzu says, "When a man is careless and lazy and forgets himself, that is when disaster occurs." What examples do you have from your reading or from your experience that will bear out this observation? Hsün Tzu refers most specifically to the process of education, taking it seriously and keeping one's attention on the principles and the execution of each step in one's education. Can you verify his observation from your personal experience?

3. Consider the aphorism in paragraph 8: "In old times men studied for their own sake; nowadays men study with an eye to others." How true is this observation? If true, how does that affect the entire project of education? Write an imaginary letter to Hsün Tzu that takes this aphorism for its thesis, and explain to him what people do in their studies "nowadays." Tell him what you observe as the truth about what is happening in modern education.

4. Hsün Tzu mentions the desirability of making use of the erudition of others. Choose one of the subjects of your own study, and describe the ways in which you are making use of the erudition of others. Does that process ever result in people making use of your own erudition? Explain how you go about making use of the erudition of others and what the result of that process has been for you. Try to make a significant point about education by making use of the erudition of others.

5. Write an essay of your own titled "Encouraging Education." Write your essay to someone whom you know may not value education as much as you do, and who therefore needs a good deal of encouragement. Decide what methods you will use to convince your reader, and see if using some analogies in the style of Hsün Tzu can be helpful in getting your points across. Choose a thesis that either begins your essay or becomes embedded in one of your early paragraphs. Consider the importance of education to your audience and the rewards that your audience can expect from a good education. Study the main points of Hsün Tzu's argument, and see which of them is most useful in talking to a contemporary person.

SENTENCE OUTLINE: See p. 138 of this manual.

BIBLIOGRAPHY: See p. 181 of this manual.

JOHN DEWEY
Thinking in Education (pp. 555–569)

The more I read Dewey, the more compelling I find him. One reason I included this piece is that it is close in date to Maria Montessori's selection, and it shares some of the same issues and concerns. There is nothing here as intensely concrete as Montessori's disquisition on school furniture, although I feel confident Dewey would agree with her. But the thing that attracts me to Dewey is the clarity of his thought and the progressive nature of his prose. It resembles the step-by-step approach of some philosophers, such as Spinoza or Kant. Fortunately, it is less abstract than their arguments; nonetheless it has a seriousness that is imparted by the structure he chooses.

The pragmatic principles he maintains in this essay are important because they introduce into education a then-current philosophy based on results and practicality. Pragmatism developed in the late 1870s with the work of the American philosopher Charles Sanders Peirce (pronounced *Perse*), who was one of Dewey's teachers at Johns Hopkins. William James was also part of the pragmatist group. In essence, they evaluated ideas in terms of their consequences rather than by any abstract values. In this sense they were empirical, depending on observation and perception of effects. Dewey called his version of pragmatism "instrumentalism" or "experimentalism." He felt he could evaluate an idea in terms of what experience warranted as reasonable. In any event, the emphasis on the empirical works readily in examining the effectiveness of the classroom. A method that begins with providing experience to the student, from which then develop problems to be solved, which then demand information or data to help solve them, leads naturally to a situation in which the child will learn.

Dewey felt that knowledge depended on experience and that when an idea had good results it could be considered true. This kind of thinking depended on a larger view of society and the body politic, as implied in the title of his book, *Democracy and Education,* from which this selection comes. Democracy obviously spreads out the authority in the classroom. The student takes an active, not passive, role and thus helps direct his or her education.

People have called his approach "progressive education," and one of the natural results of his theories is to downplay the role of authority in the classroom. As he says, in a good situation the student may teach and the teacher may learn. Setting up an environment in which this can occur is an ideal that I and other teachers aspire to in the classroom, but rarely achieve.

Of course, I am not sure how much Dewey was thinking of the college classroom when he was writing in 1916. I am not sure how his theories would apply to the kinds of courses we teach, but that is a question you can pose to your own students. It might provoke a lively debate.

SUGGESTIONS FOR CLASS DISCUSSION

1. Would Dewey's ideas work well in the classes you now attend?
2. Do you think that Dewey's theories might account for the permissiveness some people feel is common in our current society?
3. Judging in the manner that Dewey judges, would you say that the result and outcome of his theories on education are good or bad?
4. How does Dewey define "ideas"? (para. 12)
5. Dewey writes about learning as a sense of discovery. Is this what learning has meant in the classrooms you are most familiar with?

SUGGESTIONS FOR BRIEF ESSAYS

1. Dewey describes how the value of ideas is recognized. Write a brief essay in which you clarify his thinking on the value of ideas, and offer your own way of evaluating ideas. How does your viewpoint differ from or agree with Dewey's?
2. In what classroom did you, as a child, have the most Dewey-like experience? Do you feel it was a positive learning experience? What was positive or undesirable about it?
3. Do you agree with Dewey's statement that "[i]nformation is vitalized by its function; by the place it occupies in the direction of action" (para. 19)? Give some examples from your own experience that demonstrate the importance or validity of his view.

SUGGESTIONS FOR LONGER ESSAYS

1. Describe the kind of classroom learning process that Dewey would absolutely condemn. Have you had any experience, either first- or secondhand, of such a classroom? What are the likely results of the process that Dewey would condemn? Do you agree with him that it should be condemned?

2. Write an essay that clarifies Dewey's concept of thought and thinking in education. How does thinking in education occur? What is its value? What is its result?

3. Read *Democracy and Education,* and try to describe the most important ideas that Dewey considers in designing a classroom for grade school students. Judging from your own educational experiences, how influential do you think Dewey has become? How important is the concept of democracy to Dewey? How does it inform his theories on the ways in which children should be permitted to act in the classroom?

4. Dewey constantly suggests that the problems students set for themselves are far more important to their education than any problems the teacher sets in advance. What problem do you see that invites an interesting solution? How does the solution to that problem contribute to your education?

5. Dewey asserts that thinking begins in experience, the perception of events. Others assert that thinking is abstract, not connected to action but totally intellectual in nature. Analyze your own thought processes, and try to come to a conclusion about the real nature of thinking. You may need to discuss this project with others to get a sense of what they understand to be the nature of their own thought processes. Reflecting on thinking is not as simple as it might at first seem. Be sure to refer to Dewey's description of thinking.

SENTENCE OUTLINE: See p. 139 of this manual.

BIBLIOGRAPHY: See p. 175 of this manual.

MARIA MONTESSORI
The Montessori Method (pp. 571–585)

This selection is taken from Chapter 1 of Montessori's classic book, *The Montessori Method,* published in 1912. I have focused on the second part of the chapter and her argument in favor of giving children more freedom, more space in which to explore and learn.

The first part of the chapter is filled with references to contemporary Italian scientific studies that impinge on the education of children. To some extent she is reacting to the prevalence of scientific inquiry in Italy at the time—"scientific pedagogy" was a term frequently used. However, it is important that we recognize that Montessori was a scientist and that her use of science in the study of children is the result of training that emphasized observation of the subject. Her complaints about science in the first part of the chapter focus on measurement—first of the physical body (with an emphasis on measuring the head) and second of the child's psychology, in the form of tests. The most important point she makes is that none of the scientific investigators took into account the behavior of the child in a learning environment. And to raise the stakes, she considers the question of the inner child, the spirit of the children in her school.

The success she had with *Casa dei Bambini* was remarkable. The students she worked with were slum children who were thought to be hopeless, but the environment she provided, along with the methods she used to train them and develop their intellect, created a marvel for the time. In other words, empirical evidence demonstrated the value of her program.

Because Montessori schools are ubiquitous in North America, you may well have a number of students who attended one. It might help to poll your class and see if there is anyone who experienced the Montessori method, and if so, ask at what level in his or her education. As in the case of the selection by Emerson, I am interested in the personal experiences of the students who read Montessori. What is their take on the likelihood of success or failure of her ideas in contemporary schools?

There is one other interesting detail that does not show up in the selection. Montessori constantly referred to her project in terms of "communitivity" because she wanted the children to be part of a larger entity consisting of themselves and their teachers, parents, and neighbors. Her attitudes may seem to anticipate communism, but she had no concept of the Stalinist version of history. She was in Barcelona in 1936 when it was a stronghold of antifascism, which implies that she had Communist sympathies. But her views were focused on schooling in relation to the support that all learning environments need in order to succced.

SUGGESTIONS FOR CLASS DISCUSSION

1. What would happen if a college course were taught in a manner that would please Montessori?
2. Do you think of your early schooling as having been a form of slavery? Did you feel confined and limited in the early years of school?
3. What is Montessori's attitude toward progress and its connection with education?
4. Did you experience restrictions in your early education that you now think may have slowed down your process of learning?
5. What do you imagine a teacher would do in a preschool Montessori classroom?

SUGGESTIONS FOR BRIEF ESSAYS

1. Write an essay that evaluates the use of school prizes in early education. How valuable are they? What might be their drawbacks? Do you consider college scholarships to be a form of school prize? How would you evaluate scholarships? Are they all alike?
2. Critique the environment in which you currently study and for which you currently use this book. Does it have any of the problems that Montessori found in traditional classrooms in Italy? Do her concerns about the school environment hold true in your current circumstances?
3. In paragraph 37 Montessori states, "Our joy is to touch, and conquer souls, and this is the one prize which can bring us a true compensation." Write a brief essay that attempts to define what she means by this statement.

SUGGESTIONS FOR LONGER ESSAYS

1. The selection ends with a quotation from Giuseppi Sergi: "Today an urgent need imposes itself upon society: the reconstruction of methods in education and instruction" (para. 46). What urgent needs do you perceive our own society faces in "methods in education"? Would any of Montessori's suggestions help us realize an improvement in contemporary education?
2. This selection is only part of Chapter 1 of her book, *The Montessori Method.* Read her book and offer an analysis of what you feel its most important points are. How much of what Montessori argued for in 1912 seems to have been incorporated into modern education as you have experienced it? How much more do you think we need to incorporate in order for our educational system to be truly excellent?
3. In paragraph 43, Montessori refers to the end purpose of education as understood by society. She suggests that in her time it had "no definite end." What do you think the end purpose of education is? Consider the experiences of Frederick Douglass and the theories of Ralph Waldo Emerson. What do they imply are the true ends of education?
4. Write an essay that takes into account some of the same principles and concerns as does Montessori, and title it "My Method." What do you feel is truly needed for education to progress and for improvements to be made in current schools? As much as possible, rely on your own experience or the experience of friends and acquaintances. Use comparison and analogy where possible, and focus on at least one concrete aspect of the educational environment. In the process, make your recommendations for a better educational system.
5. Montessori sees a connection between the rigid immobilization of children in Italian schools and the rigid immobilization of civil service office workers. She does not say directly that the situation of the adult worker is a product of the conditions of early education, but she definitely implies that this may be so. What would you suggest as the likely result of the current methods of early education in your society? What does early schooling prepare the adult to accept as normal in the work environment?

SENTENCE OUTLINE: See p. 140 of this manual.

BIBLIOGRAPHY: See p. 187 of this manual.

CARTER G. WOODSON

The Mis-Education of the Negro (pp. 587–603)

You may feel your first job is to suggest that this essay is not only about the "mis-education" of African Americans, but that it is about the fact that any minority group—especially any non-European group—may feel that it is being disserved by the education system in place either in the 1930s or today. While teaching in programs for minority students, I have heard students and some people working in the programs complain that the education system is for whites and that it does not serve the needs of minority students. These opinions essentially echo Woodson's arguments. For that reason, it is important to give students a chance to discuss this essay at large, particularly in relating it to their own experiences. Some students will be very much in Woodson's camp, but there will be many more who will counter his view with their own sense of how education has benefitted them.

It will be interesting to hear what your students think about Woodson's argument. Some, I am sure, will say that it is no longer relevant, if it ever was. Others will see it as partly significant but say that things have changed. Others may actually feel that the changes in education, such as those implied in the success of Black History Month, are no longer necessary. Still others may resent the fact that there is a Black History Month and will disagree that there should be a month set aside for the history of any minority group. The range of possible responses to this discussion will depend on how you conduct the class and on how open the students feel to controversial discussion.

In contrast with Hsün Tzu, Woodson discusses industrial education, which could lead you to a discussion of the relative virtue of an education that trains you for work and one that trains you to think. I'm sure you'll have plenty of conversation on this point. You might ask whether minority students would profit more from an industrial education than a classical education. While discussing this point, remind students that Woodson says learning to think is the chief goal of education.

SUGGESTIONS FOR CLASS DISCUSSION

1. Should there be one kind of education for majority students and another for minority students? If so, which kind is appropriate for each?
2. Woodson says that current education is Caucasian education and that "the Negro" student is being educated to be "white." Is this true? Was it true?
3. In paragraph 6, Woodson suggests that school essentially serves up propaganda. Based on your own experience, can you verify or discount this statement?

SUGGESTIONS FOR BRIEF ESSAYS

1. In paragraph 4, Woodson says that almost all the "successful Negroes" of his time were uneducated or had little or no formal education. Can this be said today of any minority groups? What do you think is the connection between education and success in today's world? Do you think that the connection is different for minorities today than it was in Woodson's time? How would you counter or support Woodson's interpretation of the relationship of education to success in the minority community?
2. How are individual students in today's secondary schools affected by having their ethnic cultural achievements either ignored or valorized? Woodson describes the effect on the African American student of European values being valorized. What effects have you observed on any ethnic group when the achievements of another ethnic group are valorized or ignored?
3. How has your education served your gender? Has it made you feel proud of your gender, or has it made you feel sometimes inferior? Has your education been gender neutral? If so, is that a good thing? Should education be gender neutral? How could an education be gender neutral?

SUGGESTIONS FOR LONGER ESSAYS

1. Look up the Freedmen's Bureau of 1865 to see what was done for freed slaves after the Civil War. What provisions were made for their education, and how successful was the program of

the bureau? Write an essay that gives your reader some insight into the historical background of Woodson's essay.

2. Woodson discusses classical education in terms of learning about "the Hebrew, the Greek, the Latin, and the Teuton and to despise the African" (para. 1). When Woodson went to school it was normal to learn Latin and Greek and sometimes Hebrew. Is it true that a modern classical education (which today may be considered the standard liberal arts curriculum at most colleges) must by definition "despise the African"? Should minority students necessarily avoid a classical education?

3. Woodson is very specific about condemning highly educated "Negroes" because they ignore their African culture when teaching history or literature or the sciences. Their training is in European, not African, traditions. Thus they are of little help to their African American students. Write an essay that either agrees—including highly educated members of any minority group—or disagrees with Woodson's view on the effectiveness of any specific member of a minority group on students. What is the problem? Is there a literature on this problem? Should these educated people not be teaching? Should they not be educated in a European tradition?

4. In paragraph 40, Woodson says: "There can be no reasonable objection to the Negro's doing what the white man tells him to do, if the white man tells him to do what is right; but right is pure relative." What does Woodson mean by saying that what's right is relative? Do you agree that in matters of education what is right is relative? What kinds of studies do not admit a relative "right"? In what areas of study is relativity inadmissible? If Woodson says that it's okay to do what someone tells you to do if it's right, but that what's right may be relative, then how can anyone know what's right?

5. Decide whether or not the educational experience you have had up to now has prepared you to be white, as Woodson says it does. Construct an argument that you feel will convince a skeptical reader that your position on this subject is right.

SENTENCE OUTLINE: See p. 141 of this manual.

BIBLIOGRAPHY: See p. 194 of this manual.

JONATHAN KOZOL

The Uses of "Diversity" (pp. 605–617)

Kozol's letter is interesting in part because it poses as an argument demonstrating the absence of diversity in the schools, yet the putative audience for his letter does not need an argument to be convinced of his views. He is preaching to the choir because it is Francesca who set the standard for the entire discussion. I have no idea whether this was an actual letter. Some of the material seems to be adapted from his earlier work, especially his article in *Harper's Magazine* in 2005: "Still Separate, Still Unequal: America's Educational Apartheid." So I think that like so many literary letters, this one is carefully crafted to appear to be casual, but clearly it is not. However, no such reservation can invalidate the views that Kozol maintains in this selection. The data he and others have gathered reinforce his view that the schools are largely segregated, although not by legal means.

You will probably want to discuss some of the personal experiences of your students to see how many of them will verify Kozol's views or take issue with them. The entire question of diversity is still being argued, and you will find some students who may have the courage to speak out against it even though they know it is a rallying cry of some educators. If there are arguments against diversity, you will have a lively class discussion. Of course, all your students will know that there is a politically correct answer to any questions about racial discrimination, segregated schools, or the need for diversity. Getting them to open up and speak their mind will depend on the atmosphere in the class. Some classes will feel much more comfortable with this material than will others, which in itself would make an interesting subject to write on.

If you read some of the reviews of *Letters to a Young Teacher,* you will find some interesting responses that you can use in your discussion.

SUGGESTIONS FOR CLASS DISCUSSION

1. What are the advantages of diversity in the schools?
2. To what extent is diversity essential to a democratic nation?
3. Do most students today have an equal opportunity to get a good education?

SUGGESTIONS FOR BRIEF ESSAYS

1. Laws have been in place since 1954 to promote diversity in the schools. Why does it seem impossible to legislate diversity in the schools? What are the limits of the law, and how can a nation ignore the spirit of the Civil Rights Act and *Brown v. Board of Education*? How have the laws been avoided?
2. Kozol points out that teachers "are participating in deception of their students" (para. 16) by not telling them they are studying in segregated schools. Should teachers tell their students such a thing? Should six year-olds be told there is no diversity in their school and that they participate in an apartheid education?
3. Write a brief essay in which you defend or attack the proposition that most students in your state are in a "racist education system" (para. 31), whether they know it or not. Explain your position on this question by relying on personal experience as well as on any data that you can find regarding the educational system you know best. Be sure to conduct interviews with teachers and students and ask their views on this question.
4. Look up the background of *Plessy v. Ferguson*. What prompted the debate in 1896, and what compromises were made at that time? Were the compromises made with goodwill, or were they essentially cynical and politically motivated? What was the outcome of the legislation? Did the legislation work? Was it a good law, or would Thoreau have disobeyed it?

SUGGESTIONS FOR LONGER ESSAYS

1. Kozol went to school in Newton, Massachusetts, in classes that were almost entirely white from grade school to high school. There was little or no diversity in that school system. Why would people not complain of lack of diversity in such schools? What would be missing from the educational experience of white students in an all-white school system? Would they be aware that they were missing anything at all? Why would such a system not be desirable, and why would it need to change?
2. Do some research and learn what you can about *Brown v. Board of Education*. What did the resultant laws respond to in the environment of 1954? What were the arguments in favor of and against the laws that were enacted? Was this a regional issue limited to the South, or was it a national issue relating to all parts of the nation? What were the hopes of the people who were in favor of the outcome of the law? How long did it take to initiate action to begin integrating the schools? What were the reactions of the citizens, black and white, across the country? Which groups of citizens were most hopeful for a good outcome? Which were most enthusiastic in passing the law? Which most enthusiastic in upholding it?
3. What is the "secret curriculum" Kozol refers to in paragraph 38? Have you experienced the kind of innuendo that he describes, or has the secret curriculum taken a different form? Based on your experience in education, what is the secret curriculum that you are most aware of as you study? Are others aware of it? Is it just part of the "system," or is it something that is limited to individual teachers, students, or administrators? Do those who are part of the system seem aware that there is a secret curriculum?
4. Kozol's argument centers on all black and Hispanic schools in pockets of poverty in inner cities. The lack of diversity there tends to reduce the amount of money and the support necessary for a first-class education. If there were a school that was all black and Hispanic in a wealthy neighborhood with substantial funds, supplies, and technology and truly gifted teachers, would that school still need diversity to consider itself successful? Would such a school be able to deliver a first-class education to its students? Would Kozol praise such a school?

5. In paragraph 16, Kozol talks about "the moral progress that our nation has made." What moral progress is he talking about? What are the moral issues involved in this discussion of diversity in the schools? Why does he talk about moral issues at all? If you have studied any of the selections in Part Three, "Ethics and Morality," bring to bear the thinking of Douglass, Murdoch, or Appiah on this question. Is it realistic to cite moral issues in relation to the needs of children in primary education?

SENTENCE OUTLINE: See p. 143 of this manual.

BIBLIOGRAPHY: See p. 183 of this manual.

HOWARD GARDNER
Designing Education for Understanding (pp. 619–643)

The chapter from Gardner's *The Disciplined Mind* that appears in *A World of Ideas* (Chapter 6) does not really do total justice to the entire argument of Gardner's book. I chose it because it is a carefully argued chapter that emphasizes the kind of education that I think all children can profit from and that in some cases many children do not really receive. What is not present in the chapter are some of Gardner's central issues as presented in his book. For example, he mentions several times that he hopes to impart a deep understanding of truth, beauty, and goodness in the children educated by his system. He also emphasizes that it is better to study a few things in depth than many things superficially. Naturally, he agonizes over what must be left out if that procedure is followed.

Gardner focuses on three main issues that figure in the rest of his book, but which are not entirely obvious in the chapter presented here. He does not suggest a program for mathematics, but he does suggest programs of study for the other three areas that he emphasizes. For example, for science, he proposes a very careful and detailed study of the principles of evolution. This may be controversial in some areas of the country, but because of "erroneous conceptions" about evolution, Gardner feels it essential to study the idea in depth. In the area of the arts, Gardner suggests a program of study of the music of Mozart, particularly *The Marriage of Figaro*, an opera that has a social quotient. Finally, in the area of history, he recommends a close study of the Holocaust, if only because there have been many misconceptions of this event, and most students have only a vague awareness of its importance. You can see a bit of his program in paragraph 57 in the selection.

One source of controversy that may stimulate classroom discussion has to do with his portrait of the principles of the University of Phoenix, which emphasizes job preparation and training rather than broad education. It is a practical education taught by practitioners rather than scholars. Gardner is aware of the virtues of such education, but he feels it is inappropriate as a basis for general education. Some students will argue about this point, and it would be good to let them explain their position and then to contrast it with Gardner's.

SUGGESTIONS FOR CLASS DISCUSSION

1. Gardner says many educational systems have floundered. Why is this so? (See para. 8–9.)
2. Is it true that people whose names are in the first half of the alphabet are at greater risk for cancer?
3. What pitfalls undermine historical thinking? (See para. 39.)

SUGGESTIONS FOR BRIEF ESSAYS

1. Which of the areas that Gardner cites—mathematics, science, arts, or history—is most comfortable for you? What do you notice about your own ways of thinking that make that discipline most comfortable? Are you aware of a disciplinary way of thinking that makes the subject of that discipline come alive and makes you more likely to develop accurate notions rather than misconceptions about it?

2. Why does the University of Phoenix deem it unnecessary for students to study liberal arts? Why does Gardner feel that it is essential to study the liberal arts? Where do you stand on this issue? What are the most important areas of study for you at this point in your life? Do you sense a difference between being trained and being educated?

3. In paragraph 28, Gardner discusses how teachers are complicit sometimes in promoting educational misconceptions, saying that "the villains include a text-test context," which he condemns. What is he talking about, and how frequently have you yourself experienced that kind of approach in your classes? Is there any way you as a student can effect change in such an approach to learning?

SUGGESTIONS FOR LONGER ESSAYS

1. Examine the four approaches to achieving an education for understanding, beginning in paragraph 44. Consider each in turn, and decide how likely each is to create the kind of educational experience that Gardner hopes for. What are the weaknesses of each of the suggestions, and what additions can you make to the program? How would these approaches have improved or hindered your own personal education? Would you want these approaches in effect for your own children?

2. Starting with paragraph 15, Gardner introduces his "alternative educational vision." What kind of education is his program an alternative to? What are the most important elements of Gardner's educational vision? Do you think his plan would be feasible in your primary and secondary school system? How would it differ from your own education? Would you have preferred Gardner's plan, or do you feel your own schools' plans were just as desirable?

3. Do some research and find out where Ruby Bridges Hall is today and what her education has helped her achieve. What seem to be her principles of education today? What seem to be her current hopes and expectations for the schools?

4. Beginning in paragraph 33, Gardner raises the interesting claim about science that "correlation does not mean causation." This is an important point because so many people think simplistically about what causes certain occurrences. Research the causes of lung cancer and the relationship of smoking to lung cancer. Consider what Gardner has to say about causation, and find out all you can via medical Web sites, books, and other sources about lung cancer causation and what theories of the disease's causation may be erroneous or questionable.

5. In paragraph 80, Gardner talks about technology as a helper. This is one of the "other players" he refers to as essential or helpful in achieving a quality education for students in the primary and secondary levels. What is your position on the use of technology in the schools? Some school systems simply do not permit the students to use computers or other technological devices. Other school systems invest many thousands of dollars on computers, iPads, and video systems to help students, even those in the early grades. Consult some of the online literature on technology in schools, combine that research with your own experiences, and establish what you feel is the ideal approach to using or not using technology in the primary and secondary schools.

SENTENCE OUTLINE: See p. 144 of this manual.

BIBLIOGRAPHY: See p. 180 of this manual.

RALPH WALDO EMERSON

On Education (bedfordstmartins.com/worldofideas/epages)

The first part of Emerson's essay, which I have omitted, is relatively general and addresses the overall project of education in the state. For example, Emerson points out that the United States, "for aught I know for the first time in the world," has instituted universal education, "thus deciding at the start the destiny of this country." He also discusses some of the subjects he feels are important, such as the sciences and literature. Some of his views are limited and limiting, and I have chosen to include what I feel is the "meat" of the essay, the second part.

Emerson was famous as a speaker and was loved by his students and the parishioners in his Unitarian church. He began reading Eastern philosophy and learning about Eastern religions, and eventually he reacted against the essentially Puritan background that had been transmitted through his father and other ministers who had helped train him. He delivered the famous "Divinity School Address" on July 15, 1838. The address was expected to be inspirational to the senior class; instead, it laid out his misgivings about some of the basic tenets of Christianity. As a result, Emerson, famous though he became, was not welcomed back to Harvard for some thirty years. He had scandalized the university.

One thing you will note from the questions and suggestions for writing at the end of the selection is that I chose to aim this essay at your students and ask them to qualify it in terms of their own experiences. Much that Emerson says is basic, but almost cryptic. For example, the injunction to "respect the pupil" can be interpreted in any number of ways, and it will be interesting to see how your students respond to that idea. Likewise, Emerson's constant hymn to nature, a theme he maintained all his life in prose and poetry, is worth close examination and analysis. I confess that Emerson's views have me thinking carefully about my own methods as a teacher. His concern for how teaching the masses results in addressing the slower students rather than the brighter, more independent students has made me review the ways in which we need to structure our classes, whether large or small. I think it worthwhile for us to discuss these basic issues with our students in an effort to help them take their own education very seriously.

SUGGESTIONS FOR CLASS DISCUSSION

1. How different are modern students from the students Emerson describes?
2. How would Emerson react to the style of teaching that you encounter in your classes?
3. Emerson describes some of the problems facing the average teacher. What are they? Do these problems persist today?
4. Describe the ideal student. Describe the ideal teacher.
5. What have you personally learned about nature, and how did you learn it?

SUGGESTIONS FOR BRIEF ESSAYS

1. In writing about education for the masses, Emerson sees problems. He insists that education should be one on one. How do you react to this idea? What have been the most positive experiences you have had with mass education?
2. In paragraph 14 Emerson states that the secret of learning is patience. Describe your own positive (or negative) experiences in education involving either your patience or the patience of someone else. How did patience affect the outcome of whatever learning endeavor you took part in?
3. In paragraph 15 Emerson seems to focus on suggestions for improving education in grade school. How well would his suggestions work? Which ones seem most likely to be effective, and which ones seem most to represent his most basic values regarding education?

SUGGESTIONS FOR LONGER ESSAYS

1. Emerson is not entirely in favor of rules. He states, "A rule is so easy that it does not need a man to apply it; an automaton, a machine, can be made to keep a school so" (para. 13). Assuming that he may be right, how well does the computer (a machine) teach? What are your experiences in learning with the computer as your teacher? Does the machine have any of the virtues of the kind of teacher Emerson would approve? Can the machine nourish your soul, the way Emerson feels that fine teaching can?
2. One of Emerson's most famous essays is "The American Scholar." It was written in 1837 and represents a kind of declaration of his intentions in life. In it are many of his ideas on education and on the uses of education. Read "The American Scholar" and write an essay that examines it from the point of view of helping to expand Emerson's views on education. Does he seem to be the kind of teacher from whom you would have learned a great deal?
3. Write an essay in which you explain what Emerson means by his constant emphasis on the natural way to education. What are your views on how the basic nature of students can be best used

to help in their education? Do you think the structure of education as you have experienced it respects these views? If possible, read the descriptions of curricula for various grades, and ask yourself whether the material progresses in a natural way to help the student.

4. Write an essay in which you describe what you have learned from someone who is not by training or vocation a teacher. How much of that learning depended more on you than on that person? How much did that person actually teach you, and what was the result of that teaching? Do you consider that situation a good model for education? Why or why not?

5. In one of his complaints about education, Emerson states, "In education our common sense fails us, and we are continually trying costly machinery against nature, in patent schools and academies and in great colleges and universities" (para. 8). (A patent school is run by a town or state.) To what extent does common sense fail contemporary education? What costly methods or "machinery against nature" are being developed that seem to contradict common sense? Do you feel that common sense has a real chance in modern education?

SENTENCE OUTLINE: See p. 146 of this manual.

BIBLIOGRAPHY: See p. 176 of this manual.

PART SIX

GENDER AND CULTURE

On the surface, the question of gender seems simple enough. Most people are comfortable with the assigned gender roles of men and women in our culture, but the seven authors in this section bring some of our preconceptions into question. Some cultures do not assign gender roles based on the sex of the individual; some cultures have assigned limiting gender roles that limit, as John Stuart Mill tells us, the opportunities of a large part of society. As a utilitarian he argues that modern society wastes the productive work of women, who constitute half the culture. Margaret Mead examines the varieties of primitive cultures in their attitudes toward gender obligations. Germaine Greer argues that masculinity is a cultural construct, not a biological imperative. Judith Butler examines the case of a boy raised as a girl—a case that calls into question many assumptions about gender. Finally, Karen Horney describes certain habits of mind that may be thought of as culturally induced but that may also reflect genuine differences in individual minds.

MARY WOLLSTONECRAFT

Of the Pernicious Effects Which Arise from the Unnatural Distinctions Established in Society (pp. 653–667)

This is a very difficult piece to work with—at least for many students. The problem is not in what is being said so much as in the way Wollstonecraft says it. Her style, typical of much eighteenth-century prose, may seem turgid to twenty-first-century readers. Facing up to that issue at the outset can help smooth the way to a good discussion. In any event, the difficulties are not serious, and a careful examination of the points raised in the essay will generally overcome any difficulties with style.

You might point out right away that this is one of the earliest and most important documents in the movement for women's liberation. You may find it useful to comment on Wollstonecraft's background: she was known as a relatively free-thinking person regarding marriage and religion. She and her sisters began a girls' school in England at Newington Green. It ultimately failed for financial reasons, but she did write a book on education, *Thoughts on the Education of Daughters* (1786). She also wrote travel literature and wrote about the French Revolution after observing it firsthand. Her essay reprinted here is the product of a generally inquisitive mind.

Wollstonecraft lived with the American adventurer Gilbert Imlay, had a child by him, and attempted suicide when he left her for an actress. When she met William Godwin, well known as a radical thinker, she fell in love, made an unusual marriage (they kept separate circles of friends), and subsequently died from complications in childbirth.

SUGGESTIONS FOR CLASS DISCUSSION

1. You might review Claire Tomalin's *The Life and Death of Mary Wollstonecraft* (1974) and present some details of her biography. Students are inevitably fascinated by the liveliness of Wollstonecraft's life. They have little concept of how anyone in the eighteenth century lived, so it is certain to provoke discussion.
2. It is generally easy to generate discussion on the question of women's independence and liberation from this piece. You might ask your students how intense they feel Wollstonecraft's emotional commitment is to women's independence.

3. The cool, rational tone of Wollstonecraft's appeal may surprise some students. It is worthwhile examining her argument to see how logical it appears to most students. You might experiment by asking whether they think she is governed more by her head or by her heart. Mention the usual prejudices against women on this point.

SUGGESTIONS FOR BRIEF ESSAYS

1. Define the phrase *pernicious effects* on the basis of what is stated in the essay.
2. Is it possible to compare women with property on the basis of this essay?
3. Clarify in what way the "unnatural distinctions" affecting women in society cause them to behave as Wollstonecraft says they do. Do you feel it is a genuine cause-and-effect relationship?
4. After reading a biography of Wollstonecraft, do you find her essential message in this essay more understandable? (This, of course, could also be a longer essay.)

SUGGESTIONS FOR LONGER ESSAYS

1. How much have things changed since Wollstonecraft's day? Are the problems that beset women in the eighteenth century completely solved? Are you surprised at what Wollstonecraft says about the situation of women?
2. The question of what a woman's duties should be pervades the selection and especially dominates paragraphs 15, 16, and 17. As clearly as possible, clarify what Wollstonecraft feels a woman's duties are. Do you agree with her views? Try to use the rhetorical technique of allusion in writing on this question.
3. Ironically, Wollstonecraft died in childbirth. Establish Wollstonecraft's attitudes toward motherhood, particularly in reference to paragraphs 7 and 16. Have these attitudes changed radically in our time? Do you or your friends share her basic views? By using episodical observations, make a case for accepting or rejecting her views.

SENTENCE OUTLINE: See p. 147 of this manual.

BIBLIOGRAPHY: See p. 194 of this manual.

JOHN STUART MILL
The Subjection of Women (pp. 669–687)

One thing I did not mention in the text is the nature of Mill's paragraphing. It is obvious that he likes paragraphs that are sometimes two pages long, a practice that has been long abandoned. You might want to talk with your students about the kind of attention that these paragraphs demand and the rhetorical advantage in his time—and the disadvantage in our time—of not breaking the page visually. As I have said elsewhere, paragraphing is a relatively new invention in writing, and except for the training we receive in grade school and high school, there are no real rules to guide a writer. The business of the topic sentence is a case in point. One thing you might ask your students to look for is the topic sentence in some of the larger paragraphs. It would also be an appropriate challenge for them to discuss with you what they see as the rationale for Mill's paragraphing. Obviously, they would be grateful for the subheads that Singer and Mason or Leopold use, and you might point out that their practice is a result of their adhering to journalistic principles of writing.

The selection here is the first part of Chapter 4 of *The Subjection of Women.* I have tried to focus on the key elements in this chapter, much of which is devoted to the differences between men and women and between husbands and wives. I think the most important issues are the ones I cite in the introduction: simple justice for a large part of the human race and the avoidance of wasting the natural resources of half the race. Freeing women to participate in the general work of the world seems so obvious to most of us now that it hardly needs to be argued. However, you will see immediately in your classroom that Mill's view is an ideal and that not all your students will agree with it. Some will disagree with great seriousness.

You may also see some disagreement in your class about the question of whether our society has in fact rid itself of the subjection of women. Some of the women and perhaps some of the men in your class will want to qualify the nature of social progress in that area. But I think the most discouraging thing you are likely to encounter is the essential indifference of women to this argument. My sense is that the excitement of the feminist movement of the 1970s and 1980s has waned so considerably that it may be a struggle for you to get the point across that Mill is talking about the 1860s, but that the situation he describes could still be relevant to the twenty-first century. I hope you have a wide variety of opinions in your classroom. If you do, you will find this a stimulating essay.

I'm taken, too, by Mill's antagonism toward charity. He seems so much in agreement with Carnegie that I'm a little surprised. This is a key point in this selection if you extend your discussion of charity to our current practices, both private and public. Some women, especially single mothers, depend heavily on charity in our time, and it might be said that the practices of welfare tend to keep them dependent and make it all but impossible for them to climb out from economic subjection. The question of charity in our time is often politically loaded, so it would be a very lively discussion if you have a class that has a diverse political constitution.

Then, of course, you will also find both men and women in your class who will protest that there is no real subjugation of women in our society, except in limited situations. You will be fortunate if others in your group take issue with that point of view. But apathy toward the question may be the worst thing you face. For your sake, I hope there is enough controversy in this selection to avoid anything like that.

Incidentally, I ask a question about Mrs. Grundy below. She was a character in Thomas Morton's play *Speed the Plough* (1798). She was the guardian of propriety, a tyrannic imposer of proper behavior, and became a stereotype that lasted into the twentieth century.

SUGGESTIONS FOR CLASS DISCUSSION

1. If you think women are now free, do you feel that humanity is better off?
2. Mill says, "Marriage is the only actual bondage known to our law" (para. 2). Is that still true?
3. How effective is Mill's argument concerning justice for women?
4. What is the moral influence of women?

SUGGESTIONS FOR BRIEF ESSAYS

1. In paragraph 8 Mill talks about men's desire to be admired by women. He mentions a display of courage as one quality women admire. What other qualities have you discovered that women admire? If you are male, do you possess the qualities women admire? Do you think the qualities women admire are really desirable in a man? If you are a female, what qualities do you most admire in a man? Do you find many men with those qualities? Do men value those qualities as much as you do?
2. What concrete evidence do you have from your personal experience that tells you that women's opinions definitely affect men's behavior? Try to use examples from your immediate environment and from people you talk with. Have you seen women's opinions change men's behavior in any public venue, such as television or politics?
3. To what extent have you found the issues raised in this selection to be no longer relevant to our modern way of life? Interview men and women who have read this selection, and quiz them on what their views are. Are they as concerned about the subjection of women as Mill was? Talk with some people who have not read the essay, and ask them if they are aware of the subjection of women in modern culture. What are their views? Do they corroborate your views?

SUGGESTIONS FOR LONGER ESSAYS

1. In paragraph 13 Mill says, "It is often said that in the classes most exposed to temptation, a man's wife and children tend to keep him honest and respectable." What are the classes most exposed to temptation? Is it your view that a man's wife and children tend to keep the husband honest and respectable? Scour the national news for scandals, and see to what extent a man exposed to temptation is kept free from trouble by a wife and children.

2. In paragraph 14 Mill says, "Whoever has a wife and children has given hostages to Mrs. Grundy." Find out who Mrs. Grundy is, and then decide exactly what Mill means by his statement. Look up Mrs. Grundy in the library or online, and decide exactly how she fits into the argument that Mill defends. Then decide whether or not you think Mill was correct in his own time and is correct today. Who are the Mrs. Grundys of our time?

3. Judging by Mill's descriptions of good and poor marriages, what seems to be an ideal marriage from his point of view? Try to accommodate all the issues that Mill raises in relation to marriage, and describe the kind of marriage he would have most approved. What for you describes the ideal marriage? Try to be as specific as possible in determining not just the qualities of a mate, but the qualities of the relationship. Mill talks about many kinds of marriage that seem essentially to portray two people just putting up with each other. How can one hope to avoid such an outcome in marriage? Use examples of marriages that you have known to help you establish what you feel is the best kind of modern marriage.

4. Find a copy in the library or online (http://ebooks.adelaide.edu.au/m/mill/john_stuart/m645s/) of John Stuart Mill's complete book, *The Subjection of Women,* and read some or all of the first chapter. Comment on the way in which Mill establishes his position, and decide whether or not he addresses men or women or both. Ask yourself if you feel the argument is threatening to us today or if you think it might have been threatening to people in Mill's own time. The original publication was met with disbelief on the part of some and disregard on the part of others. What would have produced a negative reaction to his book in this first chapter?

SENTENCE OUTLINE: See p. 148 of this manual.

BIBLIOGRAPHY: See p. 187 of this manual.

VIRGINIA WOOLF

Shakespeare's Sister (pp. 689–705)

This is a famous essay, and deservedly so. I find that it is an especially relaxed way into some of the issues that have plagued talented women up to today. Perhaps the word *talented* is one that your students will pick up and then try to expand upon. However, you might point out that the book from which this essay comes, *A Room of One's Own,* was built upon two invited lectures given to the women of Girton and Newnham Colleges, Cambridge. These were the first colleges to admit women at Cambridge, and therefore one can assume that in speaking to these women Woolf was especially interested in talking about talented women and the extreme frustrations that accompany the gifted who are restrained from using their gifts.

Consider the question of how Woolf perceives her "basic capabilities" and her "combined capabilities," as well as the relationship of her capabilities to how she actually functions. This selection is interpretable in terms of justice because Woolf implies that in order to be able to realize her potential, she must have the necessary basic requirement of a place to work and an outlet for her work. You might ask your students to decide whether Virginia Woolf is talking about the question of justice, and not just the question of feminism.

I'm quite taken by the style of this piece, and I think that a discussion of tone is very appropriate. A discussion of some of the writers that Woolf mentions would be appropriate as well. In the early part of the essay, in paragraph 3, Woolf introduces some of the great women characters in literature, beginning with Clytemnestra, who murders her wayward husband, Agamemnon, when he returns home from

Troy with his mistress. The list ends with Madame de Guermantes, the woman ultimately rejected by the homosexual Charlus in Proust's *Remembrance of Things Past*. Woolf is very careful in all the details of the essay, a point that might be of some help to young writers.

Her figurative language is also very impressive. Her careful use of description as well as some of the metaphors are both worth discussing. When Woolf begins the narrative of the life of Judith Shakespeare, her writing is so detailed and careful that, as I said in the introduction, she virtually convinces her audience that such a woman existed and went through the ordeals that she describes. Her skill as a novelist shines through in this section; pointing this out will help clarify the varieties of style possible in an essay that is essentially nonfiction.

The question of how much a feminist tract this will be for your students must be answered by them. Some of your students will feel it has not gone far enough, and some will feel it is not feminist at all. Margaret Drabble considers the entire book to be a feminist essay, so you can weigh in with one outside opinion (besides my own). However, you can also use any disagreement that arises in class to stimulate a lively discussion.

SUGGESTIONS FOR CLASS DISCUSSION

1. It is useful to point out that this essay was originally delivered to women students at two Oxford colleges. Ask your students to identify what evidence there is to suggest Woolf was aware of the nature of her audience.
2. What do the chapter headings from Trevelyan's *History of England* (para. 6) reveal about historians' concerns?
3. What would Woolf propose as the most important changes in society that would alter the situation most talented women find themselves in? Why does talent make a woman's situation especially difficult?

SUGGESTIONS FOR BRIEF ESSAYS

1. In paragraph 8 Woolf says, "Genius like Shakespeare's is not born among laboring, uneducated, servile people." In a brief essay, establish why you can say with confidence that this is an ironic statement.
2. Choose one of the female characters that Woolf mentions in paragraph 3, and write a brief essay on how she is portrayed in literature. Why does she stand as an example in this essay? What is this character's cultural significance?
3. Given Woolf's comments on the unnamed bishop, what would you guess is her attitude toward organized religion? What does the bishop represent in English society?

SUGGESTIONS FOR LONGER ESSAYS

1. Examine the references Woolf makes to Shakespeare and his plays. What can you tell about Woolf's regard for Shakespeare from those references? Which female characters in Shakespeare's plays does she mention, and how does their behavior reinforce her argument? You may have to read or reread at least one of Shakespeare's plays in order to answer this.
2. Woolf went to "the shelf where the histories stand" and found that they said virtually nothing about the plight of women in history. Try her experiment: go to the history shelves in your school's library, and see what books now exist eighty-four years after *A Room of One's Own* was published. Are there more books on women in history? What kind of chapter headings do they have? How much have things changed? What do these books reveal about the conditions of women that would augment Woolf's view?
3. In *A Room of One's Own*, Woolf cites not only the need of a room but the need of "five hundred a year" to support a gifted woman in her effort to express her talent. The sum would change in each era, but the point remains. Independence must be financial as well as social. Do you agree?

SENTENCE OUTLINE: See p. 149 of this manual.

BIBLIOGRAPHY: See p. 195 of this manual.

MARGARET MEAD

Sex and Temperament (pp. 707–723)

Your students will probably not know that Margaret Mead was a popular columnist and media maven. Indeed, many of her critics seemed to find fault with her largely because of her popular success. However, her work is still a pleasure to read, and her major books on the South Seas are authoritative and fascinating. Charges that she disdained those she studied—sometimes pushing toward a charge of racism—have been made, but they seem unwarranted. Photographs of the period, showing her in local costume, living the local life, imply that she was willing to be one with the people. Most of her critics have not had such experiences.

Some critics have argued that she ignored biological determinism in her research. The most interesting of modern critics is Derek Freeman, author of *Margaret Mead and Samoa* (1983), who went to some of the cultures Mead studied, talked with some of the people who informed her, and reported that some of her respondents lied to her. Freeman tried without success to get his book published during Mead's lifetime and even sent her a copy of the manuscript, but it arrived when she was very sick and near death. I mention this only because you can give students who disagree with her at least one source they can consult to learn more about potential counterarguments.

Given our culture and the reinforcements we get from popular music, popular films, television crime shows, and virtually all the other shows as well—not to mention the popular magazines aimed at men and aimed at women—it is no wonder that your students will have a very hard time accepting the basic argument that Mead presses forward. You will want to have your students explore the larger implication of the culture we live in and its resources for shaping behavior and expectation.

One problem I note here with paragraph 8 is that Mead says, "There are at least three courses open to a society that has. . . ." I have scoured the text and have a very difficult time finding what the third course is. If you or your students find out, let me know.

In any event, I am sure you will find this selection stimulating in the classroom. It seems to me that your students will already have a clear position on the question and will have a hard time changing their views.

SUGGESTIONS FOR CLASS DISCUSSION

1. What are the temperamental traits of women? Of men?
2. What price does a society pay for restricting the opportunities of one sex or the other?
3. Given that our culture has standardized temperamental expectations for each sex, what price does the opposite sex pay for that standardization?
4. Why should our modern industrialized society be concerned about the ways of "primitive" cultures?

SUGGESTIONS FOR BRIEF ESSAYS

1. What role do popular magazines play in aiding society to fashion male and female personalities? Choose a group of men's magazines and analyze them to determine precisely what kinds of behavior the magazines promote, expect, and inculcate in their reader. Do the same for a group of women's magazines. Do they overlap in any specific ways?
2. Emerson said, "Whoso would be a man must be a nonconformist." How can a man be a nonconformist in a culture such as ours with its specific expectations of male behavior? What price does an individual, male or female, pay for being a nonconformist in terms of gender-linked behavior in your immediate social circle? Use examples where possible.
3. Mead says, "Regimentation of one sex carries with it, to greater or less degree, the regimentation of the other also" (para. 10). To what extent is this statement true in the society that you know best? If you have experience with a culture other than that of North America, can you validate her statement in terms of behavior you have known or heard of?

SUGGESTIONS FOR LONGER ESSAYS

1. Popular music in the twenty-first century seems to affect the behavior of young people. What does the music you best know seem to promote in terms of gender typing? How forceful is the effect of that music? How much have your friends been affected by it? How much have you been affected by it? Study the lyrics and also the stage action, if possible, of the music you think best represents desirable behavior in either sex. Also decide what the attitude of the lead singers is toward members of the opposite sex.

2. Mead thinks of deviant individuals as people who do not have the appropriate temperament demanded by the society in which they are born. One result of such a situation is for the individual to live a life of frustration and unfulfillment. However, another pattern is for the individual to achieve even greater things than might be expected. Research the life of Gertrude Stein, Tennessee Williams, or James Baldwin, and write an essay that reveals how they dealt with their social situation and nevertheless achieved great success.

3. In paragraph 22 Mead establishes two situations. The first is the situation in which the individual suffers from rigid standardization of gender roles and gender temperaments. The second is the situation in which the society suffers a "loss in social values" when the differences in gender roles and temperament are erased. Write an essay that explores the potential loss in social values that would happen if all our current gender stereotypes were erased. What institutions would be lost? What would the effect be on everyday life? Would the result in your opinion be desirable or undesirable?

SENTENCE OUTLINE: See p. 150 of this manual.

BIBLIOGRAPHY: See p. 186 of this manual.

GERMAINE GREER

Masculinity (pp. 725–737)

A self-proclaimed anarchist, Greer has often been at the center of considerable controversy, but I do not think it essential to go into great detail about the controversy. She appeared nude on the cover of a magazine on condition that the male editors join her, but they did not. She shocked the staid dons at Cambridge, as the distinguished scholar Lisa Jardine said, by loudly discussing bras and breasts and using language they thought inappropriate. Her marriage of three weeks failed in part because she was unfaithful several times in that period. But all of that was part of her "bad girl" image, which she felt was an antidote to the suppressed and repressed female behavior of the day.

Today the excitement that feminism generated in 1970 has all but disappeared. I hope some of your students will still be able to respond to the feminist movement, but recent experience makes me less than certain that they will.

However, this particular essay is less concerned with feminism than it is with the concept of masculinity in our society. Greer's view largely agrees with the views of the other authors in this section in that masculinity is a construct, not a biological given. You may have a very difficult time convincing your students that this is true. The "alpha males" of your class may be the most difficult to convince, although it is not always reasonable to make such assumptions. You will certainly experience some surprises in your discussion in class, and that is usually worth the price of admission. It's interesting to poll your female students to see how much of what Greer describes as masculine behavior they can validate from experience.

I ask some questions about corporate structures that most of your students can't respond to from their own corporate experience, but I think it reasonable to ask them to address the organizations to which they belong, whether as employees or as members. The question of whether or not masculinity is at work in the structure of organizations is as interesting as the suggestion that paramilitary organizations like the Boy Scouts and ROTC are designed to inculcate masculinity in boys.

Most of the suggestions I make for writing hinge on students' personal experiences in part because what they will say is similar to some of the testimony Greer develops for her argument. However, my suggestions are also designed to explore the range of possibility in the creation of the masculine. Your students will have a wide range of responses and a wide range of experiences. Of course, one valuable point is that your male students will be interested in hearing what your female students think about this essay, and vice versa. I am sure you will have a stimulating time discussing this material.

SUGGESTIONS FOR CLASS DISCUSSION

1. What is the difference between the genotype and the phenotype?
2. What role do fathers have in developing self-confidence in their daughters?
3. Is belligerence a masculine quality?
4. What does Greer mean when she says, "Men do not only give orders; they also take orders" (para. 8)?

SUGGESTIONS FOR BRIEF ESSAYS

1. In paragraph 8 Greer says that "young men are the emotional center of young women's lives"? Do you think this statement is true? Do you also think it is true that women are irrelevant to the emotional center of a masculine man? Draw on your personal observations and your personal experiences to qualify these statements.
2. Greer says that one of the obligations of the masculine man is to "acquire a vast amount of lore" (para. 8), much of which is totally irrelevant to young women. Given your experience both with members of your own gender and with members of the other gender, how valid do you think this statement is? What are the areas in which the lore seems to be most important to men and most irrelevant to women? Do women acquire lore in the same way? Do they share it with men?
3. Greer points out that some women actually support the process of producing masculine men from boys. Does this seem reasonable to you? Describe what Greer says about how women contribute to the development of the masculine man. If you are a woman, do you feel that women should behave in such a way as to produce the masculine man? Or is there some alternative that you feel is more desirable?

SUGGESTIONS FOR LONGER ESSAYS

1. "Masculinity requires the creation of dangerous situations, actual or symbolic" (para. 10). What dangerous situations have you been in that may have required masculinity? Why would a masculine male be needed—or would a masculine female be sufficient? Why is danger such an important issue in developing masculinity? Describe the different kinds of danger that you feel are most important.
2. Obviously, not everyone will agree with Germaine Greer. If you find yourself angry or dissatisfied at her portrayal of masculinity, construct an argument that takes issue with her points and demonstrate your own views. You might want to qualify the nature of masculinity by offering your own definitions, but your definitions need to be complex and relate to specific behavior. You may use your own experience and observation of masculine behavior in order to counter Greer. You may also find some scientific research that takes an opposite view and analyze it in the process of your argument. Research and testimony will help your argument.
3. Greer seems to imply that not all men can become masculine men. What is the fate of those who cannot answer the call of masculinity? Examine your own experience, and describe the behavior of men you have known who were not "alpha males." What are their opportunities in life? Is it clear that masculine males are much more successful in life than those who are less masculine in behavior? What is your ideal in male behavior? Does it come close to the ideals of masculinity that Greer describes?

SENTENCE OUTLINE: See p. 151 of this manual.

BIBLIOGRAPHY: See p. 180 of this manual.

JUDITH BUTLER

From *Undoing Gender* (pp. 739–760)

This is a difficult selection in part because Butler uses some uncommon vocabulary, such as *dramaturg, supervenient, ablate,* and *incommensurability,* though these words show up mainly in her analytical passages. When she narrates the story of David Reimer her style is fairly clear. Butler has frequently been criticized for the impenetrability of her prose, but she defends herself by arguing that clarity in expression often hides the complexity of an idea. In any event, this selection from *Undoing Gender* is one of her clearest expositions, and I think it is useful for students even if it's difficult for them (or you) to explain the meaning of individual sentences. The overall point here is that in Reimer's case the difficulties of assigning gender are profoundly complex, and those difficulties reveal something important about the limits of socialization of gender norms.

You may be interested to know that while David Reimer was being treated by John Money, Money was publishing articles and follow-up articles about his progress, declaring that the treatment was totally successful. However, Reimer's own reports, even as very young child, indicated that Money was not paying attention to his feelings or to his acute unhappiness while he was being raised as a girl. Other girls taunted him because he was physically much more like a boy than a girl: he had broad shoulders, a masculine gait, and a roughness to him that the other children reacted to. As a young child Reimer fought with his brother over their toys, preferring his brother's guns and trucks to the dolls he was given. When Reimer was finally told that he had been born with a penis and that it had been destroyed accidentally, he dropped out of Money's treatment and underwent another surgery. At that point Money stopped writing about Reimer without any further public explanation.

Reimer arguably became the best-known example of sexual change in the scientific literature of his day. One can only imagine how difficult a life he must have led during his childhood, but he somehow managed to make a life for himself for some time as an adult. He got a job working as a janitor in a slaughterhouse—a job that he liked—and after a number of false starts he found a wife who loved him and tried to reassure him when he fretted over his sexual inadequacies. But he became depressed when he lost his job, and thereafter his life was very difficult, in part because he was conned out of a great deal of money. In the depths of his depression, he killed himself with a sawed-off shotgun.

SUGGESTIONS FOR CLASS DISCUSSION

1. What obvious markers do you rely upon to determine a person's gender?
2. To what extent is gender determined by anatomy?
3. Can you think of any contemporary groups of people who tend to use their appearance to blur gender distinctions? Are there any groups who find such blurring troublesome?
4. How important is the concept of a gender norm to your friends? How important is it to you?

SUGGESTIONS FOR BRIEF ESSAYS

1. Judging from popular entertainers in the worlds of music and theater, how important do you believe is the idea of "gender essentialism"? How elastic is the concept of gender in the world of entertainment? Consider the same questions as applied to major figures in the world of sports. Why would there be a difference?
2. David Reimer was worried about whether people would think his worth was connected to his gender definition. What is the role of gender definition in determining one's self-worth? Do people you know worry about their gender as defined by others?
3. In paragraph 19, Butler says that pediatricians who examine David Reimer's case argue that "David is really male, and that he was, even when he was Brenda, always male." Examine Butler's discussion in paragraphs 8, 9, and 10, and determine whether you agree with the view that there is "an essential gender core" to David even though he had no male genitalia between his legs. Consider too whether there can be a sense of gender even when genitalia are absent.

SUGGESTIONS FOR LONGER ESSAYS

1. Butler refers to the XY chromosomes, which are the standard male chromosomes. Do some research and write an essay that clarifies what is known about the XY chromosomes and why they may be important for understanding gender construction. Connect what you learn to the story of David Reimer as Judith Butler tells it.

2. Read John Colapinto's book *As Nature Made Him: The Boy Who Was Raised as a Girl* (Harper Perennial, 2001). Compare his narrative of the experiences of David Reimer with Judith Butler's account. What are Colapinto's concerns about this case? How do they differ from Butler's? How much more do you learn about David Reimer from reading Colapinto, and how much of what you now know was omitted from Butler's narrative? Compare the two authors' different approaches to constructing their narratives. What do you learn about the concept of narrative by making this comparison?

3. Much is made of the toys that David preferred in his childhood. Write an essay that establishes the relationship of toys to gender. Does the choice of toys establish the gender of the child, or does the gender of the child establish the choice of toys? What do you remember about your own childhood and the kinds of toys you preferred? Is the choice of toys entirely a result of the way society sees children and the way the industry produces toys for them? Is a child's choice of toys a result of socialization or of some innate "core"?

4. Does anything bother you about Butler's presentation of David Reimer's case? Do you take issue with anything in Butler's narrative? How might you have analyzed David Reimer's own narrative of his situation?

5. In paragraph 14, Butler says that "a significant percentage of children are chromosomally various, and a continuum exists between male and female that suggests the arbitrariness and falsity of the gender dimorphism as a prerequisite of human development." Define her key terms in this sentence, and then go on to argue for or against the concept of a continuum between the extremes of male and female gender qualities. Your aim will essentially be to develop a useful definition of gender based on the issues that Butler studies in this selection.

6. In paragraph 23, Butler talks about David's understanding of a "norm of how he was supposed to be." What is your own understanding of your gender norm and how you are supposed to behave in the social environment you inhabit? What are the gender norms that your parents seem to subscribe to? What are the gender norms of your peers? How comfortable do you feel in accepting and professing these norms? Do these norms ever make you uncomfortable? How so? How important is it to you and your peers that you live up to these norms? If possible, develop a narrative that helps you answer these questions.

7. What are the problems Butler faces in dealing with David Reimer's "self-description" beginning in paragraph 20? What are the usual problems with anyone's self-description? Offer your own narrative self-description, and try to satisfy Butler's concerns. Who is the audience for your narrative? How does that affect your narrative? What is your ideal audience?

SENTENCE OUTLINE: See p. 152 of this manual.

BIBLIOGRAPHY: See p. 172 of this manual.

KAREN HORNEY

The Distrust between the Sexes

(bedfordstmartins.com/worldofideas/epages)

This is a very clear and effective essay; therefore, you should have relatively little work to do in clarifying the ideas. What you probably will want to do in class is to examine its basic premises—for instance, the question of whether your students perceive hostility between the sexes at all. That is the first discussion question after the essay itself, and it may be the only one you will need for an hour's worth of debate. You might try to steer the discussion in order to include different kinds of hostility that might pertain to different age groups. There may be one kind of hostility perceived for people in the age group of your students' parents and another in your students' age group. This is a useful area of inquiry.

One important idea that must be discussed, of course, is that Karen Horney is trying to cite psychological issues and not just sociological issues. She constantly describes childhood events in order to establish the etiology of disorders that cause hostility. An important point you may wish to discuss at length is whether or not she postulates the hostility between the sexes as a form of disorder caused by childhood frustrations, mature envy, and forms of distrust, or whether she feels that hostility between the sexes should be considered a normal condition. Is it a product of two "kinds" of mind?

For class discussion, this essay is useful for helping students to clarify their thoughts on the issues, since it is likely that all of them will have plenty of personal experiences to share in class. Most of the writing assignments as well, both in the text and below, leave room for personal experience to illustrate a point or points. Beginning with a concrete narrated experience is a good way for a student to start dealing with such a suggestive series of insights into the human mind.

Finally, the relationship between the sexes has political overtones, no matter how much you may want to keep them out of the discussion. It may be wise to confront them directly, perhaps suggesting that some of the political issues are rooted in psychology, as Karen Horney has described. This discussion may lead to the question of whether there is a separate psychology—or ought to be—for women and for men. The idea that Freud may be describing a masculine psychology and Horney a feminine psychology should not be ignored or avoided. That idea could lead to the discussion of whether there is a male mind and a female mind—a conclusion that might be an extreme reaction to the essay, but one that will seem reasonable to some I people.

SUGGESTIONS FOR CLASS DISCUSSION

1. This essay comes from a book called *Feminine Psychology.* Ask your students if they feel there is a feminine psychology that is separate from psychology in general.
2. At one point Horney states that passion is rare because "we are loath to put all our eggs in one basket" (para. 6). Have students discuss whether this is true from their own experience. How do people they know feel about this issue?
3. To what extent are sexual anxieties at the root of any distrust between men and women?

SUGGESTIONS FOR BRIEF ESSAYS

1. In paragraph 2 Horney says, "The relationship between men and women is quite similar to that between children and parents, in that we prefer to focus on the positive aspects of these relationships." Is this an appropriate analogy? Is it true that people generally want to be positive in their discussion of the relationships she describes? To what extent is it difficult for us to be negative?
2. The image of the Madonna, the Virgin Mother, is cited as one that men are comfortable with when they think of women. Is this true? To what extent do you see evidence to support this contention? What other images do men have of women? Establish in what way the images men hold of women may affect their behavior toward them.
3. Some people, as Horney implies, may have absolutely no inkling that there is any hostility between the sexes. What might that mean? Under what circumstances might people be unaware of hostility? What conditions might prevail? Establish a scenario, drawn from your own or someone else's experience, in which a person might be unaware that there is hostility between the sexes.

SUGGESTIONS FOR LONGER ESSAYS

1. How clear an archetype, in Jung's sense of the word, is the Madonna figure as Horney describes it (paras. 13–14)? Jung had a view that the mother archetype is one of the most powerful we know. Horney establishes the power of the mother as an abstract idea in this essay. If the mother is an archetype, how would you describe it? You may wish to examine Jung's essay on the mother archetype in *Archetypes and the Collective Unconscious,* in Volume 9 of *Collected Works.* Is Horney substantially in agreement with Jung, or does her view stand in contradistinction to his?

2. Write your own essay on the subject of "The Distrust between the Sexes." Establish the important psychological differences between the sexes, and, with reference to examples as much as possible, describe what you feel is important about these differences.

3. Do you agree with Horney when she says that "man's fear of woman is deeply rooted in sex" (para. 13)? Interview women especially to see if they agree with this idea. Then interview some men to determine if their views coincide. Are they dramatically different or just mildly different? In your essay begin by clarifying Horney's views as much as possible. Present the views of those you have interviewed; then present your own views, based on your reflections on the material you have gathered and on your own experience.

SENTENCE OUTLINE: See p. 154 of this manual.

BIBLIOGRAPHY: See p. 181 of this manual.

PART SEVEN

LANGUAGE

The seven selections on language begin with a demanding theoretical excursion by the distinguished philosopher, Susanne Langer, and then move to a couple of lighter selections by Mario Pei and Bill Bryson that were designed for a general audience. These popular pieces are important, but also provide an entry for students thinking about language for the first time. James Baldwin writes out of a sense of anger during a period of controversy. Neil Postman writes out of a sense of urgency because he sees how the uses of language can shape our sense of reality. Noam Chomsky offers a dense but approachable analysis of the state of linguistic research at this time. Finally, in e-pages, Alexander Pope's thoughts on poetic criticism, while a far cry from the other selections in this section, offer a critical point of reference for assessing the rest of the chapter's authors.

SUSANNE K. LANGER

Language (pp. 769–781)

Susanne K. Langer was a brilliant teacher at Connecticut College and gave luster to its faculty for an important decade beginning in 1952. In 1921, the year after finishing her undergraduate degree, she married William Langer, who eventually became a professor of history at Harvard. Langer herself also taught there for a while, but at the time there were no women professors at Harvard, so Langer was ranked only as a tutor. Her career eventually took her to full teaching positions at other universities (and eventually her marriage dissolved, although the couple had two children together).

Her book *Philosophy in a New Key* was very influential in the 1960s and 1970s, because it connected a great many areas of intellectual interest in terms of her views on the power of symbols in thought. Her work in aesthetics is still very important, and her interrelation of disciplines of thought is one of her work's greatest strengths.

This essay should give you a chance to ask students to do some research into Victor, the feral boy who probably influenced Rousseau's theories of the noble savage. Itard's published work on Victor is available in most libraries, and there is a good deal of information online that students will find interesting. You may wish to read enough of Victor's story to help stimulate discussion and give your students some direction for their own research. Much of my questioning asks students to respond from their own experience, which I hope will help them connect with Langer's theories—especially since she herself offers her own experience in the process of discussing how infants acquire language.

SUGGESTIONS FOR CLASS DISCUSSION

1. Langer mentions "audible actions" in paragraph 13. What are they, and why are they important?
2. What is a phoneme, and how does it differ from lalling?
3. What does the term *Gestalt* mean in paragraph 16?

SUGGESTIONS FOR BRIEF ESSAYS

1. Early in her essay Langer refers to Helen Keller. Who was Helen Keller, and why is she an important figure to talk about when one considers language acquisition? Why was it so difficult for Helen Keller to learn language, and how did she ultimately succeed? Who helped her and how? Is her story important to helping us understand Langer's theories of language?

2. In paragraph 18, Langer says, "The fact is that our primary world of reality *is* a verbal one." To what extent do you agree with her, and to what extent do you disagree? Why has she made this statement at this point in the selection? What important point is she trying to make with this statement?

3. Langer calls "dream, ritual, superstitious fancy" forms of symbolistic thinking (para. 20). Explain what she seems to mean, and then test her views by examining your own dreams, rituals of behavior, and any superstitious fancies that you are aware of sensing or holding. What symbolic values do you find in any of these mental activities?

4. If what Langer says in paragraph 9 is true, that "the vocalizing and articulating instinct of babyhood is fostered by response," then what are your recommendations for parents of little children? Remember that in the nineteenth century it was said that a child should be seen but not heard. Is this still good advice for raising a child whom you would like to be proficient in language?

5. What do you think is the best way to teach a child language? If you plan to have children, how will you go about helping your child understand language now that you have read this essay?

SUGGESTIONS FOR LONGER ESSAYS

1. In paragraph 17, Langer says, "To name things is a thrilling experience, a tremendous satisfaction." She uses nature as an example, reminding us that people who like flowers insist on knowing their names. To what extent is Langer correct in understanding the power of naming things? How does your experience in your school reinforce her point? What names have you learned in your studies that you need in order to better understand the principles of each discipline? How important is naming in higher education?

2. Gestalt psychology was very important when Langer wrote this selection. Do some research and explain what the value of Gestalt psychology is and how it affects the ideas that Langer presents to us in this passage. Why would the concept of the Gestalt help us interpret the complex means by which infants begin the process of learning language? Do you feel that the insights of Gestalt psychology are still relevant? Are they in any way particularly relevant to you?

3. Langer says, "The transformation of experience into concepts, not the elaboration of signals and symptoms, is the motive of language" (para. 19). Write an essay that explains what Langer means here, and clarify what signals and symptoms are and how they differ from concepts. Given Langer's views on language and its relationship to symbols, why is it of first importance that experience must be transformed into concepts through language? Is this the key to understanding the difference between human understanding and the understanding of animals who interpret signs and signals? What examples might you bring to bear that could help clarify her point?

4. Examine Langer's personal observations about her childhood in paragraphs 11 and 12. Why is she telling us the story of her own experiences with armchairs? What do her childhood experiences reveal about her theories of language acquisition? How did her childhood awarenesses differ from those of most adults? How did they differ from yours? Are those awarenesses somehow a key to language acquisition?

SENTENCE OUTLINE: See p. 155 of this manual.

BIBLIOGRAPHY: See p. 184 of this manual.

MARIO PEI

Theories of Language Beginning (pp. 783–793)

This is one of the easiest selections in this book. Pei was writing for a very general audience in *The Story of Language*, which of course meant that he ended up with a best-seller. In some ways, this piece is a bit lightweight, but its ideas of language origination are intriguing, and Pei's style makes the issue interesting to most people. He was himself a competent scholar whose work on his dissertation included important studies of Sanskrit, which indicates an early interest in language origination. Given the ways in which young people use language today, you may be able to stimulate conversation by talking about words or expressions that your peers used that would mean very little to your students, or you may be able to contrast your own language with that of your parents. Language is always interesting enough to stimulate good discussions.

You might be interested in knowing that late in his career Pei studied politics and wrote *The America We Lost: The Concerns of a Conservative* (1968). In this book he referenced his memories of a childhood in Italy in which as he said, "The government was everywhere." The ambitions of young people were limited to finding jobs in the bureaucracy. The Italian government owned large businesses and controlled the country, something he deplored. This seems to have been an interesting change from the translation he made in 1928 of De Fiori's *Mussolini: The Man of Destiny.*

SUGGESTIONS FOR CLASS DISCUSSION

1. Why is it so difficult to theorize about the origin of language?
2. What words have changed in their meaning since you were young?
3. How are words used differently by different people in your family?
4. What are call words, and how do they seem to persist in languages? What call words do you use most frequently?
5. How much credence do you give to the "sing-song" theory that language developed from "primitive inarticulate chants"?

SUGGESTIONS FOR BRIEF ESSAYS

1. If languages change most at the "crossroads" of cultures, then where would you expect the most changes to take place in your language today?
2. People in the north of most countries tend to speak differently from those in the south. They also use some words differently and employ expressions differently from each other. If you have had experiences in both the north and the south of a country, what observations have you been able to make in detecting such differences? Are those differences likely to be caused by climate differences? Are they caused by differences in geography?
3. What is the Tower of Babel, and what has it to do with what Pei is talking about? Research the term and look into what myths have grown up around it. If we were to believe that the Tower of Babel is a true story, then what would we know about the origin of language? Would this be what Pei calls a "mystical explanation"?
4. What language was spoken in the Garden of Eden? Many people have proposed many languages. What are the most interesting proposals? What seems to motivate people to propose one language or another? Which language would you defend as most likely? Is it possible that no language was spoken in the Garden of Eden?
5. In a brief essay, offer your own original theory of the origin of language. Why is your theory just as good as any of those mentioned in Pei's essay?

SUGGESTIONS FOR LONGER ESSAYS

1. In paragraph 10, Pei says that E. H. Sturtevant claims, "Since all real intentions and emotions . . . get themselves involuntarily expressed by gesture," the real purpose of inventing language was to lie and deceive others. This theory, Pei says, has some merit. Examine what Sturtevant said, and decide just how convincing his theory is. Consider the power of gesture to reveal what you really think is true and the possibility that gesture could be deceptive. How effective is language in deceiving others? What experience have you had in observing people trying to hide their "real intentions" with language?
2. In paragraph 11, Pei mentions that several experiments were made in trying "to isolate children before they began talking to see whether they would evolve a language of their own." He mentions

the Egyptian king Psammetichos, Frederick II of Sicily, and King James IV of Scotland. Look those figures up, and see what they tried to do with children and how well it worked. How did their experiments work in contrast with the Wild Boy of Aveyron, mentioned by Susanne K. Langer in "Language"?

3. Several times, Pei refers to the Indo-European languages. What are they, and why does he feel it useful to refer to them? Look up Indo-European language, and write a brief essay that explains why language experts feel that our modern Romance languages all derive from Indo-European roots. What support does your research give Pei in his suppositions about how language works?

4. There have been several recorded instances of two children, twins or merely siblings, who actually create their own language for communication exclusively between themselves. Given the fact that Victor, the Wild Boy of Aveyron, mentioned in Susanne Langer's "Language," was totally alone growing up, is it possible that community is the most crucial ingredient to understanding the origin of language?

5. Mario Pei was a proponent of Esperanto because it contains elements of most modern languages and can thus be fairly quickly learned. If you find yourself interested in how Esperanto works, find a Web site such as *lernu* (http://en.lernu.net/), and take a basic course in Esperanto. You may also locate an Esperanto dictionary online to help you write a brief essay in Esperanto. See if your teacher can understand what you wrote. You may wish to keep an English translation just in case.

6. If Esperanto proves too challenging, write an essay on your critique of Mario Pei's selection, using the language called E-Prime. E-Prime is English, but it never uses forms of the verb "to be." So you cannot use the words *is, was, were,* or *been* in any sentence. This forces you to use language in a very different way from what you usually do. You may wish to write about the experience of writing in E-Prime.

SENTENCE OUTLINE: See p. 156 of this manual.

BIBLIOGRAPHY: See p. 189 of this manual.

JAMES BALDWIN

If Black English Isn't a Language, Then Tell Me, What Is?
(pp. 795–803)

There is a degree of irony in this essay because James Baldwin does not use what he describes as black English to write it. He is a master of standard English, one of the great essayists of the second half of the twentieth century. Yet he was tormented by the ways in which people in publishing and elsewhere attempted to define him through their own language, which sometimes impinged on his in the process of editing. In his biography *James Baldwin* (1994), David Leeming talks about the ways in which Baldwin was annoyed by writers working on film and other projects who took what he wrote and revised it to suit themselves, while in the process losing the character and rhythms of his prose. He was deeply offended by these people and spent more than a decade defending his prose.

Baldwin's masterful prose also garnered him some hostility from other black writers. In the late 1960s, during the intense riots in Harlem and elsewhere after the assassination of Martin Luther King Jr., Baldwin was disregarded by militants such as Amiri Baraka. He was considered uninvolved in and distant from the black community. Later, Baldwin and Baraka became friends and began to see how they were working jointly on behalf of black Americans, but it took some time for them to resolve their differences.

You may have an interesting time with Baldwin's essay because your students will almost surely have some differences of opinion on the existence of black English. Some students will doubtless want to discuss rap music in all of its variant forms. Some people will see it as distinctly black English; others will not. You may get some useful responses from all sides of the question.

SUGGESTIONS FOR CLASS DISCUSSION

1. In paragraph 3, Baldwin says, "What joins all languages . . . is the necessity to confront life." What does he mean? Is he right?
2. If you have trouble understanding English in films (or TV shows) made in England or Ireland, what seems to give you problems? Why don't those filmmakers try harder to help you understand?
3. What people in your immediate environment seem to "pay a price" for the way they use the language?
4. What can you tell about people by the way they use the language?

SUGGESTIONS FOR BRIEF ESSAYS

1. Examine all the points Baldwin makes in paragraph 11 about the relation of black children to education and the people who educate them. Can you validate what Baldwin is saying in this paragraph on the basis of your own experience? One of his main points is that the system is asking a black child to "repudiate his experience." Is it possible that schools ask all children to do so?
2. In paragraph 1, Baldwin says, "People evolve a language in order to describe and thus control their circumstances, or in order not to be submerged by a reality that they cannot articulate." Write a brief essay that supports or modifies this view. How does language control circumstances in your family? How does it control circumstances where you live? How does your use of language help control your circumstances?
3. If you are white, what problems arise if you try to use black English? If you are black, what problems arise if you try to use white English? If you are Latino, which version of English is the most difficult for you to use? What characteristics do you observe about any of these groups and the way they use special language to describe everyday events?
4. Is there such a thing as white English? What are its qualities, and how does it use identifying words in a different fashion from the ways other groups use words. Do Asian Americans have a special approach to language? Would Baldwin approve of it?

SUGGESTIONS FOR LONGER ESSAYS

1. Look up Congo Square, the open space in New Orleans where slaves were permitted to gather occasionally to socialize. This was a place in which people from different tribes would meet and try to communicate. What does the history of this place tell you about black English?
2. Read another of James Baldwin's essays in *Notes of a Native Son,* and comment on the nature of Baldwin's use of language. What is revealed about his character? Does he write using black English? How effective is his argument, and how passionate do you feel he is in writing? Do you find yourself convinced by his argument?
3. Research Baldwin's early essays and his early biography, and explain how his experiences in church affected his writing. The standard biography is *James Baldwin* (1994) by David Leeming. What did Baldwin's preaching in church teach him about writing? What did it do in shaping his phrases and patterns of word usage? Why would preaching at an early age affect Baldwin's writing? Would it also affect his speaking?
4. What is the clearest evidence you have that there is a black English and that it is somehow present throughout the general society? Would Baldwin be happy about the way the language has developed? What seems to be the purpose of the language? Does it protect a specific group? Does it attack a specific group? Do you feel that Baldwin attacks a specific group? Does his essay make you feel good about yourself? Do you think Baldwin imagined the effect his essay has had on you?

SENTENCE OUTLINE: See p. 157 of this manual.

BIBLIOGRAPHY: See p. 171 of this manual.

BILL BRYSON
Where Words Come From (pp. 805–823)

In many ways this piece is very different from the other selections in this book. On one hand, Bryson is a researcher and freelance writer rather than an originator of ideas. On the other hand, Bryson is also a major prize winner in the area of science writers and is certainly no lightweight. This chapter from his book, *The Mother Tongue,* is valuable in a number of ways. Your students will find it naturally attractive and perhaps a relief from the intensity of some of the other essays in this section of the book. Their curiosity will be aroused, and they may find Bryson to be a favorite.

For me, I find the rhetorical strategies that Bryson uses to be simple, effective, and easy to teach to other writers. Categorization is time-honored and particularly characteristic of the works of Aristotle and other classical authors. Modern writers also use the technique, although perhaps not as baldly as does Bryson. Nonetheless, Bryson uses the technique to his advantage, and with the supply of so many examples in each of his categories, he makes the most of his strategies.

Another advantage of this selection is that the introduction of so many words, both exotic and familiar, will stimulate the growth of your students' vocabulary as well as their awareness of the varieties of meaning that so many words may have. It will make them more aware of the ways in which they gather words (Beowulf's "word-hoard") throughout their years of study. It should also make them aware of how they change the meanings of words as they acquire and use them.

SUGGESTIONS FOR CLASS DISCUSSION

1. Why is it so difficult to theorize about the origin of words?
2. What words have changed in their meaning since you were young?
3. How can an exception prove a rule?
4. Which words do you use differently from the ways other people use them?
5. What differences in language usage do you notice between older people and people who are much younger than you?
6. Which population group seems to create the most new words?

SUGGESTIONS FOR BRIEF ESSAYS

1. Which of Bryson's categories for creating words do you find the most interesting? How many other words can you add to Bryson's examples? Relying on intuition or the suggestions of other writers on language in this section of the book, create a sixth category for the creation of new words.
2. Using a magazine that is directed at a very specific audience—such as muscle builders, high performance automobile enthusiasts, or lovers of antiques—determine how the specific vocabulary appropriate to that audience differs from the general vocabulary of everyday speech. What insights into word creation are evident from your research?
3. Write a brief essay that relies heavily on terminology that is usually used by specialists. Draw on your own special interests, such as chess terminology, computer language, military communications, or some other field or hobby. In the process, try to use the language in ways that you think are novel. Be sure to try to communicate with people who are not specialists in your area and are not familiar with the ways in which the language in your area is used.

SUGGESTIONS FOR LONGER ESSAYS

1. In paragraph 4, Bryson makes a reference to levels of culture, categorizing them into popular, literary, and scholarly. What does he mean by "levels of culture"? How different are the vocabularies associated with each of these categories? Write an essay that evaluates his reference to levels of culture, then write detailed passages using different ways of saying much the same thing but in each of the three categories Bryson has established.

2. Consulting the *Oxford English Dictionary* (available in your school library), find a word, common or uncommon, that has a great many entries—at least five pages worth. Write an essay that tries to clarify the extraordinary range of meanings for that word. Account for the authors who have used the word in the past (there will be a list with entries) and account, too, for the etymology of the word (which will be listed as well). What do you learn from such an examination?

3. If you have studied a foreign language—or if you are a native speaker of a language other than English—consult a dictionary of that language and find a list of at least a dozen words that are borrowed from that language and are now used in English. Categorize them as having similar meanings in both languages or as having diverse or even opposite meanings in English.

4. Bryson points out that the words describing parts of military tanks were derived from parts of naval ships because the British navy originally developed tanks. Consider forms of early transportation—such as horseback riding, stagecoach and other coach transportation, as well as early sailing ships—and collect the terms appropriate to those experiences that have been put into service in describing parts and functions of automobiles and parts of airplanes. Why do you think it is so easy to use the older terms for such novel forms of transportation?

5. Choose a writer of early English poetry, such as Geoffrey Chaucer or Edmund Spenser, and find copies of his work as it appeared in his own time (in other words, avoid any modernization of their language). Choose a dozen or so unfamiliar words from his work, and examine the range of their meaning in the context in which the author uses them. The *Oxford English Dictionary* will help you if you cannot fathom the meaning of a word. Comment on the usefulness of those words today. How different are they from the words that today might express similar meanings? How effective and useful are those words, and how likely are you to be able to use them in everyday conversation? Is it possible to see how those older words may have changed form or meaning and still be in use?

SENTENCE OUTLINE: See p. 158 of this manual.

BIBLIOGRAPHY: See p. 172 of this manual.

NEIL POSTMAN

The Word Weavers/The World Makers (pp. 825–841)

Postman maintains the virtue of clarity throughout his essay. He raises important questions about meaning and the uses of metaphor that could be applied to many of the selections in this book. But they can also be applied to the world of language outside this book. Postman's lifelong devotion to teaching and finding ways to bring serious issues into K–12 classrooms makes him ardent in trying to show us how our understanding of language and our choice of words affect the way we understand the world we live in. It may be difficult at first to convince students that the language they use shapes their understanding of the physical and emotional world they live in, but the better student writers will begin to figure it out as you talk about the ways people make themselves comfortable by choosing euphemisms to describe painful events.

The section on Korzybski may seem a bit too long here, but Postman wants to introduce us to the thinker who affected him most deeply and in whose footsteps he traveled. Korzybski was very big news when Postman began teaching and when S. I. Hayakawa was writing. Ironically, it was the newspaper and television media that made Hayakawa and Marshall McLuhan popular. The media also loved semantics and reported fully on the stars of the field. But today the very same media have degraded semantics into a term that implies insignificant differences in meaning of a word or words. In other words, that which was of such importance to Postman is now treated as if its essence is trivial.

SUGGESTIONS FOR CLASS DISCUSSION

1. What does Postman mean by his term *abstraction*? (See para. 21.)
2. Why is Alfred Korzybski important to Neil Postman?

3. Postman says that metaphor is "an organ of perception" (para. 6). How can metaphor be an organ of perception?
4. Why does Postman raise the question of over- and underachievers in schools?
5. What territory do you map on a daily basis? What words help you map that territory?

SUGGESTIONS FOR BRIEF ESSAYS

1. Write an essay on a political subject using metaphors developed from farming and gardening. Choose a political figure, and make him or her the center of your focus. What is the effect of relying on one category of metaphor on the presentation of your material?
2. What is the definition of a joke? Decide which rhetorical strategies you should use in order to define the term *joke.*
3. Examine paragraphs 6 and 7 carefully, and respond to Postman's challenge that we perceive the world through metaphors. Give some examples of the ways in which people interpret everyday experience through metaphors that shape their fundamental beliefs.
4. Review children's television programming and films made for children. What seem to be their aim? How do they map the world that children live in? Consider their use of metaphor and the kinds of questions they tend to raise. Consider, too, the questions that are presented to children as well as the answers they may sometimes provide. Is children's television as damaging to children as Postman feared?

SUGGESTIONS FOR LONGER ESSAYS

1. Choose an area in popular culture, such as popular music. Examine the language choices, particularly in terms of metaphor, and decide whether or not the language specific to that area shapes the way people see the world. You may also consult any specialty magazine that caters to readers interested in that particular area of culture. How does the language of that culture shape the readers' attitudes toward women, toward gays, toward men? How does it shape their attitudes toward the old, the infirm, the crippled, or other minority groups?
2. Consult Helen Keller's *The Story of My Life,* and look particularly at the early stages of her learning language. Keller was born deaf and blind and did not learn language in any normal way nor at any normal time in her development. But her record of how language changed her life is worth examining. Compare what she says about language with what Postman says, particularly in relation to the way language shapes our understanding of the world. How did Keller learn to "map" her world and her environment?
3. In an essay that examines meaning in words, establish the meaning of these terms: *truth* and *falsehood, theory, fact, inference, assumption, judgment,* and *generalization.* Postman refers to these terms in the last paragraph of his essay and, while doing so, contends that they are essential terms that are never really examined in school. Is he correct? How difficult is it to establish clear meanings for these terms? Do the meanings you develop begin to help you define the terms? Can they be satisfactorily defined as they might appear in a vocabulary list?

SENTENCE OUTLINE: See p. 159 of this manual.

BIBLIOGRAPHY: See p. 190 of this manual.

NOAM CHOMSKY

New Horizons in the Study of Language (pp. 843–855)

This is clearly a very difficult essay, and you will want to encourage your students to get from it what they can. They need not worry over some of the more technical and specialized terms or more complex explanations. Your students' goal should be to get the gist of Chomsky's basic theories that there is a specialized area of the brain designed for the acquisition of language and that no other animal species has it. This is a gigantic claim, and your students should be wary of accepting all that Chomsky has to say.

So far there has been no clear demonstration of Chomsky's claim. For fifty years linguists have labored to realize the claim through psychological, cognitive, and biological (genetic) means without completely settling the matter. Obviously, the claim that all children can learn any language with ease implies that there is a general grammar that all can grasp while also dealing with the surface elements of any given language. That is a compelling piece of information, and it tends to bolster Chomsky's claim. However, other linguists, such as Daniel L. Everett in his book, *Language: The Cultural Tool* (2012), disagree with Chomsky and emphasize the power of culture in league with the natural systems inherent in the brain and human physiology to make the acquisition of language possible.

Some of your students may be interested in Washoe, the chimpanzee, who learned sign language well enough to express a great many needs and ideas. If so, they may wish to take issue with Chomsky's view that language is species specific.

Other students may be very excited by the thought that there could be a specialized function in the brain that is designed to handle language (among other things). The idea of being hardwired for anything is appealing to many people. For example, how does one explain the so-called "gift" of someone like Mozart, whose understanding of music was certainly innate and expressed at the same age that other children are learning language? Is music somehow a language? It possesses discrete infinity, so does that help it qualify for language status? Remember that numbers also possess discrete infinity, so might they qualify as a language?

Finally, Chomsky's metaphors are marvelous, and they give you a great opportunity to talk about the power of metaphor to convince readers who may be skeptical.

SUGGESTIONS FOR CLASS DISCUSSION

1. What might be the surface qualities of language? Which can be considered its deep structure?
2. What are the virtues and difficulties implied in Chomsky's metaphor of a switch box that distinguishes languages by throwing switches? Who or what throws the switch?
3. In paragraph 14 Chomsky says that "the child knows vastly more than experience has provided." Why is this important to his ideas about language?

SUGGESTIONS FOR BRIEF ESSAYS

1. How does the example of Washoe, the chimpanzee who learned sign language, affect Chomsky's theories? Does Chomsky's view that language acquisition is species specific suffer because of Washoe's achievement?
2. What is the significance of Chomsky's view that language acquisition is something that happens to a child rather than something the child does? Examine your own experience, both as a child and as you are now, and qualify Chomsky's statement. Is language still happening to you, or are you "doing" it in the sense that you are making vocabulary lists or acquiring sentences in the same way you might be learning a new language?
3. To what extent do you feel the child's environment plays a major part in language acquisition? What kind of environment do you think is best for a child to help make language acquisition both speedy and of high quality? Chomsky says children learn one word an hour when they are at their peak period of growth. How would environment best help this process? What behavior do you recommend to parents and others in contact with children at their peak period of growth in language acquisition?
4. Chomsky discusses what he calls the "initial state" of language, by which he means the most fundamental features that reside in the brain and make it possible to build any specific language using its basic grammatical structure. In a brief essay, describe what you imagine would be essential for this initial state to possess in order for any language to be built from it. You may want to try a "back-formation," and analyze what you know from your language study. Choose three or four basic qualities that must be in the initial state in order for it to supply the features of any language.

SUGGESTIONS FOR LONGER ESSAYS

1. Chomsky refers to a "cognitive revolution" beginning in paragraph 11. Search the term online, and explain what the cognitive revolution is and why it might be important to Chomsky's argument. Does it seem that there is more than one cognitive revolution?

2. Generative grammar is one of the most important concepts in Chomsky's argument. It establishes that there are infinite ways to express ideas. The Renaissance philosopher Desiderius Erasmus (1466–1536) expressed a similar idea in his book, *On Copia,* in which he shows how many different ways there are of expressing the same idea. Take the basic idea in the statement Erasmus used to illustrate his point, "I was so happy to receive your letter," and write a dozen variations. Then comment on your achievement, especially on its difficulties and its pleasures. What does this tell you about the infinite possibilities of language?

3. One of the interesting debates in anthropology concerns the ability of the Neanderthal to use language. Chomsky suggests that language is species specific, which means that it is specific to *Homo sapiens,* not necessarily to *Homo neanderthalensis.* Do some research into the most current thinking about the Neanderthal, and decide whether or not there is enough evidence to claim that Neanderthals could use language or not. Given that language is a remarkable evolutionary tool for human survival, is it likely that our species alone possessed it?

4. Are child prodigies examples of people whose brains are "hardwired" for some special function? What characterizes a child prodigy, and how long do their prodigious achievements last? Do they cease to be prodigies at a certain age? In which fields do prodigies generally seem to show up? How do they differ from savants and idiots savant? How do these people affect Chomsky's basic argument for an innate language organ in the brain? You may wish to research both prodigies and idiots savant.

SENTENCE OUTLINE: See p. 161 of this manual.

BIBLIOGRAPHY: See p. 173 of this manual.

ALEXANDER POPE

From *An Essay on Criticism*

(bedfordstmartins.com/worldofideas/epages)

The selection omits only the last stanza of Book II. I mention that because I try to avoid extensive ellipses or unnatural breaks in these selections, primarily because such cuts annoy me and usually do disservice to the piece itself. As it is, Book II stands alone very well and offers some good insights into poetry. The interesting thing about this selection is that it is poetry talking about poetry.

You might spend a little time talking about your students' reaction to *An Essay on Criticism* as poetry. One of its virtues is its couplet rhyme. With the current mood toward poetry—I'm thinking of poetry slams and rap artists—rhyme and rhythm define poetry in the minds of most people who do not study it. Pope's rhyme is strong, and his rhythm is steady.

One thing that would help your students would be to explain the basic form of iambic pentameter and have some of the lines read out loud with a special effort to find the iambic stresses. This will help students grasp the concept of the "numbers" that Pope talks about.

I strongly recommend that you give your students plenty of opportunity to talk about the general message Pope offers regarding criticism. One of his injunctions, against evaluating the part rather than the whole, will be pertinent to our own practices regarding the evaluation of our students' essays. If some students raise the issue of nitpicking in corrections, you might remind them that the grade or comments you offer reflect the paper's overall success, while the detailed criticism gives students a chance to improve and learn the basics.

While commenting on the critics and their criticism, you might try to move your students toward considering what Pope recommends regarding good practices in poetry. He offers us a model in his own work. Pope would recommend rhymed iambic pentameter couplets, which are very supple in his hands, but couplets are especially useful for poems that have a message or a didactic purpose, such as *An Essay on Criticism*. Pope recommends a very direct language, and a close examination of lines 105 to 136 would be useful for discussing writing of any kind.

SUGGESTIONS FOR CLASS DISCUSSION

1. You might begin with considering one of Aristotle's concerns—the relation of form to sense. Aristotle is less concerned with form than with sense and points out that in poetry you can't have one without the other. However, it is worthwhile to look at the pleasures that your students derive from the form of their favorite couplets and the messages those couplets contain. Discuss the way in which the couplets add pleasure to the message of the poem.
2. The opening stanza treats the subject of pride, but it also treats the subject of knowing oneself. Discuss the role of pride in criticism. Discuss also the couplet in lines 13 and 14.
3. Some students feel they have problems with any poetry. Ask them if they find this poetry gives them problems, and if it does, explore what they are and why your students have problems.

SUGGESTIONS FOR BRIEF ESSAYS

1. In line 115, Pope discusses "true Expression." What is true expression, and why does it do what Pope says it does"
2. Pope says in line 165 that in poetry, "The sound must seem an Echo to the sense." Is this important advice for a poet? Which lines in this poem best carry out Pope's advice?
3. Is the advice to "Avoid Extremes" (l. 184) generally good for people to follow? Pope suggests ,hat advice for critics, but is it applicable in general? Why would Pope give this advice, and why would anyone feel it is generally useful for people?

SUGGESTIONS FOR LONGER ESSAYS

1. In line 215 Pope refers to "Quality," by which he means aristocracy. The next ten lines talk about the fact that some poems would be ignored by a critic if the critic thought they were written by someone ordinary, like Pope himself. But if the critic thought they were written by a lord or lady, then they would suddenly be "exalted stanzas." Is there a sense in which a similar pattern of behavior works in modern criticism? If so, describe it, and comment on its nature. You may consider film criticism or pop music criticism for this project.
2. Offer your own advice to critics. If possible, use a metrical line of ten syllables, and if you wish, use rhyme.
3. Write your own "Essay on Poetry." You need not use rhyme and meter, but discuss the main issues of poetry and how they should be managed. Discuss the question of conceit (use of metaphor and simile), language, "numbers" (rhythm and metrical effects), and the thought that the poem maintains. What are your recommendations concerning each of these? If possible. include samples that illustrate your point.

SENTENCE OUTLINE: See p. 162 of this manual.

BIBLIOGRAPHY: See p. 190 of this manual.

DISCOVERIES AND THE MIND

The way the mind works in the face of problems, both within and outside the individual, is the subject of the six selections in Part Eight. The means by which we think clearly about issues in our world depend on how carefully we prepare ourselves to examine the evidence before us and on which questions we choose to ask. Psychologists ask questions that lead us inward to an understanding of our own nature and our personality. Investigators of the natural world lead us outward to help us know the truth and avoid superstition and the kind of error that leads to ignorance and its destructive social consequences. As Plato and Bacon show, we are sometimes easily misled.

PLATO

The Allegory of the Cave (pp. 865–877)

It is probably best to begin with the essentialist nature of Plato's thought. Students are fascinated by Plato's ability to develop his argument so fully from the limits of his allegory. Students will often agree that the senses can be erroneous reporters of fact. But it is also worth pressing the point to stress what Kant and many later philosophers observed—that it is impossible to know about the world except in terms of its appearances to the senses. If the senses are unreliable at times, then so is our knowledge of the world. I point out that Plato and other Greeks described the observable details of things and experience in terms of accidents. What we see is accidental to an object. But as a way of postulating a reality underlying the accidents of experience, Plato had to conceive an essence. Students find this puzzling, and many of them want to get on with the commonsense business of daily life. The question persists: How can we ever know the essential nature of things? Well, first we have to suspect that there is one. The people continuing in their everyday rounds are like those chained to Plato's wall. I remind my impatient students of that and watch their reaction.

Frankly, the entire question of the value of sensory experience is one that fascinates students, and it should help make your classroom discussion exciting and perhaps even frenetic. Oftentimes, when discussing Plato, I need to attend closely to the class, helping to select ideas that could be made into successful essays. My students perform best when they react intensely.

SUGGESTIONS FOR CLASS DISCUSSION

1. Raise the issue of what it is we know when we rely on our senses. Is sensory knowledge as unreliable as Plato thinks it is?
2. Are we materialistic when we praise sense perception? What are the alternatives to any such materialism arising from overvaluing (or solely valuing) sense experience?
3. If we could perceive the world beneath sense experience, what would it be like?
4. I often ask my students to choose a sense that they do not already have and add it as a sixth sense that cannot be a merger of any of the five. It has to be new—not smelling, seeing, or hearing from a great distance. If nothing else, this exercise helps them begin to realize how hemmed in we are by our senses—particularly when I point out the ultimate similarity of touch, taste, and odor, three of the five senses that constitute virtually one sense with three "flavors."

SUGGESTIONS FOR BRIEF ESSAYS

1. Using Plato's cave as your basic reference, define *allegory.* Include a discussion of its usefulness and its effects along with a description of its nature.

2. Plato opens by talking about the extent to which we are enlightened. What is the effect on our enlightenment of the allegory he presents? What does an understanding of the allegory cause us to realize about ourselves?
3. What general human situation fits the circumstances that the prisoners in Plato's cave experience?
4. How successful is Plato's allegory for describing our awareness of how the mind works? How does it jibe with human experience?

SUGGESTIONS FOR LONGER ESSAYS

1. Consider whether Socrates is right when he says, "The truth is that the State in which the rulers are most reluctant to govern is always the best and most quietly governed, and the State in which they are most eager, the worst" (para. 61). Try to formulate a series of questions that might cast some light on this issue. Try to structure your essay in dialogue form.
2. In paragraphs 49 through 52, Socrates discusses a "clever rogue" whose mind is in the service of evil. He suggests that if circumstances were otherwise, the rogue might serve the good. What does this example say about Socrates' view of human nature and its relationship to education? Is personality a fixed thing? Is it fluid? What might affect it? Are Socrates' views on human nature and the personality modern or antiquated?
3. Write a new dialogue in which Socrates discusses a subject of keen importance to you or your friends. Include yourself as a speaker in the dialogue and any student friends you like. Try to make your dialogue sound as Platonic as possible.

SENTENCE OUTLINE: See p. 163 of this manual.

BIBLIOGRAPHY: See p. 189 of this manual.

FRANCIS BACON

The Four Idols (pp. 879–895)

Bacon is a favorite of mine; I always enjoy teaching this selection. I try to give my students a bit of background concerning the Elizabethan court and how individuals made their fortunes—often by being granted some exclusive right or monopoly by the crown and then exercising enormous power for as long as they could hold it. Fortunes were made quickly and lost quickly. Son of a distinguished man, Nicholas Bacon, lord keeper of the great seal and related to the powerful Sir William Cecil, Lord Burghley, Francis Bacon had close connections with Elizabeth's government. I don't usually describe the details of his rise through his influence with Robert Devereux, Earl of Essex, followed by his willingness to help in the government's prosecution of Essex for treason. Some biographers paint Bacon blackly for that deed, but I generally avoid mentioning it unless a student has happened to read up on Bacon.

Rather, I emphasize the fact that he lived in such turbulent times that succeeding almost meant looking first to Machiavelli's advice. Bacon rose in King James's court, becoming Lord High Chancellor in 1617 probably through the influence of George Villiers, the infamous Duke of Buckingham. But Buckingham was not as strong or as true a friend as Bacon thought, and when Bacon's enemies began to attack in November 1620, after the publication of his *Novum Organum* had swelled Bacon's reputation among some, Buckingham did not intervene. If anything, he profited from Bacon's downfall by taking over some of his choicest London property. Eventually, Buckingham helped him by lifting a ban virtually exiling him from London; meanwhile, Bacon had found contentment in his own writing. He said that his real career began in 1620, after his disgrace.

"The Four Idols" is especially important to teach to first-year college students because it includes so much they need to know. Most are innocent of the knowledge Bacon imparts. They find that they can immediately relate to each of the idols. I usually ask students to cite instances of the idols in action, and they rarely have trouble doing so. Sometimes we can actually spot them in action in the classroom, and there are even times when a student will—weeks later—catch me using one. I have not asked students to collect examples in newspapers or magazines, but such a project might be useful and might even produce a good subject for writing.

Naturally, I spend a good deal of time going over each idol to define it clearly. Bacon makes them so clear that I need hardly do it again. Still, a few moments confirming that the idols are understood will pay good rewards.

I am particularly interested in Bacon's rhetorical strategies—a paragraph for defining the idol and then several for developing its characteristics and analyzing its qualities. Enumeration is a powerful rhetorical tool, and because Bacon represents the clearest example in the book, I like to emphasize it here properly.

SUGGESTIONS FOR CLASS DISCUSSION

1. Ask students where they have last encountered one of the idols. This can be prefaced by asking whether the idols are still at work. The answer is obviously yes, but some people may want to talk about it.
2. It is important to discuss the ways in which the idols interfere with the study of natural phenomena. If possible, see whether your students know examples of discoveries that might not have been made if a given idol of thought had persisted.
3. Ask students which of the idols they feel is most likely to restrict scientific inquiry into the nature of nature.
4. Questions about Bacon's rhetorical structures will pay off well. Because this is a translation from Latin, style isn't usually an issue, but I do consider clarity, and how structure contributes to it, a sound topic for discussion. I ask students what they feel they can learn from examining Bacon's structure.
5. Point out the summary paragraphs so that students can get a good idea of how to use them in their own work.

SUGGESTIONS FOR BRIEF ESSAYS

1. Define the word *idols* in the sense that Bacon seems to use it. Is the word *idol* a good term to use for the idea that lies behind it?
2. Compare the importance of one idol with that of another. Is it possible to determine which is more likely to prevent the acquisition of true knowledge?
3. Which of the idols are the results of social intercourse, and which are the results of individual reflection? Would a person be more likely to be free of the tyranny of the idols if he/she were restricted in society? Is it possible that a hermit would be completely free of the idols? Or would he become more free the more he socialized?

SUGGESTIONS FOR LONGER ESSAYS

1. Bacon tells us that the idols are not innate but that they march plainly into our minds. How is it, then, that they are so universal? If they are not innate, they are certainly persistent. Explore how people acquire these four idols, using personal experience where possible. Have any new ways of learning these idols arisen since Bacon's time?
2. What circumstances relating to tribe, cave, marketplace, and theater make them useful as categorical titles for the idols? Invent a fifth idol whose name relates to our society as well as these four relate to Bacon's.
3. If you know of an inquiry into nature that is restricted because of adherence to one or more of the idols, describe it and establish the manner in which this inquiry has been hampered.

SENTENCE OUTLINE: See p. 164 of this manual.

BIBLIOGRAPHY: See p. 170 of this manual.

CHARLES DARWIN

Natural Selection (pp. 897–913)

I have found that many science majors graduate from college without ever having read Darwin, as if higher education were treating him as a literary rather than a scientific figure. That may be reasonable in some ways, particularly because he is indeed rather literate. But I also have found that virtually everyone I have heard denounce the theory of evolution has not read Darwin either. I have met no one who denounces the theory and who has also both read Darwin and done extensive research into evolutionary biology. I encourage my students to read Darwin with as receptive a mind as possible, looking for the details that build his argument and establish his views. This passage is an excellent model for the kinds of research students might conduct in their own college careers. It postulates careful questions, marshals a good deal of evidence—gathered from many sources—and poses a conclusion. I try to point out to my students that this is a useful model for a project that demands research and evidence gathering.

There is a definite controversy at this time over the theory of evolution itself. Steady rejection of the theory has occurred since 1859, and I point this out to interested students. Frankly, however, I am not interested enough in the controversy to encourage my students to discuss it. So far, I have had no students who have demanded equal time for the creationist viewpoint. Should your students raise the issue, I would simply ask them to present the evidence for the other side. But I would insist that the student read Darwin carefully.

SUGGESTIONS FOR CLASS DISCUSSION

1. Because I am interested in Darwin's evidence gathering, I call my students' attention to the kinds and quantity of evidence in this chapter. I ask them whether they are convinced by the nature of the evidence and whether they feel more evidence of a different kind might be needed.
2. Ask about the persuasive quality of the passage. I remind students that this is only part of one chapter in a fairly large book but also that it is one of the pivotal moments of the entire argument in favor of evolution because it describes the mechanism of evolution. If students are not convinced of the possibility of natural selection, then they cannot be convinced of the theory.
3. I like to ask my students whether there is anything offensive or repulsive about the theory of evolution. Do they feel it is demeaning for human beings to be a part of an evolutionary process?
4. Social Darwinism is also an exciting subject to discuss. I generally quote John D. Rockefeller, who defended his ruthlessness in building Standard Oil by saying that thc way onc breeds an American Beauty rose is to pluck all the small roses from the stem, leaving one. This represents the survival of the fittest, naturally, but in this case John D. Rockefeller, not nature, was making the choices.

SUGGESTIONS FOR BRIEF ESSAYS

1. Define the phrase *the survival of the fittest* (the title of this chapter in a later edition of *On the Origin of Species by Means of Natural Selection*). Look for ways in which its implications can be fully understood. Look, also, for examples by which it can be illustrated.
2. Compare the breeding of animals with natural selection. Which is more directed? Which is more dominated by chance? Which is more efficient? Which is more important?
3. How does cloning affect Darwin's views? Is cloning likely to undo the beneficial work of natural selection?
4. How does human social policy affect the survival of the fittest? Are modern medicine and modern social welfare agencies causing humans to be less fit? (You might keep in mind that all such human agencies actually help make us less animal-like and more human. But it is fun to watch students make this discovery on their own.)

SUGGESTIONS FOR LONGER ESSAYS

1. If you find any of Darwin's conclusions hard to accept, offer an analysis of his argument and examples. Based on your analysis, take a clear position and defend it. You may wish to reject the concept of natural selection or to accept only a part of it. Try to give examples—even if only "imaginary" ones—and structure your argument by using careful definitions and by considering opposing views.

2. Analyze Darwin's writing for instances of yielding to or avoiding any or all of Bacon's four idols. Which of the idols are likely to be most threatening to the acceptance of Darwin's thinking? To which is he likely to be most susceptible? You might consider the extent to which Darwin, who definitely read Bacon, profited from his reading.

3. Readers in Darwin's age resented several implications of his theory. One is the wastefulness of nature, permitting myriad useless variants to die in order to produce one that survives. Another is the savage portrait of nature implied in the battle for survival. That chance, rather than a thoughtful plan, governs evolution is, of course, still a sensitive point. Finally, the inclusion of humans in the evolutionary scheme was particularly offensive. Using the technique of enumeration, treat each of these points from the point of view of a person contemporary with Darwin. How much do these points still affect the modern age? Have our views changed?

4. Analyze Darwin's rhetorical strategies in this essay. Consider his structure and organization, his use of the common topics, and his attitude toward his audience. Add style and tone—keeping in mind that Darwin was anxious to convince his audience of his views but cautious not to overstep himself and incur the wrath of those who were disposed against them.

SENTENCE OUTLINE: See p. 165 of this manual.

BIBLIOGRAPHY: See p. 174 of this manual.

SIGMUND FREUD

The Oedipus Complex (pp. 915–925)

This selection appears very deep in Freud's *The Interpretation of Dreams.* However, it is useful to know that it is part of a larger section titled "Typical Dreams," in a subsection called "Dreams of the Death of Persons of Whom the Dreamer Is Fond." There are quite a few such typical dreams that can be accounted for by the Oedipus complex. Interestingly, the preceding section is titled "Embarrassing Dreams of Being Naked." If your students want to read more, that would be an interesting place to start.

One of the real advantages of this selection is that Freud not only writes clearly, but he avoids his usual habit of citing authority after authority (usually German) in the process of making his own insights plain. He uses very little jargon and thereby is better able to communicate with a general reader. Also, this is a very short selection, which will make it easier for your students to spend some time rereading as necessary.

Some of your students will have read both *Oedipus Rex* and *Hamlet.* Those students should be encouraged to comment on what they perceive in these plays that would have some importance for Freud's views. If possible, have the students who have read the plays summarize what they see as the key issues that have a relevance to the Freud piece, which will help the students who are unfamiliar with either or both plays. You may find yourself having to summarize the plays' key points, but given the detailed way in which Freud discusses them, you should not have to do more than reinforce what he has said.

The question that will probably be most important is whether or not the entire idea of the Oedipus complex is plausible. Your students will certainly find it a difficult concept. Most will have no sense of it as having been possible in their own mental life. However, those students who have young children in the family may have some observations that would help reinforce Freud's views. Freud used his own patients as the basis of his generalizations, so it is reasonable to ask your students to refer to their own personal experience in observing others to see if they can add to Freud's views.

SUGGESTIONS FOR CLASS DISCUSSION

1. Do you feel your dreams have a significance that would be useful to understand?
2. What dreams most mystify you?
3. Which dreams are frightening? Describe a recent frightening dream.
4. Why do you think most people forget their dreams?
5. Is dreaming a mental activity?

SUGGESTIONS FOR BRIEF ESSAYS

1. If dreaming is a mental activity, who or what controls it? Some of our mental activity is controlled by our ego, our conscious mind. Are dreams connected to the conscious mind? Are they in any way controlled by it?
2. In another essay, Freud says that dreams can be "inserted into the chain of intelligible waking mental acts." If you have had a recent dream that you know can be connected to events in your waking life, describe the dream carefully and make the connection clear. What is the relation of that dream to your waking life? How do you interpret it? Does it seem to involve fear or shame?

SUGGESTIONS FOR LONGER ESSAYS

1. Describe a dream that is definitely not an anxiety dream and that has absolutely no Oedipal content. Try to be specific in your description, with attention to the people in the dream, the colors you remember, the sounds, the odors, the textures you "touched." Describe the action in as much detail as possible. How might Freud have interpreted this dream? How do you interpret it?
2. If you have read *Hamlet* recently, examine it again for the likelihood of Hamlet's having an Oedipus complex. This point has been argued ever since Freud raised it in this selection, but the question has never been completely resolved. Examine Hamlet's scenes with his mother and the scenes in which he contemplates his father and his uncle. How accurate was Freud in his estimation of Hamlet's state of mind? Would Freud's view have an impact on the question of whether Hamlet was mad?
3. Do you think that animals dream? If you do, write a short essay on what you think a specific animal would dream about. Consider that some of the same mental issues that operate in us operate in, say, pets. For example if we are repressing certain guilt-producing events, is it possible that a dog who is prohibited from using the furniture (but does so when left alone in the house) could develop enough sense of guilt to experience repression?
4. To what extent do you think children's love/hate of their parents is normal? Freud implies that such feelings exist in all children. Do you think that is likely? If so, what would contribute to those feelings? Should children worry about them? Or are they just normal feelings resulting from their having very little power in the family setting? Argue a case that suggests that the mental states Freud describes are essentially normal and nothing to worry about.

SENTENCE OUTLINE: See p. 166 of this manual.

BIBLIOGRAPHY: See p. 178 of this manual.

CARL JUNG

The Personal and the Collective Unconscious (pp. 927–941)

Jung's work is never easy to understand, but this piece is one of his more accessible excursions into the nature of the mind. He follows Freud's lead in part by accepting his basic views of the unconscious. However, Jung's innovation concerns the investigation of the archetypal symbols that he asserts are part of the collective unconscious of every individual.

Depending on your students, you may find yourself discussing the very existence of the unconscious, especially in light of the fact that the person of common sense is not likely to be aware of any such thing. But even if your students agree that there is an unconscious, the concept of the archetype may be totally obscure to them. The dream that Jung analyzes is valuable for the fact that it presents one clear archetype—that of the divine. In *Archetypes of the Collective Unconscious* (1934) Jung begins with a note that one of the earliest references to the term *archetype* is in Philo Judaeus (fl. 10 B.C.) in his term *imago dei,* or the image of god. Among Jung's archetypes are the mother and the father, and if you are interested in pursuing this line of thought, you might collect your students' experience with these archetypes by having students define them as best they can.

The most interesting thing about this selection, however, is the thought that there may be such a thing as a collective unconscious revealed to us in terms of myth. Jung believes that we inherit the collective unconscious rather than acquire it from experience, and if that is true, we have a very interesting description of the mind. When I discuss these issues with students, I make every effort to avoid committing myself on the absolute truth of Jung's hypothesis. I prefer to maintain it as a hypothesis and to permit my students to work with the idea until it becomes evident to them one way or the other.

For me, one of the most important details Jung treats here is the question of self-knowledge. I try to direct students toward examining the ways in which a deeper knowledge of their unconscious can help them become more fully aware of themselves—to develop more self-knowledge. One way to do this is by asking students to write down their dreams, although there are always many who cannot remember them. Asking them to examine their dreams for the presence of archetypes of the most basic sort can be useful. Likewise, comparing students' dreams—looking for basic patterns that might be thought of as archetypal and thus revealing of a collective unconscious—is also interesting.

SUGGESTIONS FOR CLASS DISCUSSION

1. One useful strategy is to begin by questioning the existence of an unconscious mind and then go through the class finding examples of the unconscious at work. Dreams are among the most obvious examples, but there are also many examples in the "Freudian slip" department—when by accident someone says exactly what should not be said (usually revealing an unconscious association, such as during an argument calling your friend by your father's name).
2. Although it might be difficult, one potentially interesting approach is to discuss the myths that students know that might be universal in their importance and that therefore may qualify as archetypal. Fairy tales offer a source of archetypes, but so do the popular books by Tolkien. I also think that Rambo in the eponymous movies represents an archetype, although I usually connect it to wish fulfillment as much as to archetypal patterns. Western films are another source of mythic content.

SUGGESTIONS FOR BRIEF ESSAYS

1. If you know of examples of psychic content that has been repressed and that ultimately revealed itself (Jung says "reassociated with") to the conscious mind, describe the process. Use the narrative technique that Jung favors in telling your story.
2. If you have been able to create a dream, describe the dream and the means by which you were able to create it.
3. The conscious mind can will action. The unconscious mind can "only wish," according to Freud. If you feel this is untrue, offer your reasons. If you feel it is true, explain why the mind works in that fashion: Why is the unconscious unable to act?

SUGGESTIONS FOR LONGER ESSAYS

1. After researching the term *transference* in a textbook on psychology—or in the literature of psychoanalysis—explain the current thinking on this phenomenon. In what circumstances does transference occur? When is it healthy? Is it ever unhealthy?
2. Argue against Jung's position. How would you demonstrate that his hypothesis of the collective unconscious is unproven? Examine the weaknesses in his argument, and offer a counterstatement.

3. Assuming that Jung's view of the collective unconscious is demonstrable, how could an individual actually have such an unconscious? Must the individual be born with it as something resembling a genetic inheritance? If not, how could it be communicated to the individual without passing over the "threshold" of the conscious?

4. Examine a collection of children's literature. What archetypal images appear in the material that we might interpret as central to a child's psychic development? Do you think children are aware of the archetypal content of that literature? Were you as a child given the opportunity to absorb a wide range of children's literature? What do you think you absorbed from that literature? What could the cultural function of children's literature be for any culture?

SENTENCE OUTLINE: See p. 167 of this manual.

BIBLIOGRAPHY: See p. 182 of this manual.

RENÉ DESCARTES

Fourth Meditation: Of Truth and Error

(bedfordstmartins.com/worldofideas/epages)

In his translation of *Discourse on Method,* F. E. Sutcliffe points to "something of a paradox": Descartes has generally been considered a writer whose utmost clarity was taken for granted; yet in many ways his work is obscure. I think Sutcliffe is right. There are several moments of obscurity in Descartes's writing and in this selection. However, you can use these moments in your discussion to point out how important it is to fill in the ellipses that writers unconsciously permit in their writing. For example, in Descartes's time the existence of God was virtually a given. It was not a problem for Descartes to move from postulating a perfect being to declaring the existence of that being on the basis that such a postulation had to have a cause, and that cause could only be a perfect being. If there were no such being, he could not postulate it. Today, we may want something more convincing.

This Meditation is related to Discourse Four. If you have a copy of *Discourse on Method* nearby and can compare the two, you will see that most of the concerns in "Fourth Meditation" are echoed throughout. In Discourse Four, Descartes states his famous quotation, "I think, therefore I am." In this Meditation he explores the uses of his thinking. He has kept his method of moving from the basic step to more complex conclusions, and in the process he discusses the role of memory, imagination, understanding, and will. Free will, something implied in his discussion of will, can lead to a clouded judgment and is the source of error. Descartes makes this point in order to release God from the responsibility of his making mistakes. God has given him the faculty of memory—to avoid past error—and the faculty of understanding to sort out elements of an argument and to produce reliable information. Once that pattern is established, judgment then leads to a conclusion. You might discuss with your students what process, if any, they are aware of when they try to reach a conclusion about what might be true or might not be true. How do they avoid error in their thinking?

Of course, this selection is probably most interesting because it never makes reference to any concrete or palpable thing or event. Descartes proceeds here as if he were a mathematician by not referring to phenomena, but maintaining an intellectual discussion that must be conducted with pure reason. There is no specific evidence entered into the discussion. He must "figure out" for himself the answers to his questions, and he does so by turning within and reviewing his thought processes and then using them to help achieve the end of knowledge. He is very comfortable using his mind to examine his mind, a procedure that does not work well in modern examinations of the mind and its relation to the body.

I pose a number of questions about the connections of mind and body, and I think this is a useful question to put to your students. Most of them will probably not have given it any thought, and some will think it hardly matters. But a probing discussion should uncover some of the seriousness of the distinction. Descartes says that the mind is "what I am," and you will want to explore that idea with students. I suspect you'll get a wide variety of opinions.

SUGGESTIONS FOR CLASS DISCUSSION

1. Why is doubt an important and valuable intellectual tool?
2. What is the importance of truth? Why must error be avoided?
3. How convincing is Descartes's distinction between the mind and the body?
4. Descartes says he has a weakness that makes it impossible to "keep my mind continually fixed on the same thought" (para 15). Why is that a problem, given his purposes in this meditation?

SUGGESTIONS FOR BRIEF ESSAYS

1. In a brief essay, explain what Descartes sees as the nature of God. He constantly refers to God throughout the essay and makes several claims about God's nature. What qualities does Descartes's God possess? What is Descartes's relationship with God? Given the nature of his God, how can Descartes expect to have free will? What mental qualities possessed by people make it evident to Descartes that God exists?
2. The question of the mind/body distinction is raised in paragraph 11. Descartes suggests in that paragraph that he does not know whether "the thinking nature which is in me, or rather by which I am what I am, is different from this corporeal nature, or whether both are merely one and the same thing." Then he seems to say that it hardly matters. Do you think it matters? What is your view on the relationship of mind to the physical brain? Do you feel you are your mind? Or do you feel you are your body? What would it matter which you decide?
3. What problems does Descartes leave unsolved in this discourse? Establish what you feel he is trying to say to you, then point to the difficulties that remain in your efforts to understand fully what he is trying to communicate. Why is the selection difficult to interpret?

SUGGESTIONS FOR LONGER ESSAYS

1. Descartes discusses memory, understanding, and will in paragraphs 9 and 10. Explain what he means by these terms, and interpret them in relation to your own experience. How does your memory work? How does it relate to your understanding, and how do both help you discover and maintain the truth of things? What is meant by "will" in this selection? Do you also possess the kind of will that Descartes describes, and is it as likely to lead you into error, as Descartes feels it will lead him? How do your memory, understanding, and imagination help you discover the truth and avoid error? If possible, use a concrete example from your recent experience to illustrate your argument.
2. In paragraph 8 Descartes says "that one must not consider a single creature separately, when one seeks to inquire into the perfection of God's works, but generally all creatures together." Why does Descartes insist on this principle? Explain why it is essential to consider all creatures and perhaps all creation when examining the perfection Descartes refers to rather than singling out one creature or one class of creatures or even one class of phenomena in the universe. Then consider the usefulness of his comment for the purposes of establishing the truth of any principle of importance.
3. Using the material in both the introduction to this selection and the selection itself, explain Descartes's method and what he hopes will result from its application. Then examine "Fourth Meditation" to see whether or not he applies the method himself. What kinds of truth do you feel can be learned from his method? What kinds of truth could not be discovered by the use of this method?

SENTENCE OUTLINE: See p. 168 of this manual.

BIBLIOGRAPHY: See p. 175 of this manual.

SENTENCE
OUTLINES

The following sentence outlines are presented
in the order in which they appear in the text.

ARISTOTLE
Democracy and Oligarchy (pp. 59–73)

Paragraphs 1–3: Diverse forms of government exist because states are made up of many different kinds of people, including laborers, families, and the wealthy. The composition of states and the distribution of power among classes within a state also differ, and there are as many forms of government as there are ways of arranging the offices of power within a state. Democracy and oligarchy, however, are the two main forms of government, and everything else is a variation of these. The free rule in democracy, while the rich rule in oligarchy. More specifically, a government is a democracy when the rulers are free, poor, and in the majority, whereas an oligarchy is ruled by people who are rich, aristocratic, and in the minority.

4–5: The parts of a state are made up of different classes of people: farmers, craftsmen, commercial traders, laborers, warriors, administrators of justice, property owners, politicians, judges, and statesmen. These roles are not exclusive; for example, an individual can be both a craftsman and a warrior. However, a person cannot be both rich and poor. Because the rich are generally small in number and the poor large, these economic classes are antagonistic to each other. If the rich prevail, the government is an oligarchy; if the poor prevail, the government is a democracy.

6–7: In one form of democracy, based on equality, all people share in the government. In another kind of democracy, only property holders participate. There are also forms, however, where the masses have the power, rather than the law. When the laws are not supreme, demagogues gain power. In this situation, power is held collectively, not individually. The masses rule in the manner of tyrants, and everything is subject to popular vote. It is fair to say that this form of government is not really a democracy, since the law does not reign supreme.

8–9: In some forms of oligarchy, the majority has no share at all in government; in others, there is a high qualification for office. Sometimes the rule is hereditary, passed down from father to son. Another form of hereditary rule occurs when the magistrates, not the law, reign supreme. This form, like the last form of democracy mentioned above, is tyrannical.

10: In the form of democracy ruled by farmers and other laborers with little leisure time, the government is administered by law; everyone participates, but the government assembles only when necessary, and political representatives are not paid. In other forms of democracy, the only participants are those who have the time and money to do so. The most recent form of democracy evolved when cities grew and became wealthy. Everyone participates and shares in administration. The poor are paid to participate, and they gain more power than the wealthy, who cannot afford the leisure time to govern. In this form of democracy, the masses are supreme, and the poor—not the laws—govern the state.

11: In the first form of oligarchy, ruled by numerous property holders, the sharers in governance are many; therefore, the law is supreme, not individuals. The second form of oligarchy is ruled by very few property holders, and power resides in a small minority that uses the law to represent its desires. In the third form of oligarchy, the hereditary governing class accumulates great power and becomes much like a monarchy because individuals rule and not the law.

12–16: There are five forms of government: monarchy, oligarchy, aristocracy, democracy, and constitutional government. Aristocracy is rule by the most noble or meretricious men. Constitutional government is a fusion of democracy and oligarchy. In the way that aristocracy inclines toward oligarchy, constitutional government inclines toward democracy. Citizens claim a share of government on three grounds: freedom, wealth, and virtue. When free and wealthy people rule, we call this constitutional government or polity. When free, wealthy, and virtuous people rule, we call this aristocracy or rule by the best.

17: Oligarchical and democratic governments can be combined in three different ways to make constitutional government. In the first way, the laws made by both oligarchies and democracies are combined. In the second, a middle ground, or mean, between the two is found. In the third, principles are borrowed from both oligarchical and democratic forms.

18–19: In some states the fusion of oligarchy and democracy is so complete that the state can be called by either name. Some people call Sparta a democracy because education is given to all, and the rich and the poor eat the same food and wear the same clothes. But other people call Sparta an oligarchy because representatives are elected to office by vote, not lottery, and the power to judge is held by the few, not the many. In a constitutional government, elements of both oligarchy and democracy should be present, the government should be self-dependent, and all classes in the state should be willing to maintain the constitution.

THE FOUNDING FATHERS

The Constitution of the United States (pp. 75–107)

Preamble: We the people of the United States establish the Constitution for the following reasons: justice, domestic peace, national defense, prosperity, and freedom.

Article I: The Congress, made up of the Senate and the House of Representatives, shall have the power to enact laws. Members of the House are elected every two years. The population of a state includes free people and three-fifths of each slave, and excludes untaxed Indians. Each state has two senators chosen every six years. The Vice President is the President of the Senate. The Senate tries all impeachments. Each House of Congress shall determine its own rules of proceeding, and all senators and representatives will be compensated for their service. Spending bills will originate in the House of Representatives. In order to become law, bills must pass the House and Senate and then be signed by the President. Presidential vetoes can be overturned by a two-thirds vote of both Houses. The Congress has the power to collect taxes, pay debts, provide for the national defense, borrow money, regulate international commerce, coin money and punish counterfeiters, establish the post office, regulate trademarks and patents, establish lower courts, punish pirates, declare war, establish and maintain an army and a navy, organize and govern state militias, and create laws for the district that is the seat of government. Prisoners cannot be unlawfully detained. The Congress cannot give regulatory preference to one state over another. States cannot coin money or make treaties on their own.

Article II: The President has executive power. The President is elected by state electors equal to the total number of senators and representatives in each state. Only natural-born citizens over age thirty-five who have been residents of the United States for fourteen years can be President. If the President dies, is discharged from office, or is incapacitated, the Vice President will take over the presidency. The President will promise to preserve, protect, and defend the Constitution. The President is commander in chief of the armed forces, and he has the power to pardon, make treaties, appoint ambassadors and judges, and make recess appointments. The President shall give to Congress information on the State of the Union and can call joint sessions of Congress on extraordinary occasions. The Congress can impeach and remove from office the President, Vice President, or other civil officers if they are guilty of treason, bribery, or other high crimes and misdemeanors.

Article III: The Supreme Court and all lower courts established by Congress have the judicial power of the United States. The Supreme Court has final jurisdiction. All trials should be jury trials tried in the states where the crimes took place. The Congress decides punishment for treason.

Article IV: All states must respect the laws and proceedings of other states. A state cannot discriminate against the citizens of other states. Fugitive slaves should be returned to the states they escaped from. New states can be admitted to the United States, and all those states shall have republican forms of government.

Article V: By two-thirds vote, the Congress can propose amendments to the Constitution. These amendments are ratified when they are approved by three-fourths of the states.

Article VI: The Constitution is the supreme law of the land. All elected officials shall swear to support the Constitution. There can never be a required religious test for elected officials.

Article VII: Ratification by nine states will establish the Constitution. The Constitution is ratified and established by unanimous order of this Constitutional Convention.

Preamble to the Bill of Rights: The states wish to prevent abuse of government power, so the following ten amendments shall be added to the Constitution and known as the Bill of Rights.

Amendment 1:   Congress shall not establish a religion or prohibit the exercise of religion. It shall not lessen freedom of speech or the press. The people have the right to assemble and petition the government.

Amendment 2:   Congress shall not infringe on the right of the people to bear arms.

Amendment 3: Soldiers shall not be quartered in private houses without the consent of the owner.

Amendment 4: Without a warrant based on probable cause, people cannot be searched.

Amendment 5: Grand juries indict citizens for capital or serious crimes. No citizen can be tried twice for the same crime. Citizens cannot be compelled to incriminate themselves. Citizens have the right to due process. Property cannot be taken for public use without just compensation.

Amendment 6: Defendants have the right to a speedy and public trial by an impartial jury within the district where the crime was committed. Defendants have the right to face accusers and witnesses. Defendants can call witnesses. Defendants have the right to legal representation.

Amendment 7: Citizens have the right to trial by jury in civil cases.

Amendment 8: Defendants should not be given excessive bail, fines, or cruel and unusual punishments.

Amendment 9: There are other rights that citizens have outside the Constitution.

Amendment 10: Powers not granted to United States nor prohibited to the states are reserved for the states or the people.

Amendment 11: States have sovereign immunity and cannot be sued without consent.

Amendment 12: Each elector casts one vote for President and Vice President.

Amendment 13: Slavery and indentured servitude are abolished.

Amendment 14: All persons born or naturalized in the United States are citizens. No state can take away rights from citizens, nor deprive them of life, liberty, property, or the equal protection of the law. All residents are counted to determine populations of states. The right to vote cannot be denied to any male over age 21. No person can hold office who previously rebelled against the United States. All public debt is valid. The United States will not pay compensation for the loss of any slave.

Amendment 15: The right to vote cannot be denied based on race, color, or previous enslavement.

Amendment 16: Congress can collect income taxes.

Amendment 17: Senators should be elected by popular vote.

Amendment 18: Alcohol cannot be made, sold, brought in, or shipped out of any place in the United States.

Amendment 19: Women have the right to vote.

Amendment 20: The terms of the President and the Vice President end at noon on January 20, and the terms of Senators and Representatives end at noon on January 3. Rules are given for filling the office of President in case of death.

Amendment 21: Repeal of the Eighteenth Amendment.

Amendment 22: Presidents cannot be elected more than twice.

Amendment 23: Citizens of the District of Columbia can vote for President and Vice President.

Amendment 24: Congress cannot make a citizen pay a tax to vote.

Amendment 25: The Vice President becomes President if the President dies. The President can nominate a new Vice President if the office is vacant, and his nominee must then be confirmed by Congressional vote. When the President submits a written declaration of resignation, the Vice President becomes President. If the President is incapacitated, the Vice President shall be acting President.

Amendment 26: All citizens over age 18 have the right to vote.

Amendment 27: No law that changes the compensation for members of Congress shall take effect until the start of the next term of Congress.

JAMES MADISON

Federalist Paper 51: On the Separation of Departments of Power
(pp. 109–119)

Paragraphs 1–3: In order to preserve freedom, the powers of government should be separate. Each department of government should interfere as little as possible in the appointment of other departments' members. Though the people are the source of all authority, direct elections of the judiciary are problematic. Each department of government should be as independent as possible.

4–5: In order to stop the concentration of power, each department must be given the constitutional means to resist the influence of other departments—the departments must be in competition with one another. This competitive balance will guard against abuses of power. Rival interests in government will provide checks and balances.

6–7: Each department, however, cannot be equally powerful. The legislative department dominates in republics. In order to diffuse legislative power, there should be separate legislative branches with different means of election and as little connection to one another as possible. The executive, in contrast, might be too weak on ordinary occasions and too strong on extraordinary occasions. Perhaps the best way to deal with this is to make the executive dependent on the weaker branch of the legislative department. These principles can be applied to both state and federal constitutions.

8–9: In a republic, the people give power to a single government with separate powers. In America the power is divided between state governments and the federal government, and this power is then further separated into the different branches of government. The people's rights therefore have a double security against tyranny.

10: In a republic, parts of society must also be protected from one another. Citizens have different interests, and a majority can abuse the rights of a minority. There are two ways to protect against this abuse: (1) create a powerful authority outside of the majority; (2) have so many diverse interest groups in a society that it becomes impossible for an unjust majority to rule. The first method occurs in all governments with hereditary power, and it is not a very effective defense against oppression. The second method will be used in the United States, where the interests, classes, and groups are so diverse that unjust actions on the part of a majority will be unlikely. Just as many religious sects guarantee religious liberty, so do many civil interest groups guarantee civil rights. The more diversity a state has, the more security it has. A federal system is the best form of republican government. The government should protect all parties, and it should protect the weak from the strong. If the weak are not protected from the oppression of the strong, anarchy reigns; the uncertainty of anarchy leads even the strong to want government protection. The largeness and diversity of the United States make it capable of self-government. The republican cause of self-government is aided greatly by federalism, or divided government.

ALEXIS DE TOCQUEVILLE

Government by Democracy in America (pp. 121–141)

Paragraphs 1–4: Europeans should study American democracy because it has been enacted in a free and natural way.

5–17: All Americans—a highly diverse group—can vote. Some Europeans believe that universal suffrage will lead to political rule by the very best and most competent men. In America, however, this is not the case: the most outstanding men are rarely in public office. This happens because the masses work very hard and cannot devote all their time to becoming enlightened; thus, the people often make uninformed decisions when electing politicians. Also, since democratic institutions promote envy, the people can become resentful of the successful and exclude them from the offices of power. Distinguished men know this and do not seek political careers.

18–29: From times of crisis, great leaders often emerge. Exceptional men are willing to take public office, and the people put aside their envy and support the best candidates. The dramatic circumstances of the American Revolution caused extraordinary leaders to emerge. Regional values also influence American democracy, and America's different communities make very different political choices. Even the Senate and the House of Representatives have widely divergent compositions. Because of the Senate's two-tier election process, Senators tend to represent the broad and refined values of the community. The members of the House are coarser because the people elect them directly.

30–38: Americans prefer the instability that comes with a short interval between elections to the risks of revolution that come with a long interval. Even though the founders warned us about it, feverish law-making is simply a fact of American democracy.

39–53: American civil servants look like all other Americans—they are plain and approachable. Since power is a necessary evil, those who hold power do not wish to show it off; this is one reason American officials are not uniformed. Unpaid government officials are the first step toward aristocracy and monarchy. Because American officials are paid for their service, anyone can and does run for office—including coarse men of moderate desires. This leads the talented and passionate to avoid politics and pursue wealth.

54–69: Officers of the state exercise arbitrary power in both absolute monarchies and democracy. In absolute monarchies, a ruler allows magistrates great freedom because he knows they will never use their power against him. Since democracies can remove magistrates from power at any time, the people's ultimate control leads democracies to give great power to officials—a power even greater than that given to royal officials. American officials are free because the electorate merely shows them the goal; it doesn't tell them how to get there. Thus, political officials in democracies can enact more restrictive and arbitrary laws than the most despotic monarchy can.

70–73: American society leaves very few records. Newspapers are the only historical documents in America. There is a lack of historical consciousness in America—no one thinks about what happened in previous years, and American administrators learn little from the past. The instability of democracy can damage government.

74–88: Democratic republics produce much more wealth than despotic monarchies. Comparing free nations to each other will tell us about the financial systems of each country. A nation can always be separated into three classes: the rich, the comfortable, and workers with little property. If the wealthy make laws, they will not care much about spending money. The middle classes, in contrast, will not want to spend money or raise taxes, so government by them is the most economical. Government by the lowest classes will lead to lots of spending since higher taxes do not hurt people with no property; the wealthy will be taxed to benefit the poor. Only in democratic government can people vote for taxes that they do not have to pay.

89 101: Universal suffrage gives control of the government to the poor. However, as the masses become wealthier and have a greater share in their country's economy, this becomes less of a problem. Aristocracy is satisfied with the way things are, so aristocrats do not try to improve a country's lot. In democracies, though, the people are always trying to improve things. This leads to restlessness, excitement, innovations, expenditures, and new necessities. Expenses, civilization, knowledge, and taxes all rise together. The last reason why democracies are more expensive than other governments is that democracies cannot always manage money. The state constantly expands, and its expenditures are inefficient.

CARL BECKER

Ideal Democracy (pp. 143–163)

Paragraphs 1–7: Democracy is a vague word; in order to discuss it, we must define it. In the most general sense, democracy refers to a form of government by the many and not the one. Its source of authority is the people and not the ruler.

8–10: Democracy is rare. Democracies began to flourish worldwide only in the nineteenth century. Historically, democratic governments have had limited success because they are a luxury.

11–13: In order to exist, democracies must meet certain material conditions. One is ease of communication; the citizens *must* be able to share information. Another is economic security; democracy does not thrive in poor countries.

14: Democracies must also meet intellectual conditions. Its citizens should be capable of managing their own affairs and compromising. They also have to be rational men of good will who can fairly judge public policy.

15–18: Ancient democracies were pragmatic and limited. They consisted of people bound together by kinship and tradition. Modern democracies, however, are different. They are based on an ideology of universal and inalienable individual rights.

19–26: The secular intellectual revolution in the West gave rise to the modern doctrine of progress. Men had long imagined ideal worlds, but most often these were projected into a legendary past or a heavenly afterlife. Men now began to conceive a utopia founded on natural laws. Through rational principles and hard work, men could actually create this state. In fact, it became clear that man has a duty to bring his political institutions into accord with the laws of nature and nature's God.

27–28: Instead of the state, the individual was exalted. Men had self-evident and imprescriptible rights that government could not impair. Combined with reason, liberty would bring about material and moral progress for all of mankind. Since freedom and competition lead to good outcomes, the government's main purpose is to ensure as much personal liberty as possible.

29–31: The founders of modern democracy had faith in reason, good will, and public service. They were idealists. However, their vision of democracy is not the same as the democracy we actually have.

JULIUS K. NYERERE

One-Party Government (pp. 165–175)

Paragraphs 1–7: Just like the ancient Greeks, Africans conceive of democracy as founded on discussion—leaders talk until an agreement is reached. To contemporary Westerners familiar with the parliamentary tradition, though, this kind of government appears to be a one-sided dictatorship. However, democracy is defined as governance by discussion rather than force. The two-party system is only one form of democracy, and having opposition groups does not necessarily make a political system democratic.

8–12: The British two-party system evolved within a class-based society. Africa does not have the same concept of class; the colonial power is the opposition party, not other Africans. The struggle for independence has left the people of African countries united, but the difficulty of post-independence nation building will demand even more solidarity.

13–18: The essentials of democracy are individual well-being and freedom. Democracy is as much an attitude as it is a form of government. We have asked what attitude the government will have toward its opposition. We must also ask what attitude the opposition will have toward its government. Every government has trouble meeting all of its obligations to the people. Africans will expect a lot from their new governments, and the common African people must be listened to. Most newly free African countries are very diverse, with little internal unity, and these divisions will make nation building difficult.

19–24: New African nations will also face external pressure from foreign countries. For this reason, the new governments should act as they would in a national emergency. Because the new nations are so fragile, the opposition parties must act responsibly, and the government cannot be overly tolerant of an irresponsible opposition. Democracy in Africa has a long history, and the anti-imperialist struggle, combined with native African democratic traditions, bodes well for the future of democracy in Africa.

BENAZIR BHUTTO

Islam and Democracy (pp. 177–194)

Paragraphs 1–4: Some people think that democracy cannot work in Islamic countries because Muslims value the laws of God over the laws of men. However, humans must strive for a just society on earth in order to gain entrance to Paradise in the afterlife. Therefore, even though the terrorists who attacked me justified doing so by claiming that they acted in the name of God, on judgment day they will still have to account for their own actions. They will not be able to rely on a religious edict granted by another human being to justify taking innocent people's lives.

5–7: The Constitution of Pakistan recognizes and grants Muslims the right to a democratic government. However, the word *secular,* which refers to the separation of government and religion in the West, often translates into *atheism* in other languages, including Urdu in Pakistan. This makes democracy seem contradictory to Islam, so new terminology may be needed to realize democracy in the Muslim world. The individual aspects of democracy—free elections, an independent judiciary, respect for women's and minority rights, the rule of law, and fundamental freedoms—are compatible with the values of Islam and would be clearer to Muslims in discussing democracy than a word like *secular.*

8–13: Islam is being misused for political purposes. Militant Muslim extremists are always angry for many reasons, but that anger is always politically motivated, not spiritually motivated. They have tended to target nationalist movements to advance their agendas, yet most Muslims have not welcomed the extreme interpretation of Islam. Extremists were able to establish the Taliban in Afghanistan only because the country had already been softened by years of resistance by Afghan mujahideen. These extremists typically blame Americans for the civil war in Iraq, but the war is actually a result of long-standing tension among Muslim communities that extremists have encouraged and exploited. Pakistan is also a target of extremists: pro-Taliban forces have set up in many areas of the country and are looking to spread to the capital city, Islamabad.

14–15: I returned to Pakistan to try and move my country from dictatorship toward democracy in the 2008 elections. Extremists were threatening to take over Pakistan's nuclear program in Islamabad, and I feared the people of Pakistan would suffer because the country's dictators were focused on containing democrats instead of extremists, who are clearly the actual threat.

16–19: Despite how it is abused by extremists, Islam is actually tolerant of other religions and cultures as well as of dissenters. The Quran supports the rights of women, encourages learning, and prohibits violence against innocents—in other words, it empowers the people with rights, which is the essence of democracy. It also requires that leaders consult with their people (parliament) and that leaders serve the interest of their people or are replaced by them (accountability). Modern Muslims need to reclaim Islam's message of liberation from the extremists who abuse the religion. Only by accepting that earthly and spiritual accountability are two different matters can the true message of Islam thrive and pave the way for reconciliation with the West.

20–24: Conventional wisdom says that Islam is too authoritative to foster democracy. This simplistic thinking serves to divert attention from the West's interference in Muslim nations, which has been a major obstacle to democracy. Western policies have encouraged authoritarian governments in Muslim-majority nations. The West has given very little real support to democratic movements in Muslim countries. The gap between the West's rhetoric and its actions has led to public cynicism and extremism. Few Muslims continue to see the West as a model of freedom.

25–28: More important to Western countries than spreading democratic values has been their own economic and strategic interests. The West—especially the United States—talks about freedom as a God-given right, but selectively practices a double standard. In some places the United States supports dictators (Pakistan, Saudi Arabia, and Egypt) while overthrowing them in neighboring countries (Afghanistan, Iraq). Morality should not be selectively applied.

29–32: Clearly, there is a relationship between religious extremism and dictatorship. The West's support for dictatorships in Islamic states has led to Muslim hostility toward the West. But the lack of democracies in the Muslim world cannot be blamed on the Quran. A battle within Islam is, indeed, one part of the problem. However, the West deserves blame for the second part: its long-lasting colonization and exploitation of Muslim countries. Even though there is shared responsibility for these problems, Muslim countries are still far less democratic than the rest of the world.

33–38: Freedom and democracy are universal political values—they are not exclusively Western. We can compare Muslim and non-Muslim countries by democratic standards. By analyzing elections, political pluralism and participation, and government functions, the organization Freedom House rates governments on a scale from "totally free" to "not free." Freedom House's analytical tools work well in Muslim countries because they account for the role of religion in democratic government. The Freedom House ratings show large differences between Muslim and non-Muslim nations. Of forty-five Muslim states, only three are ranked free, while eighteen are partly free, and twenty-four are not free. The scores for political rights and civil liberties are also much worse in Muslim countries. These differences cannot be blamed on Islam but are the fault of external Western interference and the politicization of Islam within Muslim countries.

39–46: Comparing Muslim countries, we see that non-Arab Muslim-majority nations are freer than Arab ones. This suggests that the problem is not religious. Democracies often develop slowly over time. They are defined by governance as well as by elections. Shared power—not one-party rule after an electoral victory—is an important part of democratic governance. The longer a democracy lasts, the more democratic it becomes. New democracies are vulnerable; they must be nurtured. Interruptions to democratic governance can have long-lasting effects. Achieving goals peacefully is an admirable pragmatic ideal. Colonial experiences have made democracy difficult for Muslim countries. The West often stopped democratic values and structures from growing strong in newly independent countries.

STEPHEN L. CARTER

The Separation of Church and State

(bedfordstmartins.com/worldofideas/epages)

Paragraphs 1–2: Constitutional and philosophical traditions in the United States ensure the separation of church and state, but these traditions do not mean that people with religious motivations arc banned from trying to influence government.

3–6: Although religious liberty is strongly guaranteed by the First Amendment, what this liberty means in practice is complex. The notion of separation of church and state, for example, forbids government funding of religion-based social programs, a fact that frustrates supporters of such programs. Nevertheless, the aim of separation is to guarantee religious freedom.

7–8: The notion of a "wall of separation" between church and state is grounded in the Establishment Clause of the First Amendment, the clause that protects religious practice from government control.

9–10: While many controversial Supreme Court decisions based on the Establishment Clause were clearly right, other efforts to apply the doctrine have been misguided, creating what some regard as a hostility to religion in America. A strong "wall of separation" is important, but the wall should include some doors.

11–13: Since 1971, the Supreme Court has used the *Lemon* test (based on the Court's decision in *Lemon v. Kurtzman*) to decide whether a statute meets the requirements of the Establishment Clause. The test has been problematic because it protects secular politics at the expense of religious freedom and it gives lower courts poor guidance.

14–16: In applying *Lemon,* the Supreme Court has considered the religious motives of legislators (*why* they voted for a statute) rather than the actual effect of the statute (*what* it does). The notion that religious motivation makes a statute unconstitutional is an erroneous interpretation of the Establishment Clause.

17–19: Under current interpretations of the Establishment Clause, legislation motivated by proponents' religious convictions could be ruled unconstitutional even if the legislation were purely secular in effect. Such a ruling would undermine the basic concept of religious freedom guaranteed in the Constitution.

20–21: Recognizing this danger, legal scholars and Supreme Court justices have ignored the *Lemon* test, or found ways of getting around it. The Court, in effect, has ignored its own rules; it should therefore find a new way to approach the problem.

22–23: While there is no clear consensus, several scholars have proposed alternatives to the *Lemon* test. Any new understanding of the Establishment Clause should not assume that its main purpose is to protect the secular from the religious.

LAO-TZU

Thoughts from the *Tao-te Ching* (pp. 203–217)

Verse 3: The Master leads not by seeking power and control but by refraining from action and letting events unfold on their own.

17: The Master rules quietly, drawing no attention to himself; when he accomplishes something, the people believe that they themselves accomplished it.

18: When there are disorder and evil, order and goodness appear.

19: If you refrain from imposing artificial categories, good will appear naturally; let all things take their own course.

26: The Master should be steady, serenely content within herself.

29: The world is sacred and cannot be improved; there is a proper time for all things. Recognizing this, the Master remains still and does not try to control events.

30: The wise ruler does not use force; doing so only produces a counterforce. Understanding that the universe is beyond his control, he submits to the Tao and lives content within himself.

31: Peace is the greatest good. The decent man resorts to violence only as a last resort, and he does so with great sorrow and with compassion for his enemies.

37: If the powerful could center themselves in the Tao, all would be transformed, and people would be content and free from desire.

38: By not acting, the Master leaves nothing undone; by acting, ordinary men leave much undone. Loss of the Tao can lead to empty ritual and chaos; therefore, the Master concerns herself with profound truths rather than illusion.

46: In harmony with the Tao, a country lives in peace rather than preparing for war. We should put aside the illusion of fear, put aside preparations to defend ourselves against enemies.

53: When the affluent prosper and the poor suffer, balance is lost. To achieve balance, stay centered within the Tao.

57: When the leader stops trying to control, the world governs itself. The more control you impose, the less order there will be.

58: In governing a country, tolerance is preferable to repression. Attempts to force the people to change will fail. Thus the Master does not try to impose his will.

59: The best leader is moderate: open-minded, tolerant, flexible.

60: The leader should govern as unobtrusively as possible. Evil will lose its power if the leader follows the Tao.

61: The greater a nation's power, the more humble it should be. A great nation acknowledges its faults and corrects them; it tends to its own affairs and does not meddle in the affairs of others.

65: The ancient Masters taught the people to not-know, for when the people understand that they do not know, they find their own way. If you wish to govern, live a simple life so that you can lead people to rediscover their own true nature.

66: Governing the people requires humility. Even though the Master is over the people, no one feels mastered by her.

67: Those who think deeply will see that my teaching is wise. I teach simplicity, patience, and compassion.

75: When government is unobtrusive, the people thrive.

80: If a country is governed wisely, the people will be content with what they have and where they live.

114

NICCOLÒ MACHIAVELLI

The Qualities of the Prince (pp. 219–235)

Paragraphs 1–6:   A prince's sole concern and profession must be war, its institutions, and its discipline. An unarmed man is unsafe and despised among armed men. Even in peacetime a prince must keep his body and his mind in shape for war, studying terrain, strategy, and the history of successful commanders.

7–8:   To hold his position, a prince must be realistic rather than idealistic; he must learn how not to be good. He should avoid the reputation of vice, except for those vices he needs to hold his state.

9–11:   The prince who displays generosity (except in looting and sacking with his soldiers) will lose his wealth and the regard of his subjects. He is wiser to maintain the resources he needs to defend against enemies and be thought a miser than to become poor or known for rapacity.

12–18:   A little judicious cruelty shows more compassion than excessive mercy, which permits disorder. A prince must be cautious but decisive and is safer being feared than loved. He should take lives when necessary, but he should never earn his subjects' hatred by taking their property or women, even during war.

19–22:   Shrewd manipulation of men's minds is more essential than keeping promises. Men fight with laws, while beasts fight with force; but since laws often fail, a prince must be a fox to recognize traps and a lion to frighten the wolves.

23–25:   The prince need not be virtuous but only *seem* to be: he should appear merciful, faithful, and full of integrity, kindness, and religion, while in fact doing whatever is necessary to hold power. He must avoid seeming changeable, frivolous, effeminate, cowardly, or irresolute.

26–28:   Danger to a prince can be external (from foreign powers) or internal (from subjects conspiring against him). Good troops and friends will prevail over external threats; satisfying the people and avoiding their hatred will protect him from assassination and overthrow.

JEAN-JACQUES ROUSSEAU

The Origin of Civil Society (pp. 237–257)

Paragraphs 1–2: What is the basis of government? This inquiry examines human beings as they are and laws as they might be and considers justice and utility as inseparable. Being a citizen and a voter is enough qualification and reason to investigate the nature of public affairs.

3–7: Man is born free, and everywhere he is in chains. The social order and its constraints arise from conventions and not from nature. In a family, self-preservation binds children to their father; if the bond lasts after they become self-sufficient, then the family exists by choice and convention. So too with government, where both ruler and people cede their freedom only so far as it benefits them.

8–14: Some commentators, such as Grotius, take slavery as proof that political power is never exercised in the interest of the governed. In illogically deriving right from fact, they are in effect denying membership in the human race to most of humanity. Force, not nature, makes slaves.

15–18: Those who take power cannot hold it forever unless they cast might as right and obedience as duty. This is logical gibberish, however, for might is physical, not moral, and right would be invalid if it vanishes whenever might changes hands. No man is under an obligation to obey any but the legitimate power of the state—legitimacy being conferred by agreement among the people.

19–23: The argument that a people can subject themselves to a king as a slave does to a master is false—the slave surrenders his liberty for his subsistence, whereas the king subsists off the people. To be legitimate, a government must not impose more hardship than it prevents, and it must be accepted freely by each new generation.

24–30: The argument that a slave agrees to yield his liberty in exchange for his life implies that one man has the right to kill another in war. Wars, however, are between states, not individuals. We are justified in killing our enemies only while they fight as soldiers against us—that is, only when we cannot enslave them. Thus the alleged right to enslave is based on the alleged right to kill, and vice versa, proving that slavery has no validity.

31–43: Conquest may turn individuals into slaves or masters, but kingship must be conferred by the people. A group comes to function as a people by virtue of a social contract enlisting the community's strength on behalf of each individual, while preserving individual freedom. Any abridgment of individual freedom cancels the contract.

44–47: The body politic—the entity created by and comprising the individual parties to the social contract—cannot bind itself to any agreement that would violate that contract. Any attack on one of its members is an attack on the whole body, and vice versa.

48–51: The body politic need not give a guarantee to its members, as it exists at their will and for their benefit. An individual member's private and public interests may diverge, however. The body politic is therefore entitled to compel members' compliance with the general will.

52–54: The passage from the state of nature to the civil state substitutes justice for instinct in individual behavior, creates a moral basis for action, and gives reason priority over desire.

55–61: With regard to property, physical strength and the right of the first-comer are replaced by the rights of ownership under the social contract. Individuals cede their property to the state, and the state legitimates their claim to it. A person's title to land is based on the land being unoccupied and on the owner taking only as much as he needs and will use.

62: Far from destroying natural equality, the social contract substitutes for it a moral and legal equality that compensates for people's physical and intellectual differences.

THOMAS JEFFERSON

The Declaration of Independence (pp. 259–267)

Paragraphs 1–2:   When a people rejects past ties in favor of equal sovereignty, they should explain their reasons. Because all men are created equal and form governments to protect their rights, they are entitled to cast off any government that abridges their equality and rights and to replace it with a better one. Thus the thirteen United States of America cast off the king of Great Britain.

3–29:   The king has in diverse ways prevented his legislature from representing and acting in the interests of the states and has harassed and oppressed their citizens.

30–31:   The American people's petitions to the king and his subjects in Britain have been ignored, proving him unfit to be the ruler of a free people and necessitating a separation.

32:   The representatives of the United States of America therefore declare the colonies free and independent, with all the rights and powers of states, and pledge their mutual support.

ELIZABETH CADY STANTON

Declaration of Sentiments and Resolutions (pp. 269–277)

Paragraphs 1–2:   Because men and women are equally entitled to life, liberty, and the pursuit of happiness, yet women are denied these rights by the government, women now must throw off that government and demand equality.

3–18:   To establish his absolute tyranny over woman, man has deprived her of the vote, of all individual rights once she marries, of entry into the most profitable and distinguished jobs, of a thorough education, and of a voice in the church. Yet he forces her, if single and a property owner, to pay taxes supporting this unjust system. He has given her a circumscribed moral code, sphere of action, and opportunity for self-sufficiency and self-respect.

19–20:   Women, being half the population, now set out to demand their rights.

21–24:   Given that the most basic law of God and Nature entitles man to pursue his own happiness, it is hereby resolved that there is no validity in any human laws restricting woman from this right or placing her in a position inferior to man's.

25–28:   Woman should be informed of her rights and encouraged to assert them. Man should support woman as a lecturer and teacher and should follow the same high standards of behavior as are demanded of woman.

29–34:   Woman, having rights and capabilities equal to man's, must secure the right to vote and must zealously promote this and other just causes by writing, speaking, and every other righteous means.

HANNAH ARENDT

Total Domination (pp. 279–292)

Paragraphs 1–3: Totalitarian regimes seek total domination by eliminating individuality, reducing human beings to mere animals or things. This goal is achieved by ideological indoctrination and by absolute terror in the concentration camps. The camps verify the regime's ideology and sustain its power.

4–6: The elimination of individuality is possible in the camps because of their complete isolation from the outside world. This isolation explains why reports from camp survivors have an unreal quality that raises doubts about their credibility. Such doubts work to the advantage of the totalitarian regime because the enormity of the crimes committed in the camps makes the perpetrators' false claims of innocence seem more credible than the victims' truthful accounts.

7: Totalitarian regimes did not invent their methods of total domination; rather, these methods, including the use of concentration camps, have historical precedents. Totalitarian regimes borrow from the past the principle that "everything is permitted" but then move beyond that principle to a new one—that "everything is possible."

8: The concept that "everything is possible" defies common sense. Therefore, ordinary people often refuse to accept, or even think about, the inexplicable horrors that occur in totalitarian regimes.

9–10: Recalling the horrors of the concentration camps does little to help us understand totalitarianism. And such recollection cannot alter people's characters or serve as a basis for new political communities. Our fear of concentration camps should demonstrate that the most important standard for judging events is whether or not those events support totalitarian domination.

11–14: Simplistic arguments that good may come from evil are refuted by the reality of the camps, where the limited evil of murder is replaced by a more radical evil: the total elimination of human beings as if they had never existed. The division of camp inmates into various categories masks this radical evil. But the true horror of the camps is their separation of all inmates from the world of the living, an impersonal indifference to life and death that obliterates everything. The presence of this radical evil creates an all-or-nothing outlook for modern politics, a sense that the very existence of humankind is at stake if the concentration camp system prevails.

15–17: There are no parallel situations—whether forced labor, banishment, or slavery—that can help us understand the horror of the camps. The economic uselessness of the camps only heightens their incredibility and mad unreality.

18–19: This unreality makes the camps conceivable only as an imagined life after death, with three types of camps corresponding to Hades, Purgatory, and Hell. The three share one feature: they treat inmates as if they no longer exist among the living.

MARCUS TULLIUS CICERO

The Defense of Injustice (bedfordstmartins.com/worldofideas/epages)

Paragraphs 1–3: LAELIUS: For the sake of argument, make a defense of injustice.

4–6: PHILUS: I will do so, using the language of Carneades, who refuted Plato's and Aristotle's ideas of justice. These two philosophers rightly saw justice as the greatest virtue. But they wrongly claimed that justice is natural, for if it were, it would be the same for all people.

7–10: In fact, beliefs about justice vary widely from place to place, as do religious practices and ways of life. Likewise, ideas about justice change over time.

11–13: If all laws come from God, they would be eternal, but laws change, which demonstrates that they are not natural or eternal but, rather, mere human creations. The argument that all good men act justly, regardless of human laws, is false.

14–16: Those who hold political power say that their form of government is stable and just even when it is not. Compromise and human weakness are the true origin of justice in government. Each of us must choose the role we will play in perpetrating and/or being victims of injustice.

17–19: For both the individual and the state, behaving wisely is incompatible with behaving justly. Some philosophers argue that the two are compatible, saying that the "wise" man's life is good because it is free from anxiety and that no benefit gained by injustice is worth the anxiety that will result.

20–21: Given the choice of being just but hated or unjust and loved, both an individual and a state would choose the latter.

22–23: LAELIUS: True law, which comes from God, is consistent with reason and nature. It applies to everyone at all times and in all places. Those who disobey God are punished.

HENRY DAVID THOREAU
Civil Disobedience (pp. 301–325)

Paragraphs 1–2: "That government is best which governs least." Governments, like armies, are a means for the people to express their will, but they also may be used by a few against the people's interests. Governments do not act, but facilitate (or impede) action by individuals and groups.

3–6: We need not immediately abolish government but should improve it. Governments rule by majority, not by justice, and thus may improperly overrule individual conscience, turning men into tools of the government. Those who follow their consciences and resist the government are treated as enemies by it.

7–15: The present American government, which supports slavery, forces men of conscience into resistance. Those who fail to oppose wrongdoing with action, but simply voice or vote their convictions, are leaving justice to chance. A real man refuses allegiance on any level to a government that pursues immoral policies.

16–19: We should not be deterred from rebelling against unjust laws, or persuaded to wait for a majority vote to change them, by our fear of causing more harm than good. A just government would prevent such harm; in its absence, we should concern ourselves with living justly and not with reforming the government.

20–24: Those in Massachusetts who believe in abolishing slavery should withdraw their support from the state, refusing to pay taxes and going willingly to prison. Money prevents the man who has it from living in accord with his convictions; anyone who needs the government's protection is reluctant to disobey its rules.

25–37: I myself, having little property, have declined to pay various taxes and was once imprisoned overnight. In jail I saw the barriers between me and my neighbors and particularly between me and the state. My perspective on my town became that of a foreign traveler, which lasted even after someone paid my tax and I was released.

38–45: Unlike natural forces, a government of men warrants resistance. Those who pay much attention to the government, however, or work within it, are paying homage to a static manifestation of human values rather than to those values themselves. The ideal government would be just to all men and would treat every individual with respect.

FREDERICK DOUGLASS

From *Narrative of the Life of Frederick Douglass,*
an American Slave (pp. 327–341)

Paragraphs 1–2: My new mistress was a kind woman who had never owned slaves before. But the "dehumanizing effects of slavery" caught up with her and changed her quickly from warm and decent to harsh and unjust.

3: Mrs. Auld started to teach me to spell, but her husband made her stop because it was illegal to teach a slave to read. Mr. Auld's explanation that learning would make a slave "unfit . . . to be a slave" made me understand that learning to read was a crucial first step toward gaining my freedom.

4: In general, city slaveholders (such as the Aulds) treated their slaves far better than plantation slaveholders; but Mrs. Hamilton, who lived on our street, whipped her slaves mercilessly and also grossly underfed them.

5–8: While I lived with the Aulds, I taught myself to read and write. Though my mistress was initially helpful, she soon refused to let me see the newspaper to make sure I couldn't educate myself in any way. Still, I learned to read by befriending hungry white boys; I traded them bread for reading lessons.

9–10: When I was twelve I came across *The Columbian Orator*, a book including dialogues and speeches denouncing slavery as morally wrong and arguing for emancipation. The book gave me the language for ideas I had been previously unable to articulate, but it also gave me cause to hate my enslavers more and more. My master had been right: learning to read made me discontented, even tormented, for now I understood my oppressed condition but remained powerless to do anything about it.

11 12: I began to hear about "abolition" and learned from the newspaper what it meant; I also learned from two dockworkers that slaves could run away to the North, where they would be free. I resolved to do so when the chance arose and, in the meantime, to teach myself to write. I did this by copying the letters I saw carpenters write at the shipyard and then telling boys who could write that I could do it too; to prove me false, they would write more than I could, so I learned the letters they wrote. I copied from Master Thomas's copybooks as well.

13–17: When my old master died, his estate had to be divided between his children; as part of the "property," I had to return to the plantation. People and animals alike were grouped together, examined in the same callous way, assigned a particular value, and divided between Andrew and Lucretia. We were all terrified of being sent with Master Andrew, whose cruelty I witnessed firsthand when he savagely beat my little brother in front of me. In the end, I was sent back to Baltimore and the Aulds, who were as glad to see me as I was them.

18–19: My grandmother's fate vividly illustrates the barbaric oppression of slavery and the monstrous cruelty of slaveholders. When Lucretia and Andrew both died, my grandmother, who had served my old master from his birth to his death and supplied his plantation with four generations of slaves, was left by his heirs to fend for herself in a hut in the woods where she could not possibly take care of herself alone in her ailing condition.

20–22: Master Hugh's drinking caused a falling out with his brother Thomas, who took me with him to St. Michael's to punish Hugh. I welcomed the move because Master Hugh and his wife had undergone a "disastrous change." I knew I would not miss them as much as the boys in Baltimore who had taught me so much. I regretted not taking the opportunity to run away then, for it is easier for a slave to escape the city than the country. On the trip to St. Michael's, I took note of the ships' routes, and resolved to attempt escape as soon as an opportunity presented itself.

FRIEDRICH NIETZSCHE

Morality as Anti-Nature (pp. 343–357)

Paragraphs 1–2: The moral codes of the past—Christianity in particular—seek to destroy human passions. To attack the passions is to attack life itself.

3–4: People too weak or degenerate to curb their own passions are drawn instinctively to moral codes that reject all passion. When such people cannot eliminate their passions, they become even more hostile to sensuality.

5–7: Those of us who oppose this anti-sensualist morality have conquered it by spiritualizing our hostility—by acting and thinking in total opposition to Christianity. We have also spiritualized our hostility to the "internal enemy"—the desire for "peace of soul." "Peace of soul" is usually just a fancy name for something far less elevated.

8: "*Anti-natural* morality" condemns the instinct for life—makes God "the *enemy of life*." A natural, healthy morality springs from an instinct for life.

9: The rejection of life, which is fundamental in Christian morality, is futile. Anti-natural morality values only a "declining, weakened, weary, condemned life."

10–12: Conventional moralists say what man ought to be, naively ignoring what men *are*. The conventional moralist wants to condemn; we immoralists want to affirm.

13–15: The first error is the confusion of cause with effect (as exemplified by the case of Cornaro). Religion and morality mistakenly say that if a person acts virtuously (cause), then happiness will follow (effect). I say that if a person is happy, virtuous acts will follow.

16–18: The second error is false causality. People have long believed that they themselves (through acts of will, consciousness, or ego) cause things to happen. Today, though, we have dismissed this idea entirely.

19–22: The third error is imaginary causes. We fear the unknown and are therefore eager to have an explanation when something unexpected occurs. If an event or feeling has no obvious cause, we are naturally inclined to imagine one—preferably a familiar explanation that we can retrieve quickly from memory.

23–25: Religion and morality fall under the concept of imaginary causes. We attribute our pleasurable and unpleasurable feelings to particular causes, such as our sinfulness or our trust in God. But in each case, these "causes" are imaginary.

26–28: The fourth error is free will, a concept invented to make mankind dependent on authority. Because men are "free," they can be held "responsible" for their acts—and therefore judged and punished. Today, "we immoralists are trying . . . to take the concept of guilt and the concept of punishment out of the world again."

IRIS MURDOCH
Morality and Religion (pp. 359–373)

Paragraph 1:   The nature of religion and its relation to morality are proper subjects for moral philosophy.

2:   The concept of virtue is the most obvious link between morality and religion. Some still regard virtue as a valuable concept; others see it as outdated, useless, even dangerous.

3:   We might broaden the concept of duty to include the notion of living a virtuous life. I prefer, though, to define duty narrowly as "formal obligation." Whereas virtue is connected in some way with religion, a moral code based on duty requires no link to religion. (Kant, though, does connect duty with the experience of a higher good.) The moral choices we must make are complex, multifaceted, varied, and often of different or competing kinds; nevertheless, we also "have to live a single moral existence." This desire for unity is a "religious craving."

4:   Some people, even those who have lost their religious belief, say that religious images absorbed in childhood may provide some lifelong emotional benefit to an individual. Others would argue, from a more strictly rational viewpoint, that if religion is false, children should be told that it is false. Perhaps religion should be regarded as "a form of heightened consciousness" that powerfully engages the whole person emotionally and imaginatively. Because of its emotional-imaginative qualities, religion can embody high moral ideas more effectively than reason can.

5:   The diaries of Francis Kilvert illustrate the qualities of holiness and reverence that characterize religious experience. So too does an image from Wittgenstein and, in a different way, one from Julian of Norwich.

6:   Kierkegaard, with his notion of salvation as a radical rebirth, would reject the idea that morality and religion exist on a continuum. Religion offers many devices for amending one's life, including repentance and forgiveness, sudden or gradual conversion, finding a place of renewal, meeting the mystical Christ. Some people would argue that there are secular and nonmysterious equivalents to these devices—and that there are good reasons for rejecting religion as a means of amending one's life. Non-Christian religions offer alternative paths.

7:   Despite the general assumption that religion is moral, many thinkers from the Enlightenment to the present have viewed organized religion as contrary to morality and as wholly bankrupt. During this period, Western society has improved in many ways. At the same time, some aspects of moral conduct may have declined. In any event, recent thinkers have significantly altered modern conceptions of reality. One thinker, F. H. Bradley, argues that both religion and morality demand a unity that can never be achieved.

MARTIN LUTHER KING JR.

Letter from Birmingham Jail (pp. 375–395)

Paragraphs 1–4: While here in jail I read your statement calling my activities "unwise and untimely" and indicating bias against "outsiders coming in." I came here at the request of our Southern Christian Leadership Conference affiliate in Birmingham. More basically, I came to carry the gospel of freedom. Injustice is here, and injustice anywhere is a threat to justice everywhere.

5–9: You deplore the demonstrations here but not the conditions that caused them. Any non-violent campaign has four basic steps—collecting facts, negotiation, self-purification, and direct action. Our fact collecting has shown the depth and breadth of racial injustice in Birmingham. We negotiated and won promises that have been broken. We prepared for action with self-purification—a series of workshops on nonviolence. Then we planned our action.

10–11: You call for negotiations; so do we. The purpose of direct action is to dramatize the issue so that it can no longer be ignored. We are here to create the constructive, nonviolent tension necessary for growth.

12–14: You ask, why not give the new city administration time to act? No administration here will act unless prodded: freedom will not be offered voluntarily by the oppressor but must be demanded by the oppressed. *Wait* has almost always meant *never*, and given the lynchings, beatings, poverty, cruelty, and degradation we suffer, we cannot afford to wait.

15–22: You deplore our willingness to break laws. Though we urge people to obey just laws, we have a moral responsibility to disobey any law that conflicts with the law of God. Segregation is not only politically, economically, and socially unsound, it is morally wrong and sinful. Our civil disobedience shows respect for law and is part of the great Christian and American traditions.

23–24: I have almost concluded that white moderates, not rabid segregationists, are our greatest stumbling block—those who value order over justice, prefer reducing tension to achieving peace, agree with our goals but reproach our methods, and believe they can set a timetable for our freedom. I had hoped you would understand that tension must be released to be alleviated and that injustice must be exposed to be cured.

25–29: You accuse us of precipitating violence by our nonviolent actions. As the federal courts have affirmed, it is wrong to urge anyone to give up his constitutional rights because seeking them may precipitate violence. Nor will time inevitably bring redress; progress requires work. You speak of our activities in Birmingham as extreme; yet I stand between the opposing forces of passivity and hatred, espousing the nonviolent middle course.

30–36: The American Negro has become aware of his birthright of freedom and is not willing to remain oppressed. Try to understand his yearning rather than squelch it. If I am an extremist, so were Jesus, Paul, Martin Luther, Lincoln, Jefferson, and others. I had hoped the white moderate would recognize the need for creative extremists, responding to the cry of the oppressed race as a few white brothers have. Instead, some white church leaders have opposed us outright, while too many others choose caution over courage.

37–41: The early church was powerful, when Christians acted energetically in defense of their beliefs. Today it is often weak, passive, and ineffectual, a bulwark of the status quo. Yet some noble souls have broken loose and joined our struggle for freedom. I hope the church as a whole will meet this challenge. But whether it does or not, we will reach our goal because freedom is the goal and heritage of America.

42–44: You commend the Birmingham police for keeping "order" and "preventing violence," when their dogs attacked unarmed demonstrators, and the policemen are habitually cruel and inhumane to Negroes under their control. Their public display of nonviolence in defense of segregation uses a moral means to achieve an immoral end. I wish you had commended the courage and discipline of the demonstrators, who one day will be regarded as heroes.

45–47: I hope circumstances will soon make it possible for us to meet, not over civil rights but as fellow clergymen and Christian brothers.

KWAME ANTHONY APPIAH

The Case against Character (pp. 397–413)

Paragraphs 1–9: Character is very important in virtue ethics: a virtuous person has a complex mindset that combines virtuous actions, traits, and dispositions. For virtue ethicists, being virtuous makes a life good and worthwhile. Vices are the opposite of virtues and are also seen by virtue ethicists as multi-track and based on character. These are the basic points of virtue ethics—the right thing is what a virtuous person would do; a virtuous person does virtuous things, and virtues are traits that allow a person to live a good life.

10–14: Virtue ethicists' idea of character is globalist or unified; that is, a virtuous person displays all the virtues, not just one. Social psychologists, however, discovered that most people do not demonstrate all the virtues together. Character, in other words, is not consistent and context-free; it is dependent on situations and context.

15–20: Psychological experiments have shown that people behave differently in different situations. Sometimes a trivial difference in circumstances can make a huge difference in outcome. Many of us, though, still believe that underlying character, and not context, determines behavior. In fact, many people don't understand why they do the things they do, so the explanations we give for behavior are not necessarily reliable.

21–26: If these situational ethics ideas are true, then the foundation for virtue ethics is severely weakened. If people do not have full control over their responses, developing a virtuous character is very difficult. Perhaps no humans are fully virtuous.

27–29: If psychology has shown that people do not have the traits that lead to a virtuous character, a virtue ethicist faces two possibilities: the wrong character traits have been identified, or people cannot have virtuous lives. Both these possibilities are problematic; if either is true, psychology seems to be more important than philosophy, and this makes virtue ethics theory secondary to psychological experiments.

30–33: That said, situationism does not undermine the ideal of virtuous character. Perhaps these psychological experiments can even help a person become more virtuous. Even within psychological experiments there are small groups of people who behave virtuously no matter the situation. The traits studied in the experiments may not correspond exactly to the traits in classical virtue theory. Also, the situationist hypothesis does not claim that these dispositions are nonexistent. Perhaps virtue ethicists should think of virtue as an ideal that, while difficult to attain, should be strived for.

MICHAEL GAZZANIGA
Toward a Universal Ethics (pp. 415–432)

Paragraphs 1–6:   Increasing and advancing human knowledge affects everyone on earth. Much modern knowledge is in conflict with traditional belief systems. Most philosophic and religious ideas about human life are really just stories cultures tell. Historical and scientific data, however, are the foundation for modern knowledge. Even though people disagree about it, there is clearly a universal human nature with some fixed qualities—but is there a universal human morality?

7–9:   James Q. Wilson claims morality is universal, a product of evolution by natural selection and not just a social construct. Modern brain imaging appears to back up Wilson's reasoning—human moral behavior is connected to the brain's automatic emotional responses.

10–20:   Moral reasoning is good for human survival, but is it hardwired by evolution? Scientists look for moral reasoning centers in the brain by using modern brain imaging. These researchers study three main topics—moral emotions, theory of mind, and abstract moral reasoning. All of these can be connected to regions of the brain. In abstract moral reasoning experiments, subjects respond differently depending on whether the scenario is personal or impersonal. When subjects judge personal dilemmas, areas of the brain having to do with emotion and moral cognition are activated. Our ability to make quick moral decisions—those based on gut instinct—is most likely a product of evolution. Brain imaging suggests that humans have a universal morality.

21–22:   If morality were purely rational, then all cultures would respond differently to the same problems. Subjects, however, make similar moral choices, and they all have trouble justifying their actions. These responses seem to be subconscious and intuitive. We react first and then form justifications for our actions. Our brains trigger responses that we later classify as absolute truths.

23–29:   Evolution does not just save individuals—it saves the group too. Evolution has selected for the ability to read minds, or understand others and predict their behavior. One theory that explains this ability is simulation theory, or the ability to imagine another's life and circumstances. Another is theory-theory, which maintains that we use knowledge embedded in the brain to make decisions. Simulation theorists do not believe that we use previously embedded knowledge; they say that we make models of other people's behavior based on our own brain responses. Many studies support the idea that empathetic simulation increases helping behavior.

30–38:   Mirror neurons are probably responsible for understanding the actions of others. The human mirror system allows us to learn by imitation. Understanding the way human imaging works will help us understand the brain's mechanisms for perceiving and dealing with the outside world. The mirror system may have even been an important evolutionary step on the road to language. The brain seems to have been built to feel the experiences of others. Moral rules undoubtedly exist, and we should look for a universal ethics based on emotions, context, and evolutionary survival. Brain reactions are hardwired, and this makes a universal ethics possible.

ARISTOTLE

The Aim of Man (bedfordstmartins.com/worldofideas/epages)

Paragraphs 1–2:   It is correct to assume that all knowledge and all purpose aim at "the good."

3–4:   We should be careful to aim for the highest good, as that will have the most beneficial influence on our lives; this highest good is statecraft, because it encompasses all other arts and sciences and is capable of directing all citizens toward good.

5–7:   In contemplating the good, we hold it only as a general rule—it is necessarily inexact; a student of statecraft must be experienced and educated in the affairs of life and be objective.

8–9:   The aim of statecraft is happiness for all citizens; to live well and to do good deeds are the same as to be happy.

10–11:   There are three outstanding types of life: the hedonistic, the political, and the contemplative. In each of these, happiness is viewed in conflicting ways, and the degree of intrinsic good varies.

12–18:   A plurality of ends are chosen to meet other ends, but the final end—the ultimate good we seek—is never chosen for the sake of another end. Because happiness is never chosen as a means to another end, Aristotle assumes that it is final.

19–22:   It has been customary to divide good things into three classes: external goods, goods of the soul, and goods of the body. Those of the soul we call good in the highest sense and the fullest degree.

23–25:   It is reasonable to assume that happiness is god-given; if it is not god-given but attained through learning or habitation, then it is still divine in nature. It is wrong to assume that happiness—the greatest and noblest thing in life—is a product of chance.

26–32:   Happiness requires an entire lifetime for its fulfillment; this means the ultimate level of one's happiness is based on one's life's sum of virtuous activity, not that one is never happy until death.

33–39:   There are two kinds of human excellence: intellectual and moral. Both are derived from the same, which has a rational and an irrational side.

ADAM SMITH

Of the Natural Progress of Opulence (pp. 441–451)

Paragraph 1:   The major commerce of a civilized society is the interchange of goods between town and country. The country provides the town with raw materials, and the town provides the country with manufactured products. Both town and country benefit.

2:   The development of the country must come before that of the town because the country provides basic necessities, whereas the town provides conveniences and luxuries. Some towns acquire their basic necessities from the nearby countryside, whereas others must rely on more distant places. As a result of this disparity, opulence (affluence) develops at different rates in different places.

3:   Human beings are naturally inclined to prefer farming to manufacturing and trade. Those who spend their resources cultivating their own land have more control of their economic welfare than do those who engage in trade.

4:   To cultivate their land efficiently, farmers need the help of artisans (artificers), who settle together, along with various retailers, to form towns. The economic condition of towns improves in direct proportion to the increased productivity of the surrounding country.

5:   In the American colonies, where uncultivated land is plentiful, artisans use any excess goods they produce to buy nearby land, which they then cultivate. As farmers they enjoy an independence that they lacked as artisans.

6:   In contrast, in countries where little or no uncultivated land remains, artisans sell any excess goods to distant areas and thus become manufacturers.

7:   Just as farming is preferable to manufacturing, so too domestic manufacturing is preferable to commerce with foreign nations. But if a nation does not have sufficient wealth to cultivate all its land and to manufacture all its raw materials domestically, then that nation will benefit by exporting raw materials to foreign nations.

8:   And so in the natural progress of economic development, wealth is used first for agriculture, second for manufacturing, and third for foreign commerce.

9:   But this natural progress has to some degree been inverted in all the nations of modern Europe.

KARL MARX

The Communist Manifesto (pp. 453–479)

Paragraphs 1–6:   The specter of communism haunts Europe, whose powers have allied to oppose it. Every opposition party, advanced or reactionary, is labeled communistic. Therefore, Communists of various nationalities have gathered to publish their views and goals.

7–11:   The history of society is a history of class struggles. In our own epoch, society is more and more splitting into two great hostile classes: bourgeoisie and proletariat.

12–22:   The bourgeoisie sprang from burghers, became merchants, and grew into the present industrial middle class. Modern industry has established the world market, causing commerce and navigation to burgeon. Meanwhile, the bourgeoisie has swamped all other classes. It has replaced old ties and values—veiled exploitation—with the naked exploitation of treating everything as a cash transaction.

23–26:   The bourgeoisie cannot exist without constantly revolutionizing the instruments of production and thereby the relations of production, and with them the whole relations of society. In its rush to achieve, it has generated constant uncertainty and agitation. It has superseded local patterns of production and consumption with multinational industries and markets, creating new wants and dependencies among consumers.

27–30:   By improving the means of production and communication, the bourgeoisie has forced the world into its own mold. It has subjected the country to the towns and undeveloped nations to civilized ones. It has centralized population, production, and property control as well as stimulated enormous technical change.

31–34:   Although built on a feudal foundation, the bourgeoisie's development of productive forces burst the fetters of feudal property relations. In stepped free competition, with accompanying social and political adaptations. But the productive forces have grown too strong for bourgeois control and create a periodic chaos of overproduction that endangers bourgeois property and society. The bourgeoisie fights back with greater market exploitation, paving the way for worse crises and its own eventual ruin.

35–38:   The bourgeoisie has not only forged the weapons of its destruction but called into existence those who are to wield them—the proletariat. The proletariat is a class of laborers who live only as long as they find work and who find work only as long as their labor increases capital. Like all commodities, they are subject to market fluctuations. They function as appendages of machines, slaves of the bourgeois class and state, doing simple monotonous tasks.

39–46:   Old workers, children, women, small tradespeople, and those with specialized skills all sink into the proletariat. Their initial struggle with the bourgeoisie is individual and local; workers attack the instruments rather than the conditions of production, seeking to restore their feudal status. As the proletariat becomes concentrated and aware of its commonality, workers form broader geographic unions, in which lie their ultimate strength.

47–55:   The bourgeoisie, embattled on numerous fronts, needs help from the proletariat and therefore gives workers weapons against itself. Sections of the ruling class also fall or jump into the proletariat. Unlike all previous classes, the proletarians have nothing of their own to fortify; their mission is to destroy the existing system of individual property. Unlike all previous historical movements, theirs is not a minority but a majority upheaval.

56–59:   The proletarian-bourgeois struggle is national at first. It begins as a veiled civil war and then breaks out into revolution and the proletariat's violent overthrow of the bourgeoisie. The bourgeoisie is unfit to rule because it cannot even ensure its slaves' existence within their slavery but lets their situation degenerate to where it must feed them. As industry ends laborers' isolation and competition with each other, the fall of the bourgeoisie and the victory of the proletariat are inevitable.

60–93:   The Communists are not separate from or opposed to other working-class parties but work on behalf of the proletariat worldwide. They favor the overthrow of the bourgeoisie and the abolition of private property, ending the dominance of capital and enriching the life of the worker. They do not aim to sweep away freedom and individuality, only the bourgeoisie and their system of buying and selling.

94–110:   Bourgeois culture, laws, and institutions, like bourgeois productivity, exist only to benefit the ruling class. The exploitive bourgeois family will vanish along with wage labor when capital vanishes; the bourgeoisie has already destroyed the proletarian family. Those who criticize communism for planning to make women, like the means of production, common to all, ignore that bourgeois marriage is in reality a system of having wives in common.

111–126:   National divisions are already obsolescent and will vanish under the supremacy of the proletariat. Bourgeois religion and philosophy also must disappear along with the capitalist system to which they correspond.

127–133:   The victorious proletariat will centralize all instruments of production in the hands of the state. Private property, inheritance, and child labor in factories will be abolished; a heavy income tax will be instituted. The state will take over property, credit, communication and transportation systems, and education. Everyone will be equally liable to labor. The distinctions between agriculture and manufacturing, between town and country, and between classes will disappear.

134–145:   The Communists have established a role in relation to existing working-class parties in England, America, France, Switzerland, Poland, and Germany; but they focus chiefly on Germany because that country is on the eve of a bourgeois revolution that will be followed immediately by a proletarian revolution. The Communists everywhere support all revolutionary movements against the existing order, emphasizing the property question and the international union of workers.

ANDREW CARNEGIE

The Gospel of Wealth (pp. 481–497)

Paragraphs 1–5: Within a few hundred years, science and capitalism have brought immense and welcome changes to human life. The living standards of poor and rich alike are much greater than our ancestors could have imagined. However, there is also great friction and inequality between classes. The problem of our time is to harmonize the relationship between rich and poor.

6: We owe our improved material conditions to competition, which is inevitable and beneficial to the human race. Inequality, though, results from competition. Talented men secure greater rewards than the masses. Eventually, in a free economy, the most successful men will accumulate far more capital than they can spend on themselves. However, this accumulation benefits the whole human race.

7: Anyone who opposes the natural law of competition opposes civilization, which depends upon the sacredness of property. Communists and socialists want to change human nature, but that is a waste of time. Economic laws may appear imperfect or non-ideal, but they cannot be altered. Even though they give wealth to the few, competition and capitalism also do the most good for the most people.

8–11: How can vast fortunes be administered? The rich can leave money to heirs, but this is often wasteful and can even harm the recipients. The wealthy can bestow fortunes for public purposes, but this money may not be used correctly.

12–16: Governments are wise to tax estates upon death because this encourages the wealthy to use their money properly. The most useful way to administer a fortune is for the rich man to dispense of it while he is alive. Administering wealth for the common good elevates mankind and leads to less inequality.

17–22: Rich men can dignify their lives by imitating the spirit, though not the life, of Christ. A rich man should live unostentatiously, and he should leave a moderate amount of money to his heirs. He should then view all his surplus capital as a way of benefiting the community and helping the poor. His charity should not be indiscriminate. Handouts do not help the poor. Assistance should be useful and not wasteful. Parks, works of art, and all kinds of public institutions are the best ways to benefit the community.

23: In this way, the rich can help the poor and increase the wealth of the whole community. Because the wealthy man is talented, he can administer his money better than anyone else. This will solve the problems of inequality without changing the laws of competition and capital accumulation. Rich men who die without administering their wealth for the public good die disgraced.

24: This is the true Gospel of Wealth, and it will bring peace on earth and good will among men.

JOHN KENNETH GALBRAITH

The Position of Poverty (pp. 499–511)

Paragraphs 1–3:   Alfred Marshall suggested at the turn of the century that solving the problem of poverty is the central concern for economists. In modern America, however, the poor are considered more as a reason for economists to go on working than as an urgent national issue. Economic expansion has changed poverty since Marshall's time from a majority to a minority affliction.

4–5:   People with enough income to survive are still poor if they cannot afford to eat, dress, and live at a standard the community considers decent. Though this degradation is better understood now than formerly, poverty has not been eliminated.

6–11:   Case poverty derives from an individual's inability to master his or her environment. Insular poverty exists throughout a community, creating a poor "island" within the larger society. Case poverty is easily blamed on the sufferer's deficiency and also presumably easily solved with charity. Insular poverty is more widespread, harder to explain, and most common in rural and urban slums. Though it is often characterized as geographic, no correlation in fact exists between the natural resources of an area and its residents' tendency toward poverty.

12–13:   Race, which restricts mobility and thus access to jobs, is clearly a contributing factor. So are poor educational facilities and the disintegration of family life. A general rise in income therefore will not cure insular poverty (or case poverty) because the poor cannot share in it.

14–16:   As poverty shifted from a majority to a minority position, it became a less attractive issue to politicians.

17–18:   An affluent society that is also both compassionate and rational would ensure a decent standard of income for all its members. Such a policy also would prevent parents from passing on poverty to their children. When the poor were a majority, guaranteeing a minimum income to all was unrealistic. Now it is an essential first step in the attack on poverty.

19–21:   If we continue to assume that the only remedy for poverty is helping people to help themselves, we miss the chance to improve the living conditions, and thus the future prospects, of poor children. Those outside the insular poverty community need to invest in high-quality schools, health services, nutrition, and recreation for children whose parents cannot provide such necessities. In addition, plentiful decent low-cost housing and mass transit, plus a safe environment and health care, would help poor people overcome the restraints imposed by their situation. Case poverty, too, might be alleviated by such remedies.

22–24:   Though we search for social explanations of the urban ghetto, partly in hopes of avoiding a huge investment in the public sector, only money is likely to solve the problem. Allowing poor people to participate in the economic life of the larger community also would increase their productivity as well as the nation's. The survival of poverty in a country as affluent as the United States is a disgrace.

ROBERT B. REICH

Why the Rich Are Getting Richer and the Poor, Poorer (pp. 513–531)

Paragraph 1:   In the United States, a worker's role in the economy determines his or her financial success: symbolic analysts (people who identify and solve problems) are succeeding, whereas service workers are doing badly, and routine production workers are doing worse.

2–3:   In the past, regardless of their role in the economy, most American workers shared similar fortunes, based on the health of the nation's economy as a whole. As the middle class grew and bought more of the products it produced, the national economy flourished.

4–10:   But as new technology permits quick, efficient, and inexpensive transmittal of information around the world, many major American companies are using cheaper labor that is readily available in other countries. As a result, not only are there fewer jobs in the United States in both heavy industries (such as manufacturing) and light industries (such as data processing and computer programming), but the wages and benefits for those that still exist are declining. This pattern is occurring not just in the United States but all over the world.

11–15:   While production workers in developing countries benefit by getting more and better jobs, workers in advanced economies suffer. Unions and collective bargaining agreements that used to protect these workers are no longer effective, in part because of the decline in the traditional unionized industries.

16–18:   Lower- and middle-management production jobs are also disappearing. Foreign companies are doing *some* production here using American workers, but technology is making many of these workers obsolete.

19:   The decline in routine jobs has hurt men more than women because men's jobs in manufacturing traditionally paid more than women's jobs in textiles and data processing; the gender gap in wages began to close in the early 1980s, not because women were making more money but because men were making less.

20–24:   Service industry jobs are also in trouble, although less dramatically. Service workers, who earn less than production workers and have fewer (if any) benefits, now have to compete with former production workers, people who would have looked for production work were it available, and immigrants. Like production workers, service workers are also threatened by labor-saving machinery and technology.

25–26:   The fortunes of service workers will temporarily improve due to changing demographics. But the standard of living of service workers won't really improve because the people demanding their services won't have enough money to pay for them; therefore, the workers themselves will bear the brunt in the form of taxes and social security.

27:   The service workers' standard of living also depends indirectly on the standard of living of those they service; if the latter do well in world commerce, they'll have more money to spend on service workers.

28–36:   The outlook for America's symbolic analysts, in contrast, is bright, especially for those at the highest levels. Demand for their ideas has grown steadily as new technologies allow them to communicate their ideas clearly, rapidly, and cheaply. Symbolic analysts include anyone who works with images and ideas. Symbolic analysts not only make large sums of money but, unlike those in production and service jobs, enjoy their work.

37–41:   At mid-twentieth century when America was a national market dominated by major corporations, there were constraints on the earnings of people at the highest level. No one was supposed to make too much or too little; this way the workers had money to spend, and national economic growth continued. But by the 1990s, symbolic analysts' earnings were unlimited.

42–44: Major American corporations were vanishing by the 1990s, as were the ethics associated with them. As American corporations sold goods and services all over the world, there was no connection between the bosses and their workers, many of whom were not in this country. The purchasing power of American workers became far less relevant to a company's economic survival, and top executives are getting richer while the workers are getting poorer.

MILTON AND ROSE FRIEDMAN

Created Equal (bedfordstmartins.com/worldofideas/epages)

Paragraphs 1–2: Are the ideals of equality and liberty consistent with each other? Can they be realized in practice? The attempt to answer these questions has shaped American history.

3–5: Equality once meant "equality before God"; later, it came to mean "equality of opportunity." Both meanings were consistent with liberty. Recently, it has come to mean "equality of outcome," which does conflict with liberty.

6–8: The assertion that "all men are created equal" does not mean that every person has the same capabilities. Rather, it implies that we all enjoy "personal equality"—equality before God—and the liberty to lead the life we choose, regardless of our various abilities.

9–11: Personal equality requires that no individual or group impose its will on others. The American founders believed that government must therefore be limited: it should promote the general welfare while protecting the individual from domination. Likewise, the French thinker Tocqueville saw equality, not majority rule, as the best feature of American democracy.

12–14: In recent decades, the U.S. Democratic Party has worked to strengthen government in order to promote a concept of equality at odds with the ideals of Jefferson and Tocqueville. Of course, the actions of the American founders did not always live up to their ideal of equality. For example, the practice of slavery led to the Civil War.

15–17: After the War, emphasis shifted from personal equality to "equality of opportunity"—the idea that a person's abilities, not factors such as race and religion, should determine his or her opportunities.

18–20: Like personal equality, equality of opportunity allows for individual differences and is consistent with liberty. But like every ideal, equality of opportunity cannot be fully realized.

21–23: After the Civil War, U.S. economic policies emphasized equality of opportunity by supporting a free market system that valued the accumulation of personal wealth. This system expanded opportunities for social mobility and increased charitable activity.

24–25: Despite government policies, however, many were still excluded from economic opportunity because of class, race, or religion. And government policies limited foreign trade in ways that were inconsistent with equal opportunity.

26–31: "Equality of outcome" gained ground in the twentieth century. Supporters say that government should ensure "a fair share for all," but the *ideal* of "fair shares" and the *ideal* of individual liberty are at odds. Government efforts to achieve "fairness" diminish liberty.

32–34: Many feel that it is unfair for the children of rich parents to have an advantage. But the complex ethical issues raised by various types of unfairness cannot be resolved by simplistic formulas such as "fairness for all."

35–37: We often benefit from the essential unfairness of life. Those blessed with physical beauty or talent provide pleasure to millions of people. Would it not be unfair if, in the interest of equality, Muhammad Ali's earnings were limited to that of an unskilled dockworker?

38–39: In life, as in games of chance, we make choices that involve risk, and we bear the consequences—good or bad. By contrast, if we expect the government to protect us from certain risks, we must also expect to give up a measure of our personal freedom.

40–44: In our economic system, individuals have traditionally taken their own risks. This system has created great wealth for some and benefited society as a whole by providing new jobs, products, service, and philanthropic activity (either private charities or government assistance).

45–50: Politicians, intellectuals, and the public at large claim to support equality of outcome, but their actions—such as support of legal gambling or an unwillingness to redistribute their own wealth—suggest otherwise.

51–54: Those who believe that society should enforce economic equality can practice what they preach by joining egalitarian communes, but few people do so. Public support for the graduated income tax, another democratic practice, is similarly lukewarm.

55–60: Since World War II, the British have aggressively promoted equality of outcome, but the result has been to create a new privileged class, not to achieve greater equality. The British experiment failed because it thwarted people's basic instinct to improve their lots in life.

61–62: The drive for equality in Britain has caused many of its most able citizens to leave the country and has retarded overall economic growth. Some of the negative effects of promoting equality of outcome are also evident in the United States.

63–67: Free market capitalism—what we call equality of opportunity—has been blamed for increasing the gap between rich and poor. But, in fact, that gap is widest in societies that do not allow the free market to operate (e.g., Communist states like China and the former U.S.S.R.).

68–70: By contrast, ordinary people, even more than the rich, have benefited from industrial progress. What John Stuart Mill said in 1848—that the mechanical inventions of his day had not eased human toil—is no longer true in modern capitalist societies.

71–72: A society that places equality of outcome ahead of freedom will have neither equality nor freedom, but one that places freedom first will have greater freedom and equality.

HSÜN TZU

Encouraging Learning (pp. 543–553)

Paragraph 1: Learning should never stop. If a person is not familiar with ancient wisdom, he is not truly educated. All people, however, have different customs and are educated in different traditions. Transforming yourself by studying the Way is the greatest achievement of all.

2–3: Thought is not as important as study—everyone needs help to improve. Tools allow you to do things better, but you must pick the right tools and the right place to use them. Be careful in choosing where you live and who your friends are.

4–6: There is a cause for everything that happens. People's character is reflected in their reactions to the bad or good things that happen to them. Strong people can handle adversity, while weak people cannot. Flaws within the self invite the attacks of others. Be careful how you present yourself. You make a long journey one step at a time, but you will never get there by giving up. Keeping your mind on one thing—staying focused—helps you reach your goals. Doing small, good things can lead to grand achievements that people recognize.

7–10: Learning does not end until death. A program or curriculum of learning may end, but no one must ever give up learning as a goal of life. Learning shows itself in a person's actions and words. A gentleman studies for himself; a petty person studies for others. Don't talk too much or answer too many questions. Surrounding yourself with learned people is the quickest way to become educated. You should also honor traditions and the rituals of the past. If you are educated but do not honor ritual, people will look upon you as a shallow know-it-all. Deal only with people who behave in proper, respectful ways. Be cautious when choosing whom to talk to.

11–12: A good scholar understands morality and behaves righteously. Learning means achieving this benevolent oneness. Do not be a dabbler. Things that lack completeness cannot be called beautiful. Study in order to become a part of the Way. Loving what is right will bring great pleasure. If a person loves the Way, no amount of pressure or persuasion can move him off its path. Constancy of virtue allows a person to order himself and help others: he will then be a complete man.

JOHN DEWEY

Thinking in Education (pp. 555–569)

Paragraph 1:   Teaching that puts the acquisition of skills, the acquisition of information, and training in thinking in separate categories is ineffective. Schools can do only one thing for students: improve their ability to think.

2–3:   All thinking is grounded in experience. Teachers mistakenly assume that they can teach a subject before students have direct personal experience to build from. But the first exposure to any new material must be experiential.

4–6:   Therefore, to encourage thinking, students' introduction to any subject should be as nonacademic as possible, giving them "something to do, not something to learn." What students are asked to "do," of course, must prompt them to solve problems—to think. Moreover, the problems should be real, not simulated.

7:   Unfortunately, most schoolrooms are not equipped to provide the kinds of situations that children encounter outside of school. In schoolrooms that provide such situations, students display greater curiosity and more facility in solving problems.

8:   In classrooms removed from everyday life, students learn to solve problems *only* as students, not as human beings. They learn to find out what the teacher wants, not to think in ways that apply beyond the schoolroom.

9:   To prompt thinking, a problem must draw on the student's previous experience while, at the same time, presenting a new difficulty.

10–11:   While each has its limitations, direct observation, reading, and listening are all useful sources of material for thinking and problem solving. Information, however, is not an end in itself; excessive emphasis on accumulating information can work against teaching students to think.

12–14:   Thinking consists in moving from the known (facts, data, information) to the unknown (ideas). Thinking is creative, or inventive, not because it constructs something from nothing but because it puts everyday things to new uses. Therefore, "*all* thinking is original."

15:   Only in grappling with issues firsthand does the student think. Teachers should therefore engage students in shared activities that require thinking, not merely provide students with ready-made ideas.

16–17:   Ideas are an intermediate step in learning, not an end in themselves; they must be applied to the circumstances of actual experience before they have full meaning.

18–20:   Students often perceive the ideas and information they learn in school as artificial and detached from the reality of the world. Schools equipped with facilities for reproducing real-life situations have an opportunity to remedy the separation of ideas from experience—if they are willing to use the facilities they have.

21:   Even when such facilities are not available, teachers have opportunities to connect the subject matter they teach with the experiences of everyday life.

22:   All teaching should be focused on developing students' ability to think.

MARIA MONTESSORI

The Montessori Method (pp. 571–585)

Paragraphs 1–3: The aspiring teacher must prepare for his work by observing children. He should conduct his observations with the self-sacrificing spirit of a scientist and the reverent love of a disciple.

4–7: Placing a teacher in a school with children who have lost their spontaneity and individuality is like asking a scientist to work with dead butterflies mounted in a case. If teaching is to be reformed, teachers must observe "free, natural manifestations of the child."

8–11: Such manifestations are unknown in schools today. An example is the continued use of restrictive benches and desks based on misguided scientific principles.

12–15: People in the future will find it incomprehensible that during a period of social liberation such harmful desks were used in the name of "science."

16–21: The trend toward social liberation continues for working people. In the meantime, the schools continue to require physically harmful desks for children. Change is badly needed, but the schools seem blind to this need.

22–23: If the child is educated in conditions so unnatural that they harm his body, what effect must those conditions have on his spirit?

24–26: Despite some reforms, schools today continue to use a rigid system of prizes and punishments that enslaves the student's spirit and frustrates his natural development.

27–28: Society continues to make gradual progress toward ending slavery and servitude, but in the schools such progress is not apparent.

29–30: Many government employees, like schoolchildren, work mechanically for petty promotions and punishments, with no sense of human dignity or larger purpose.

31–32: Fortunately, most of the nation's employees resist this system, and their natural instinct for liberty continues to move the world ahead.

33–36: Those who achieve great goals, who create new things, who further human progress, are motivated by inner force, not by external rewards. Pursuing prizes may cause us to miss our true vocation, our natural calling.

37–38: The only meaningful prize is the joy we feel in personal accomplishment.

39–41: Punishment is useful only to repress criminals. For the ordinary person, real punishment is a sense of personal shame.

42–46: In schools today, degrading prizes and punishments and inflexible official curricula are the norm. We should feel shame that this situation exists, and we ought to work to change it.

CARTER G. WOODSON

The Mis-Education of the Negro (pp. 587–603)

Paragraphs 1–5: Educated African Americans have been taught to admire other cultures and histories and despise their own. It is as if Africa and African Americans have no history. At every level of education, and even at black colleges, the inferiority of African Americans is taught. The most successful African Americans are self-educated or uneducated. Teaching self-hatred in school is a form of lynching. Indeed, the struggle against a biased education system is more important than even the anti-lynching movement.

6–10: American universities present a limited and ineffective view of the humanities and economics to African American students. Primary schooling has also been a failure. Mathematics pedagogy should take into account, for instance, that rural African American students are heavily disadvantaged when they start school, so they need more instruction than their white counterparts. African American students have received inaccurate and hurtful educations in economics, theology, and journalism.

11–17: African Americans have been given a Eurocentric education, sent back to the black community, and told to stay in their place. The African American graduate, however, has been given no tools to help his people. He can only teach his community to conform to the dominant white culture; he certainly cannot raise race consciousness or encourage Afrocentrism. The educated African American thinks that celebrating Afrocentrism will lead to more discrimination and segregation, but he does not realize that separation can be a good thing: it can lead to an empowered people.

18–22: The only way to understand this situation is to look at it historically. The education of black people was a philanthropic effort by the United States government. No thought was taken, however, of the oppressed and disadvantaged circumstances of these citizens who had so recently lived in slavery. The underfunded schools provided a poor education to African Americans; they were not prepared for the world they lived in, nor were they given the tools to change that world.

23–28: Educators argued about what was best for African Americans: a classical liberal education or an industrial education that included vocational training. Many industrial schools began educating African Americans. However, African Americans received outdated, faulty educations at these industrial schools—industrial training was a failure. Classical education also failed. Because African Americans are kept in the lower rungs of society, a humanities education is useless. Neither one of these systems has benefited black people.

29-37: The contributions of peoples who were not white have been excluded from the curriculum. The achievements of Africans in science, chemistry, art, folklore, and literature have been ignored. African and African American languages have been denigrated or unmentioned. Law schools and medical schools have also exhibited prejudice toward African American people and issues. Someone could study history from kindergarten to college and hear nothing but negative statements about Africa. Black people have been categorized as inferior.

38–40: Black teachers cannot fight against these falsehoods and omissions because they have no political or administrative power. African American education is in the hands of those who have enslaved and segregated them—white people. Even if black teachers had political power, they too have been educated to see Africa and African Americans as inferior. As far as the education of black children is concerned, black and white teachers are basically equivalent. The educational system trains African Americans to be white—but it also says that they can never be white. Until black and white people actually began to cooperate on an equal level, this system of faulty education and economic oppression will continue.

41–42: Black people's minds have been enslaved by their education. Most highly educated African Americans support or defend the present system, and those who do not are a powerless minority.

Highly educated African Americans are of no service to themselves or to white people. White people do not need educated black people. Educated African Americans do not need the black working class. Thus, highly educated African Americans can only teach and preach and head down blind alleys, with little hope for future change.

JONATHAN KOZOL

The Uses of "Diversity" (pp. 605–617)

Paragraphs 1–6: The way that diversity is taught in most schools is bland, boring, and non-realistic. Diversity curricula cover up the lack of diversity in most schools. The word *diverse* is often a euphemism for schools that are basically segregated and non-diverse.

7–12: Most schools teach civil rights as historical phenomena; teachers do not focus on present-day civil rights issues. The civil rights lessons focus on the desegregation of southern schools in 1950s and 1960s. Segregation should not be taught as a distant piece of history. Many schools and school districts have reverted to *de facto* segregation. The proper way to teach children about civil rights is to empower them to understand and speak about contemporary segregation.

13–18: Integrated schools are at their lowest level since 1968. Many schools in American cities have basically the same rate of segregation as the Jim Crow South. When teachers ignore this fact, we deceive children and teach them to live with a lie. These inner city schools do not even live up to the promises of "separate but equal."

19–33: Many students in inner city schools have not even been taught to question or think about contemporary segregation. Martin Luther King Jr.'s life, philosophy, and politics have been sugarcoated—he would see modern-day segregation as immoral. Many white people, including liberals, deny that this *de facto* segregation exists and prefer to remember the idealistic civil rights years of the 1960s. They are blinded to the sophisticated apartheid in place today. Teachers should not ignore the problems of the present by focusing exclusively on past victories.

34–40: Teaching can often be full of joy and humor, but it is also often full of contradiction and absurdity. For example, how does a teacher judge whether or not a student is "respectful of diversity" if that student has never been in class with students of another race? Teachers will continue to show impatience and frustration with hypocritical diversity curricula. Education is not neutral. Either we teach children to think for themselves, or we teach them to settle for official truths. We should be teaching children to speak about their realities using their own words.

HOWARD GARDNER

Designing Education for Understanding (pp. 619–643)

Paragraphs 1–6:   New kinds of nontraditional universities have arisen—for-profit, private universities focused on practical, not academic, knowledge. These universities have a utilitarian mission, not an intellectual one, and their goals are exactly the opposite of the goals I cherish.

7–11:   One way to think about education is to imagine what kind of graduates we want to produce. But many educational systems have failed. Neither all-encompassing nor proportional approaches have worked. Approaches without teacher accountability or coordination have also failed.

12–13:   I call for an approach that gives students an understanding of thinking in these disciplines—science, mathematics, the arts, and history. Students must undertake an in-depth, substantial study of topics within these fields; however, they do not need to cover the entire field. Students can study one art, science, or historical period, but the goal is not to make them into experts. This curriculum of study will allow students to understand the mode of thinking within each discipline and, therefore, to be better prepared to understand the world.

14–24:   Educators tend to favor cultural literacy over in-depth knowledge of select topics, but the cultural literacy approach is shallow and incoherent. My approach centers on understanding and application. A student who possesses understanding will be able to apply his or her conceptual knowledge to new and unfamiliar topics or situations. This understanding, however, is mostly lacking in students. New and unfamiliar materials or problems confound our students.

25–29:   The theories that children come up with on their own are part of the problem. The facts children learn in school often cover up deeper theoretical misperceptions. These theories persist—in disciplines as diverse as physics, biology, and history—even though they are mistaken. Teachers are complicit in this because they test students on content without challenging them to use the material in new ways. Only a rich investigation of a limited number of topics will let students see the weakness of their misconceived theories and allow a sophisticated understanding to emerge.

30–31:   Education must necessarily be multidisciplinary because we must synthesize approaches in order to understand why misperceptions persist. People come up with incorrect theories for both cognitive and cultural reasons; it takes knowledge of biology, psychology, and pedagogy to understand and combat this.

32–38:   Unlike naïve students or ignorant adults, experts have deep knowledge of their specialties. For example, scientists know that just because things are related to each other does not mean that one causes the other. Cause and effect can be very difficult to determine, and scientists have been trained to be skeptical. Systematic and skeptical thinking are part of the scientific enterprise. We can get students to think like scientists by letting them explore one scientific area deeply; this will be more effective than a shallow exploration of many different examples from multiple sciences.

39–42:   People simplify history all the time because they do not understand historical thinking. Rather than succumbing to presentism or exoticism when investigating the past, a historically informed individual will be able use the tools of the discipline in order to arrive at a more accurate picture. These habits of mind will not come from shallow survey courses that cover huge stretches of historical time. The ways of thinking are what matter. If students understand the modes of different disciplines, then they can apply those modes to novel problems. Rote memorization is old-fashioned; we want to teach students the modes of thinking in different fields.

43–51:   There are four promising approaches to understanding. The first is learning from instructive institutions, which would combine aspects from apprenticeship and hands-on learning to encourage students to develop and test theories on their own under expert supervision. The second approach is to confront students with mistaken conceptions. Once a student offers an explanation, experiments can be conducted to challenge the theory. In order to combat memorization of algorithms, math students will be encouraged to develop their own formulas. Students will be less likely to rely on simplistic stereotypes if they think about an event from multiple points of view. Challenges to deeply held beliefs, attempts to defend beliefs, and discoveries of better beliefs are very promising approaches to enhancing understanding.

52–55: The third approach is one that prioritizes understanding. Understanding should be thought of as a public exhibition of knowledge. From the start of their education, students should be given examples of understanding; they should also be allowed to demonstrate their own understandings. Even though understanding is a mental activity, it is not just an interior event. Athletes learn by watching more proficient athletes perform and then attempting performance themselves. These performances of understanding can be the basis of pedagogy in other academic fields, too.

56–64: In order to prioritize understanding, a teacher would first list the understanding goals of the course or unit. Next, the teacher would identify essential questions for understanding. Third, and most important, students must know how to do performances of understanding in the class and how they will be judged on these performances. The last component is ongoing assessment. Instead of relying on tests and final grades, students should receive constant feedback from teachers and time to reflect on their performances. Over time, students should learn to internalize assessment and not just rely on teachers.

65–69: This approach is not behaviorist; it is cognitivist. Obviously, the assessment must be of behaviors since mental representations cannot be judged. We favor coaching, though, that encourages students to revise and confront conceptions that stand in the way of understanding. Students must also develop new and more flexible representations. This whole program of teaching for understanding will take time to implement in the classroom.

70: The fourth approach is to find multiple entry points to understanding. People approach things in different ways. There are multiple intelligences, and there are multiple approaches to understanding.

71–75: In order to teach understanding, teachers must be comfortable with the material and value understanding in their own lives. This will help them engage students. Teachers should also keep up with changes in their own fields and the field of teaching.

76–86: Teachers must also motivate students to take responsibility for their own learning. Technology is also a tool to increase understanding. Teachers must examine their goals and figure out specific ways technology can help to achieve them. The community—including parents, businesspeople, school boards, state and local officials, and the general public—also must be aware of what is going on in the classroom. Learning takes place outside of the classroom; students need to participate in field trips, apprenticeships, work-study positions, and mentorships.

RALPH WALDO EMERSON

On Education (bedfordstmartins.com/worldofideas/epages)

Paragraph 1:   We ought to cultivate imagination in young people by encouraging them to read widely.

2–3:   In educating the child, respect his nature. Avoid strict discipline; support the child as a companion.

4:   Preserve the boy's essential nature, and build on it. Allow him to pursue freely his genius, his inspiration, his enthusiasm, his bias.

5:   Sir Charles Fellowes achieved an excellent education by following his enthusiasm for restoring an ancient Greek structure found at Xanthus.

6–7:   Enthusiasm is not incompatible with drill. Accuracy and precision are important, and learning often occurs in small steps, leading gradually to full accomplishment.

8–10:   We often impede nature by using rigid, mechanical methods of education. But our efforts fail, and we must return to natural methods, recognizing our innate desire to teach and learn and our pleasure in doing so.

11:   When natural methods are abandoned, the young lose their potential for genius and become sensual and lazy. The colleges, which are organized to accommodate such students, use systematic, impersonal methods that cannot produce excellence. Innovation in education is badly needed.

12:   Much patience is needed to see promise in an ill-prepared student. The teacher's idealism is crushed by the reality of the school: large numbers of students with disparate abilities, too little time, harsh and expedient forms of discipline.

13:   Our educational system aims to teach large numbers of students mechanically and efficiently, leaving no room for the nurturing of the individual. The rare teacher who rejects this system in favor of simple discipline and natural methods must have great character and strength.

14:   To correct our faulty system, we must abandon military efficiency and embrace Nature, whose secret is patience. Teachers must be tranquil, trusting, observant, and restrained in order to bring forth students' natural gifts.

15:   We can best reform our system by addressing individuals rather than institutions. Teachers should prefer sympathy to force; should encourage wit, imagination, and thinking; should reward students' expressions of individuality.

16–17:   Teachers, continue your noble work and maintain your high ideals.

MARY WOLLSTONECRAFT

Of the Pernicious Effects Which Arise from the Unnatural Distinctions Established in Society (pp. 653–667)

Paragraphs 1–4:   Those who gain wealth and comfort tend to become idle and fail to perform their moral obligations; thus, more equality must be established between the classes before morality can gain ground.

5–7:   Society is not properly organized; it prevents both sexes from gaining respect through virtue, affection, and the fulfillment of their moral duties, by compelling men to gain respect by acquiring wealth and property, and women to advance by using their charms.

8–19:   A woman's rank in life requires her to be dependent and charged with motherhood and denies her the opportunity to think and act for herself; men may unfold their faculties by becoming soldiers and statesmen.

20–29:   Unlike women of the lower classes, women of the upper class are not bound by the duties of wife and mother and should, but do not, have paths by which they can cease to be arbitrarily governed, share in government deliberations, and study politics, medicine, and business.

30–32:   The most respectable women are the most oppressed and usually become contemptible only because they are treated like contemptible beings in their bondage of ignorance.

33–34:   Reasonable men are called on to assist in the emancipation of women, to be content with rational fellowship, rather than slavish obedience, from women. As a result, women will learn to respect themselves and love men with true affection.

JOHN STUART MILL

The Subjection of Women (pp. 669–687)

Paragraph 1:   If women were free, would mankind be better off?

2:   We cannot be blind to the evils of marriage. Husbands hold wives in bondage. This is unjust, and it contradicts our modern principles. In fact, married women are the only remaining legal slaves.

3–5:   Why should we eliminate these inequalities and give women full citizenship? The first reason is this: the relation between men and women should be *just,* not unjust. All selfishness in mankind comes from the present state of the relation between men and women. Every boy believes that he is superior to half the human race. Men are like lords or nobility; their station comes from a mere accident of birth, and women are their vassals. This superiority complex perverts the characters of men. Modern principles demand that personal conduct alone should be rewarded. Power and authority should come from merit, not birth, but broader political changes will not happen as long as women are treated unequally.

6–8:   The second reason to give women full citizenship is the fact that humanity would have a larger pool of talented people to do work. We lose much potential labor by denying half our citizens the right to meaningful, intellectual labor. If we educated women, then they would be able to work on an equal level with men. Women would think of themselves as full and complete human beings, and they could have an even greater moral effect on humanity. Already women have softened the excesses of men, and they have always encouraged men to be courageous and virtuous. These two kinds of moral influence helped create chivalry, which was a combination of warlike qualities and generous treatment of women.

9:   Chivalry is one of the moral monuments of humanity; it was an ethos that attempted to dignify society by infusing morality into its institutions. Chivalry also represents the high point of women's moral influence upon history. Our modern moral foundations should be justice, prudence, respect for others, and self-dependence. Granted, chivalry encouraged only a minority of society to do right and not wrong, but it *was* a step in the right direction. Morality, after all, works because of punishment and deterrence. We no longer have to rely on the chivalry of the powerful; by repressing wrong behavior, modern society can protect the weak in all stations of life. This is true throughout society—except in marriage relations.

10–14:   The moral influence of women has become part of general public opinion, especially in peacemaking and charity. However, this influence is not always a positive force. Charity can relieve the poor of the need to care for themselves, and this lack of self-control can have terrible consequences. Because women are an oppressed group, they do not value self-dependence; thus, women do not encourage self-dependence when they give charity to the poor. On a personal level, women *do* exert a great influence over their husbands, especially among the classes most exposed to temptation. But if women were emancipated and given equal treatment under the law, this influence would be far greater. In higher social classes, a wife prevents her husband from falling too low but also prevents him from rising above his station. She reflects the common public opinion. A man will be wary of taking chances because he is concerned with the judgments of his wife and the welfare of his family. Society oppresses women by making their whole lives revolve around the ideal of self-sacrifice, so women do not support risk or dissent; thus, the family remains mediocre and content with respectability.

15–16:   The ideal of married life is very harmful. People who are extremely unlike one another will not share interests and will be unhappy together. Differences of opinion and tastes can lead to bad marriages. In such cases, husband and wife find themselves at odds—they work against rather than *with* each other. Because women are raised in an unequal manner, natural differences between men and women are exaggerated. Women must submit to their husbands' wishes, and this is a bad outcome for both sexes: the woman is oppressed, and the man has a servant rather than a partner. However, when two people are equal and compatible, they can enrich one another. If the sexes were not treated differently, happy marriages would be more common.

148

VIRGINIA WOOLF

Shakespeare's Sister (pp. 689–705)

Paragraphs 1–2: I decided to see what historians had to say about the lives of Elizabethan women in England. Perhaps the reason women wrote none of the great literature of that age was because of the conditions in which they lived.

3–4: Trevelyan's *History of England* says little about women, except to note that they were often beaten by their fathers and husbands and had virtually no control over their own lives. In fiction, however, women are exalted.

5–6: Historians mention an occasional queen or great lady but say nothing about ordinary Elizabethan women. Based on what little we do know, it would be very odd indeed if one of these Elizabethan women had written the plays of Shakespeare.

7: "What would have happened had Shakespeare had a wonderfully gifted sister?" She would not have gone to school, as Shakespeare did, and her parents would have discouraged her interest in books and expected her to marry young. She would have traveled secretly to London, where she would have been mocked and rebuffed when she tried to become an actress. Later, she would have accepted help from a sympathetic man, become pregnant, and committed suicide.

8–9: That, I think, is what would have become of a woman in Shakespeare's time had she had Shakespeare's genius. Had she survived the impossible obstacles facing her, the stress of living freely in sixteenth-century London would have made her writing "twisted and deformed" and compelled her to publish her work anonymously.

10–11: The circumstances of sixteenth-century life would have made it very difficult for a woman to achieve the state of mind needed to create art. From confessional writings of the eighteenth and nineteenth centuries, we learn of the enormous obstacles male artists faced in producing works of genius.

12–14: For women, those obstacles were far more formidable. Both the material conditions of their lives and the hostility of society stood in their way. Though men like Oscar Browning, who asserted that women were intellectually inferior to men, are largely discredited today, their opinions once carried great authority. Even in the nineteenth century, women were not encouraged to become artists. Men appear to hold a deep-seated desire to be superior to women, not only in the arts but also in politics.

15–17: Old-fashioned opinions about women may seem amusing today, but they caused much pain to the women of earlier generations. Artists, in particular, are sensitive to what others think of them; hurtful opinions can cloud the incandescent state of mind needed for the creation of great art—the state of mind that Shakespeare possessed.

MARGARET MEAD

Sex and Temperament (pp. 707–723)

Paragraph 1:   This study is concerned with the ways three primitive societies have grouped attitudes toward temperament about sex difference. By comparing the ways these tribes have used sex-difference, we can see which elements of sex are socially constructed.

2–4:   We cannot measure all human cultures by the same scale. When comparing societies, we cannot expect to see simple and predictable patterns or reversals. Cultures differentiate the sexes in multiple ways, including labor, dress, manners, and social and religious functioning. In some societies these roles are founded on superficial concerns and do not always reflect the society's attitude about innate differences between the sexes. However, other cultures, in the roles they assign, assert an actual temperamental difference between men and women.

5–6:   Though the Arapesh and Mundugumor tribes give men and women different tasks, neither of these tribes believes that temperamental traits are innate. They do not see traits like dominance, bravery, aggressiveness, or objectivity as either "masculine" or "feminine." Instead, these tribes view such temperaments as variations of human behavior in general.

7–10:   The realization that male and female traits are socially constructed can lead to flexible and diverse societies, yet it can also lead to narrow and regimented societies. One course is to differentiate sharply the personalities of men and women. Though this makes for a coherent and clear social ordering, it wastes the talents and gifts of men and women who do not fit into the prescribed gender roles.

11–13:   Cultures can also take the opposite course by standardizing the personalities of men and women. However, a lack of distinctions in sex-personality can lead to less complex societies. People who do not conform are frustrated, and the overall range and depth of behavior are restricted.

14–17:   Our society has always believed in sex-differences. If we begin to insist that there are no distinctions between men and women, we will standardize personality. This will lead to more conformity, less diversity of thought and belief, and a decrease in social criticism. We will be left with only one possible set of values. Society will lose the types of personality that were once exclusively masculine or feminine. Even though assigning arbitrary roles to sexes, individuals, and social classes limits individual behavior, it also allows for complex cultures.

18–21:   Deviants are better off in a complex society because they can always find a group that allows them to express their temperament. The very fact that different values exist in a complex society provides *some* support for the deviant. Even so, these are crude compensations for out-of-place individuals. These compensations do not allow the deviant to fully participate in social life, and alienation is perhaps too high a price to pay for complex societies. Can we obtain diversity and complexity without creating unhappy and confused deviants?

22–24:   A civilization does not have to simply standardize or abolish differences. It can also accept and encourage diverse capabilities in its citizens. In the past, members of the upper classes have been allowed to transcend sex-categories, but this does not lead to greater individual freedom; instead, an arbitrary standard based on sex has merely been exchanged for an arbitrary standard based on class.

25–27:   Another way to make sex-differences less rigid is to recognize individual gifts as they occur in either sex. Recognizing *real* distinctions and not artificial ones benefits both society and the individual. The same potentialities exist in men and women, but society must encourage these capabilities or they will be useless. Instead of patterns of behavior for men and patterns of behavior for women, we would have many different patterns for all kinds of people, regardless of their gender. This would create a much richer and less arbitrary society.

GERMAINE GREER

Masculinity (pp. 725–737)

Paragraph 1:   Maleness is a biological fact, but masculinity is a cultural construct. Feminists now prefer to use the term *gender* instead of *sex* because gender can and should be changed; sex, however, is less malleable.

2–4:   In 1997 David Skuse argued that masculinity was genetic, but Skuse's interpretation was clearly flawed. He did not prove that masculinity is "natural." In fact, most research shows that masculine men are *made*. Parents treat boys and girls differently. Mothers respond more rapidly to a boy crying, and boys are fed longer and more often than girls. Girls are taught patience; boys are taught instant gratification. Skuse's data reflect differences in socialization and parenting, not genetic differences between boys and girls.

5:   Father-love and mother-love affect boys and girls differently. Girls develop more self-confidence when they have encouraging fathers, but such fathers are rare. Boys' self-confidence, however, comes from attentive mothers, and attentive mothers are common. Thus, boys grow up believing they are lovable regardless of their appearance and behavior.

6–9:   Young boys are *made* into masculine men. Women do not require this. In fact, boys become masculine because of *other* boys. Males use challenges and trials to achieve masculinity. Young males group behind dominant males and prove themselves by conflict with other groups; they also fight for power within the group. A man's self-worth comes from his groups and his status within them. Gaining respect from other men is essential. A man uses his abilities—his knowledge of masculine things, his humor, his physical prowess—to secure respect. In this way, young men also exclude women from their groups.

10–11:   The myth of masculinity demands that every boy should be a strong warrior. Any man incapable of this is less of a man. The myth creates anxiety in many men who cannot live up to it.

12–14:   Masculinity is the system of behaviors that form corporate society. Corporations are full of many masculinist hierarchies. Men exclude women from these groups, or they punish women for trying to fit in. Any woman who belongs to a masculinist hierarchy does not concern herself with the interests of other women. The myth of the compassionate and nurturing female executive simply covers up the fact that these women have no real power.

JUDITH BUTLER

From *Undoing Gender* (pp. 739–760)

Paragraphs 1–2: Truth is defined and regulated in ways that limit people and what it means to be human. These are the politics of truth, which order our world and tell us what counts as truth. This brings up a question: What can I become when possibilities have been limited? And what happens when I become something for which there is not a place?

3: These are questions about justice—about what a person is and how a person is recognized within a society. The ways people are put into gender categories regulate the possibilities of the human and tell us whether individuals can even recognize themselves as human.

4–6: David Reimer was born a boy, but his penis was severely damaged during an operation. After this, he underwent surgery at John Money's institute to become Brenda, a girl, though a vagina was not yet created. Brenda, though, had a strong desire to buy "boy" toys and urinate standing up. She did not want estrogen or a vagina, and she did not like developing breasts. A new set of psychiatrists intervened, and Brenda began living as a boy again, and a phallus was created for him.

7–9: Money insisted that Brenda was happy and the project was successful; to Money, this showed that gender was not fixed at birth and could be changed by doctors. Critics questioned this and proposed that Brenda's desire to be a boy showed the opposite: gender was fixed and socialization could not reverse it. Many critics challenged the legitimacy of social construction as a theory. These critics never questioned the value of normalcy itself.

10–13: Milton Diamond argued that intersexed infants with a Y chromosome should be assigned to be male. Cheryl Chase argues that gender's relationship to biology is complex and surgery on infants to assign sex should not be done; doctors should wait until the child is mature enough to decide what he or she wants. Experts argue about whether or not gender can be constructed. On Money's side, the way a person looks determines gender identity and surgeons can remake it. On Diamond's side, gender is essential, deeper than appearance, and cannot be changed by surgery. Chase says that the doctors cannot conceive of leaving someone alone. Is surgery performed to eliminate the inconceivable? Or is surgery acceptable because these bodies are inconceivable?

14: An intersex movement imagines a world in which people with mixed gender attributes are accepted and gender is not fixed. Male and female are not hard and fast categories, and there are many people who do not fit into either binary category. Even though the entire transsexual community is not against surgical means to transform sex, there is some opposition to idealized categories of gender within the transsexual community. Perhaps transforming and becoming are what gender is.

15–16: In David's view, he was born a man and is now trying, through surgery and hormones, to return to being a man. Money believes David could have been socialized into being a woman. Diamond and the endocrinologists use transsexual surgery techniques to allow David to recover his male nature. Money believes gender norms can be imposed. Diamond believes they are mandated by nature. But there is a contradiction in each case: changeability is imposed by Diamond, and naturalness is found through artificial means by Money.

17–21: David's story does not provide evidence for the claims of either camp. There is another way of looking at this story, and it has to do with the self-reporting and self-understanding of the subject—Brenda/David. Self-reporting and self-observation—or presenting what the self is—take place before an audience. The doctors have asked David how he feels. Brenda was constantly subjected to scrutiny, and gender norms were constantly placed before her. The doctors tried to figure out whether or not the gender norm had been accomplished in Brenda. David's self-descriptions have been used to prove the point that David was always male. Given David's self-reporting, can we figure out what justice means in this case?

22–25: David's self-descriptions occur within a language that predisposes us to speak in certain ways about the self. We do justice by taking David at his word, but how are we to understand the language that he speaks? David clearly understands that norms about gender exist—he thinks he has failed to live up to the norm of femininity. But what if the norms have become the ways he sees himself? What if the norms themselves are what convey the sense of freakishness to David? Brenda expressed a dislike and used that as evidence of not fitting into a gender. But why does a dislike of a certain toy provide us with clear evidence of gender? Is this not very slim evidence to go on?

26–29: Transsexual surgery generally requires that the patient take gender essentialist positions. Brenda/David went through two transsexual surgeries. The first was about what gender should be based on the body, the second about what gender should be based on behavior and feelings. David is now clearly against the first position—to him, gender is not just body parts, and his worth does not come from his genitals. He exceeds the norm and recognizes this.

30–31: David's case cautions us against absolute gender distinctions. He has not become the norm, yet he is still speaking as a subject about himself. There is a gap between the supposed limits of the human and David's ability to speak about himself. His humanness emerges from the ways he cannot be fully categorized. Understanding of his self comes from outside of the accepted framework. When David speaks about the self's "I," he is speaking of his own lovability. He says he will be loved or accepted for other reasons that do not depend on what his genitals are or are not. David establishes a truth beyond the norms of gender reasoning. He tells us about how established norms limit the human. David is human but a human we do not yet know how to name. He is a person who speaks at the limits of what we think we know.

KAREN HORNEY

The Distrust between the Sexes

(bedfordstmartins.com/worldofideas/epages)

Paragraphs 1–3: In relations between men and women, as between children and parents, we prefer to assume that love is predominant and that hostility and other disturbances are accidental and avoidable. Yet the regularity of tension between the sexes suggests common denominators.

4–8: Much of the suspiciousness between women and men is understandable and even justifiable, considering the intensity of the emotions involved. Our instinct for self-preservation restrains us from the surrender of self that accompanies passion, while we resent such restraint in the partner. Projecting our own negative feelings onto the partner, we become distrustful. Moreover. love tends to release all our secret expectations and wishes, which we focus on the partner without realizing they are doomed to disappointment.

9: Frustrations in childhood also contribute to sexual tension. When the child's strong desires are thwarted or dismissed by adults, his pent-up anger turns into fantasies of violent vengeance. The resulting anxiety carries over into adulthood as a fear of love for what it might cause us to do to the partner, and vice versa.

10–11: Suppose that a little girl is badly disappointed by her father, causing her to deny her maternal instincts and transform her instinctual wish to receive from a man into a vindictive urge to take from him by force. She might become the kind of woman who fears that men suspect her of wanting something—that is, that they guess her repressed wish. Or she might project her wish and fear that men want to exploit her. A reaction formation of excessive modesty might mask her wish, causing her not to demand or accept anything from her husband. Or repressing her aggression might drain her energy, so that she feels helpless and shifts the responsibility for her life onto her husband.

12–13: Though men's attitudes toward women are influenced by their early experiences, some attitudes l'ban be traced historically and across cultures. The Old Testament, for example, denies and devalues women's capacity to give birth by depicting Eve as created from Adam's rib and cursed to bear children in sorrow; it also shows her as a sexual temptress who plunges man into misery. Man's fear of woman is deeply rooted in sex: nubile women are the focus of diverse cultural taboos to protect men from their dangerous magic powers. Though our culture no longer burns witches, men continue to define women in relation to themselves and to cast their differences as inferiorities.

14–15: Men venerate motherliness for it is the embodiment of the woman who fulfills all their expectations and longings. Their regard for female fecundity, however, is mingled with jealousy, inciting men to create state, religion, art, and science, and to dominate all aspects of culture. A residue of resentment has led men to glorify their genitality while devaluing pregnancy, childbirth, and women in general.

16–17: Male cultural supremacy is a fairly recent sequel to matriarchy. At present, as women struggle to regain their equality, we should not hope for female ascendancy but for an end to the conflict, which inevitably overvalues the weaker and rationalizes the discrepancy.

18: It appears likely that men's dread of women is due to their sense of yielding power during intercourse, the psychological association between the mother and death, and the greater sexual dependency of the male on the female rather than vice versa.

19–20: The other reason we focus on love rather than hostility between the sexes is love's incomparable potential for happiness. Analysts can help diminish distrust by uncovering the real motives of the struggle, by working to resolve childhood conflicts, and by attempting 10 forestall some of those conflicts in the future.

SUSANNE LANGER

Language (pp. 769–781)

Paragraphs 1–2: The essence of language is expression of concepts, not desires. Language's origins are on a lower level than communication by sounds. Experiments and evidence show us language is first used conceptually, not practically. Meaning is made out of words from a combination of name and image, not sign and result.

3–6: In the case of the "wild child" Victor, we see evidence that the utilitarian view of language is a mistake. Dr. Itard tried to get Victor to use words as signs when he wanted things, but that did not work. When Victor began using words, Dr. Itard realized that he was using them as expressions of joy, not use. For instance, Victor would use the word for milk when he was having milk, not when he wanted milk. Just like Victor, normal young children learn to speak by using words to bring concepts into their minds, not things into their hands.

7–8: Children learn to use language without being taught, but Victor could not learn because he was too old and had already passed the phase of constant vocalization. If language is not developed at a young age, then an individual will always be constrained in his or her use of language.

9–12: The vocalizing and articulating instincts of young children are supported by responses in a social environment. This is how use becomes habit. But when the instinct phase passes, many sounds that do not receive a response are lost. It is easier for children to learn to speak several languages because they have an optimal period of learning. In this period, children are very sensitive to expressions of any kind. Children attach meaning to all sorts of sensations and objects. Children are extremely aware of expressive forms—they play with association in an impractical way by attaching, say, a color to a vowel sound. Projecting feelings onto objects is a way of conceiving feelings. The idea of the self may come from this playful process of symbolically epitomizing feelings.

13–15: As a child grows up, these dreamlike associations decrease and become more practical. Sense data stay in fixed categories. Associations are probably even more fantastic when the infant is just learning language. Experiences cannot be classed in this primitive phase. The infant makes audible actions and unexpected productions of sound that he or she then repeats playfully. If adults reply to these sounds, the baby realizes that there is a meaningful connection between sound and response. Thus, the baby repeats one sound and not another. Babbling leads to the child's recognition of the babbling's product. The wild children did not create language because they were not properly socialized at a young enough age.

16–17: A new sound is a possession that is very interesting to a child. It is also an extremely free item, without any fixed relations, and can become a symbol when a symbol is needed. The next experience that coincides with hearing the sound will become identified with it; thus, a child can invoke the concept of a thing by uttering the word—this is naming. A child's main purpose in speaking seems to be, for a while, playing with concepts. Naming is very satisfying. Language and conception are deeply connected, as are language and experience.

18–20: Our primary reality is verbal. Without words, our imagination can only think of things that are present. Language transforms experience into concepts. Speech is symbolic, and it only sometimes acts as a sign. Symbolic abstraction precedes any communication needs. Language could have happened only to a species that had already developed forms of symbolic thinking such as dreams, rituals, and superstitions. In a group that uses symbols, conventional meanings would attach to once random acts. These acts would, with a little more elaboration, soon become material for symbolic expression. Ritual might precede language.

MARIO PEI

Theories of Language Beginning (pp. 783–793)

Paragraphs 1–10: We still do not know the origin of human speech, though there are many theories. Even the scientific theories are perhaps unprovable; they include theories that language started as imitation of natural sounds, cries of surprise, imitations of body movements, or for the purposes of lying.

11–16: Even children who are ignorant of human language begin using it as soon as they are introduced to it. Animal cries do not vary much over time, but human language is highly changeable. Human activity changes over time and across regions, and language changes with it. All languages change over time, but the more isolated a language and its speakers are, the more stable it is.

17–18: There are two different theories that explain why a language breaks apart into separate languages and dialects. In the "tree-stem" theory, new languages branch off the main trunk. In the "wave" theory, new languages spread out like ripples in water. Changes in language sound can arise suddenly or gradually.

19–25: Tens of thousands of years pass between the start of human society and the appearance of writing. Linguistic records come only from writing, and Sumerian—arising in 4000 B.C.E.—is the oldest written language. We have no record of the original Western language, Indo-European, since that language had broken into many tongues by the time writing was invented. Indo-European probably arose around 2500 B.C.E. Sanskrit, Greek, and Latin are the oldest written languages in the Indo-European family.

26–29: Latin-Romance languages have the most complete unbroken history of any of the world's languages. In the twelfth century, Anglo-Saxon became Middle English, which then became Modern English around 1400. Few words in modern languages can be traced back to pre-Classical languages. Similar forms for *dad* appear in many Indo-European languages, and its ultimate source is probably baby talk.

30–31: Linguists will probably be unable to find out the origin of language because written records do not go that far back. Linguists can speculate about these origins and come up with plausible explanations, but they will probably not be able to come up with scientific theories that are testable, repeatable, and predictive.

JAMES BALDWIN

If Black English Isn't a Language, Then Tell Me, What Is?
(pp. 795–803)

Paragraphs 1–2: The argument about whether or not black English is a language has nothing to do with linguistics; it has to do with the role of language. Language reveals the speaker and defines the other. People use language in order to describe and control their circumstances. The French language, for example, is spoken differently in Quebec, Paris, and Martinique—in each place, a different reality is articulated.

3–4: Peoples use languages in order to achieve identities, including racial, regional, and political identities. Language allows people to connect their private identities to a larger group. It can also reveal separateness. Language—especially in England—tells about a person's history, class, education, and heritage.

5–6: White American English would sound much different without the influence of black people. White people have adopted and changed many phrases and terms from black English. Black people should not be penalized for their language, which has told the truth about America.

7–8: Black English is the product of diverse Africans being thrown together as slaves in the American South. They spoke no common language at first. It was within the institution of the black church that black English was formed. Ancient elements were made into a new language, and the rules reflected the information it needed to convey. By necessity, black English was not understood by white people.

9–12: The power of black English is proof that it is a language; black people have not endured in America by means of a dialect. Asking black children to stop speaking black English is asking them to stop being black. It is also asking for a trust that cannot be given, since America has failed and continues to fail so many non-white people.

BILL BRYSON

Where Words Come From (pp. 805–823)

Paragraphs 1–7:   English has words for almost everything, though there are concepts that we have no single word to describe. Still, English has the world's richest vocabulary. Almost every word has many synonyms—no other language has as many. English has at least one word for every level in the culture: popular, literary, and scholarly. This abundance of words can be seen as a positive or negative. Even though we have lots of words, in English one word can have many meanings, which is known as polysemy. Words in English can also be spelled the same way yet have very different meanings.

8:   Words are formed in six main ways. They can be added to, subtracted from, or made up. They can be borrowed from other languages or created by mistake. Words can also stay the same while the meaning changes.

9–13:   Words can be created by mistake. One category is ghost words. At least 350 words in dictionaries happened because of typographical errors or misreadings. Words can also be misheard or made from false analogy. Authoritative writers like Shakespeare and Browning can introduce words by mistake.

14–22:   English takes words from many other languages. This process often drastically changes the original words in form and meaning. A single root can give birth to many new words. Some words that English absorbed do not exist in the parent languages. New words are often so thoroughly anglicized that no one would guess they are non-native. English often has native Anglo-Saxon nouns but adopts a foreign form for the related adjective; the noun *water* is Anglo Saxon, but the adjective *aquatic* is not. English is not, however, the world language that borrows the most. Even though English is a Germanic language, it has borrowed very few words from German.

23–29:   Words can be spontaneously created or invented with no other source. Sometimes words can fall out of favor for hundreds of years and then come back suddenly. Writers make up words; Shakespeare alone gave us about 1,700 words. Some periods of time are more inventive than others; the years 1500–1650 were particularly creative, with nearly 12,000 words coined. Words can also be invented for specific purposes.

30–37:   Words can stay the same while the meaning drifts or changes—sometimes the new meaning is the opposite of the original meaning. More than half of the Latin words adopted by English have meanings different from the originals. Phrases or expressions can preserve the old meanings of words; these archaic words are called fossils. Words can also change by becoming more specific over time.

38–46:   Words are created by addition or subtraction. For instance, adding prefixes or suffixes to an existing word can make a new word. English makes compounds very easily. This variety can be confusing, especially for non-native speakers. Some prefixes and suffixes are very rare, and others go through phases of popularity. Cutting off the ends can also make new words. English, like other Indo-European languages, makes new words by fusing compounds.

NEIL POSTMAN

The Word Weavers/The World Makers (pp. 825–841)

Paragraphs 1–3: It makes more sense to speak of *a* definition of a word, rather than *the* definition. Students, however, are taught to think of definitions as exact and stable. Questions are the main intellectual instruments available to humans, yet few students systematically study the art of question asking.

4–8: Though metaphors are discussed in school, students believe that metaphors are decorative language limited to poetry. However, metaphors are used in all fields to say things about the world. Writers once made their education metaphors explicit, but contemporary writers on education do not pay enough attention to metaphorical ways of thinking, speaking, and writing.

9–11: Definitions, questions, and metaphors should be studied with the highest priority in school because they show us how world making occurs through language. The way we use language affects the way we perceive the world. A doctor who says a patient has "done" a case of arthritis is saying something different from a doctor who says a patient "has" arthritis. Or a judge who says a bank robber "has" criminality is saying something different from a judge who says a bank robber has "done" a crime.

12–13: Even these simple verbs are powerful metaphors that express belief. They show habitual ways of discussing reality. If you "do" something, you have responsibility for it; if you "have" something, it is not your responsibility. All laws and moral codes are based on metaphorical ways of thinking, and any changes to law or morality require a rearrangement of the ways metaphors are used. Language habits are central to how we imagine the world. We should educate students about this so that they have more control of their situations.

14–16: School tests are used to determine how much smartness a student "has." This way of thinking, however, is as strange as thinking someone "does" arthritis. It makes more sense to speak of smartness as performance, as something someone "does" rather than something someone "has." The ways language creates perception are not usually a part of schooling because the subject is thought to be too complex and interdisciplinary to teach, but it should be a focus of teachers' professional education.

17–20: Alfred Korzybski is a language authority teachers should study. Korzybski attempted to offer a theory about the roots of human failure and achievement and a practical way to solve psychological, social, and political problems. Korzybski identified humans as "time-binders." Uniquely among animals, humans can take knowledge from the past and transport it to the future—we are time machines.

21: The way we bind time is through symbols. Our ability to symbolize depends on abstracting, which is the act of selecting, omitting, and organizing reality in order to experience the world as coherent. According to Korzybski, the world is constantly changing and we give it stability by recreating it and leaving out the differences. We abstract at all levels of thought by selecting, generalizing, and summarizing.

22: For example, a cup is an event, not a thing; it is always undergoing change on the molecular level. Our language and thought, however, ignore these changes. When we perceive, we always summarize—we make an abstraction. We see parts of wholes, but we pretend that we see the whole, and our language use reflects this.

23–25: When we name an event and categorize it as something, we are creating a map of reality. But the word *cup,* for example, does not denote anything that really exists. "Cup" is a concept, an abstraction. This language is always at a remove from reality. These symbols are a part of the way we think, but we must not take them for granted. We live in two worlds: the world of events and things, and the world of words about events and things. Language constructs concepts, but it also tells us what kind of concepts we should construct. Each language constructs reality differently.

26: Korzybski studied the relationship between the world of words and the actual world, or between the map and the territory. Korzybski believed that scientists solve problems more effectively than the rest of us because they are more aware of the abstracting process. If the rest of us would use language like scientists do, we could avoid misunderstanding, superstitions, and prejudices.

27–31: One way of freeing minds from the tyranny of definitions is providing students with alternative definitions of important concepts. Students should be taught that definitions are instruments for achieving purposes. They should ask about the origins and purposes of particular definitions. For example, it is illegal to joke when being frisked before boarding an airplane. But is there a legal definition of a joke? The only thing that matters is what someone in power thinks; being able to define things *is* power. The security guard decides what is a joke and what is not. All systems have means of judging and enforcing definitions. We should always ask where the power comes from that enforces a definition.

32–36: We should get students to study the relationship between language and reality. Students should be taught the universe of discourse within a subject matter. How are questions, definitions, and metaphors formed within the field? How have the forms of questions changed over time? The ways a question is asked determine the ways it can be answered. How are the words that signal correctness or falsehood within a field used? Students do not think much about how truth is different from subject to subject. Language education must include, among other things, a discussion of the context of truth and falsehood.

NOAM CHOMSKY

New Horizons in the Study of Language (pp. 843–855)

Paragraphs 1–3:   Language appears to be unique to humans—using linguistic signs is what separates us from animals and machines. Language is largely responsible for the biological success of humans, and it is a crucial part of human life, thought, and culture.

4–8:   Language is based on the property of discrete infinity. Sentences, like numbers, can go on forever. All humans are born with the ability to construct infinite sentences—this language organ is a part of human nature. The language organ consists of a faculty humans are born with and what they learn about language use through life experience.

9–10:   Language generates expressions or grammar. Each expression has instructions for speaking, thinking, and other things. A person speaking a language therefore has knowledge about how to make sounds and meaning, express thoughts, interpret, and use language in many other ways. The theory of this is called generative grammar.

11–15:   This theory arose during the 1950s when scientists focused on mental aspects of life as part of the cognitive revolution. Scientists were able to give accounts of the brain's ability to use finite pieces of language in infinite ways. The biological linguistic intelligence of humans became the object of scientific inquiry. Children know much more about language than their experience has provided. Language acquisition is like the growth of any organ—it is something that happens, not something the child does. The initial state of the language organ is shared by all humans. In their essential properties, therefore, all human languages are like each other; they differ only in trivial ways.

16–17:   The two conditions of a theory of language are descriptive and explanatory adequacy. Any particular language's grammar satisfies descriptive adequacy since it gives an account of the properties of that language. In order to satisfy explanatory adequacy, particular languages must also be shown to derive from the same initial state. There is tension between these two conditions. Research into particular languages shows great complexity and many diverse rules. Research into deeper language structure should show an unchangeable nature.

18–19:   The "Principles and Parameters" approach to this tension rejected overall rules that apply to different languages. That is, grammatical constructions in each language are just artifacts with no theoretical standing. They are local phenomena with no effect on the overall theory. The initial state of the language faculty is like a fixed network connected to a switch box. Switches are turned on or set by local conditions. Each human language is identified as a setting of switches. Small changes in switch settings can lead to a great variety of languages, but all languages still share the same initial properties.

21–22:   This program of research gives an outline of a general theory of language and suggests that it must satisfy both conditions of explanatory and descriptive adequacy. The main task is to discover how these principles interact. We know that the language organ is embedded in the human brain. It interacts with other systems, which impose conditions on the language faculty's generative processes. We must ask to what extent language provides a good solution to the conditions imposed on it by external systems.

ALEXANDER POPE

From *An Essay on Criticism*

(bedfordstmartins.com/worldofideas/epages)

Lines 1–14: The chief cause of poor judgment among critics is pride, which blinds them to their own shortcomings.

15–32: A second cause is lack of learning, which limits their perspective.

33–52: A third cause is evaluating by parts rather than by whole. We should judge the overall effect of a work and not the excellence or weakness of its individual parts.

53–66: Critics should consider that no work can be perfect in all its parts.

67–88: A story about a critic (knight) and a playwright (bard) illustrates the error of judging by part rather than by whole.

89–104: Some critics erroneously judge poetry for its cleverness and extravagant ornamentation (conceit) rather than for its substance.

105–136: Others overemphasize the poet's language, favoring style over meaning, expression over sense. The best language is clear and plain, neither old-fashioned nor trendy.

137–183: Still others overemphasize the poet's skill at versification (numbers), judging works by their sound rather than their meaning. In the best poetry, "the sound must seem an Echo to the sense."

184–193: Critics should avoid extremes, being neither too hard to please nor too quick to admire.

194–207: Some critics are biased toward a particular sect of writers—English or foreign, ancient or modern.

208–223: Some are swayed by popular opinion, by an author's reputation, or by their desire to flatter a powerful author.

224–229: Others are overly singular, shunning popular opinion even when it is right.

230–251: Some critics constantly change their opinions, praising a work one moment, blaming it the next.

252–265: Others value only works written by their own faction—those who share their views.

266–273: The envious may try to dim the glory of a work of great merit, but their efforts will fail.

274–307: A critic should be quick to praise a deserving work, for today even poetry of great meril enjoys fame but a short while.

308–325: Some great poets jealously guard their status, giving no suppor to lesser poets. Poets and critics should be magnanimous and good natured in their judgments.

PLATO

The Allegory of the Cave (pp. 865–877)

Paragraphs 1–14:   Imagine prisoners living since childhood in an underground den, chained so they cannot move or see anywhere but straight ahead. Behind them is a fire that casts shadows on the cave wall in front of the prisoners as people carry various objects past the fire. The prisoners, seeing nothing but shadows, assume the shadows are all there is to reality.

15–18:   If a prisoner were released and turned toward the light, he would not immediately be able to see the objects whose shadows he formerly watched. Nor would he believe that these objects are more real than the shadows but would cling to his old idea of reality.

19–26:   If the prisoner were taken out of the cave, he would be still more blinded by the sun's light. At first he would see shadows and reflections most easily, then objects, the heavens, and at last the sun, which he would reason about and deduce to be a sort of god of the visual world.

27–34:   Remembering his old life in the cave, the prisoner would pity his companions and rejoice in his own good fortune. Their contests at shadow watching and prediction, with honor and glory attached to winning, now would seem not enviable but repellent. But if he were taken back to the cave and forced to rejoin the contests before his eyes got used to the dark, his fellow prisoners would pity his blindness and keep any others from leaving the cave.

35–40:   The cave is the world of sight, the firelight is the sun, and the journey upward is the soul's ascent into the intellectual world. The sun is the idea of good, author of all things beautiful and right, the power on which men who would act rationally must fix. Those who reach this upper world dislike returning to the cave, where they are forced to argue about justice with people who have never seen it.

41–52:   The eye can be blinded by either abrupt light or abrupt darkness, but sight cannot be put into blind eyes. Rather, the soul must turn from darkness to light to use its capacity for perception of the good. A clever rogue might have been a wise and good man if his soul had been cut off in youth from sensual pleasures that lowered its vision.

53–62:   In the ideal republic, neither the uneducated nor those who never end their education will make able ministers of state. The founders of the state will compel its best minds to attain the good and then to descend again for the benefit of the state. The rulers of this state will be philosophers, enlightened and uninterested in fighting for power. The state whose rulers are most reluctant to govern is governed best.

63–65:   These philosopher-rulers will take office as a stern necessity. The political arena must offer them better rewards than power and wealth, so that those rich in virtue and wisdom will be willing to hold office.

FRANCIS BACON

The Four Idols (pp. 879–895)

Paragraphs 1–7: Four classes of idols and false notions interfere with the human mind's ability to perceive the truth. The best remedy for them is inductive reasoning. Idols of the Tribe are distortions arising from the limits of human perception and understanding. Idols of the Cave arise from individual idiosyncrasies and experience. Idols of the Marketplace are caused by the imprecision of language. Idols of the Theater result from misleading philosophies and principles.

8–16: Human understanding has several tendencies that comprise the Idols of the Tribe. We impute more order and regularity to the world than it actually contains. We ignore evidence that conflicts with our preconceptions. We base our preconceptions on those phenomena that strike us most readily, rather than on a thorough examination of our surroundings. We muddy our observations with unjustified interpretations. What we believe is colored by our wishes. We trust our senses for information that should be obtained by experiment.

17–22: The Idols of the Cave come from an individual's physical and mental constitution as well as education and experience. The most important are men's gravitation toward a favorite subject, shaping their other ideas around it; their tendency to attend too closely to either the similarities or the differences between things; their partiality to a particular age and its judgments; and their inclination to focus on the minute aspects of a thing while ignoring the large and general, or vice versa.

23–26: Most troublesome of all are the Idols of the Marketplace, misconceptions that have crept in through words and names. Words tend to oversimplify what they represent. Some words name things that do not exist or that are ill defined; others can be interpreted in a variety of ways and lack a clear, specific meaning. Different classes of words—nouns, verbs, adjectives—contain different degrees of distortion.

27–28: The Idols of the Theater are not covertly and inevitably deceptive like the Idols of the Marketplace but are presented to the mind by incorrect philosophies and methods of investigating the world. The preferable method of investigation would rely not on individual intelligence and reasoning but on objective observation.

29–34: Most philosophies abstract too much from too little evidence, or vice versa. Some manipulate the facts to conform with their ideas; others interweave science and superstition. The last is most widespread and dangerous, as can be seen in certain Greek and subsequent schools that offer religious and other nonobjective explanations for natural phenomena.

35: Human understanding must be cleansed of the Idols' misconceptions; for those who would enter the kingdom of man founded on science, like the kingdom of heaven, must come as a little child.

CHARLES DARWIN

Natural Selection (pp. 897–913)

Paragraph 1:   The principle of selection applies in nature as in human-controlled breeding. Man cannot create the numerous variations we see in domesticated species but can only preserve and accumulate those that occur. Given how many variations have benefited and been fostered by man, we must assume that many more occur that benefit the being in question and are fostered by the survival advantage they confer. This preservation of favorable individual differences and variations, along with destruction of injurious ones, constitutes natural selection, or the survival of the fittest. "Natural selection" does not refer to volition or Deity but merely to the action and result of natural laws.

2–3:   Any change in a given environment opens a niche for different species migrating in from outside or for variations in resident species, which adapt them better to their altered surroundings. Changing conditions appear to increase variability. Adaptation occurs even in a constant environment, however, for no species is ever perfectly suited to its locale.

4–6:   Man selects only those variations he can see and utilize, whereas Nature can act on any aspect of an organism, at any level of subtlety, and in any way that may improve the organism's ability to exploit its environment. Natural selection is constant, though we see it only when changes accumulate over time and become visible. For significant modification to occur, the initial favorable variation must be followed by others.

7–9:   Natural selection operates even on characters and structures that appear minor to us, as these may significantly affect an organism's survival advantage, and it can work in directions we cannot anticipate. Variations can affect creatures at any stage of their life and can change the relation of offspring to parent. Favorably adapted creatures do not always survive, but natural selection never perpetuates a variation that confers no advantage.

10–12:   Nature, like man, often alters males and females differently within a species. A variation may benefit a creature over others of its species. This sexual selection operates not by conferring a direct survival advantage but by increasing the individual's chances of producing offspring. Stronger males, and those more attractive to females, are more likely to pass on their characteristics to the next generation.

13–14:   Variations are perpetuated that occur in numerous members of a species rather than just one; a single individual, however well adapted, has little chance of passing on a trait to whole succeeding generations. Even if a particular advantageous trait is not transmitted to offspring, however, a tendency to vary in that manner may gradually strengthen within the species.

15–17:   Because most plants and animals stay close to home, any modification tends to occur locally at first, spreading wider insofar as it confers an advantage over other nearby populations. A variation that does not benefit the creature directly may be perpetuated if it increases the species' chance of reproducing, as when a plant yields nectar in such a way as to attract more pollinating insects. Characteristics such as sexual dimorphism may arise in this way. At the same time as a plant species' variations make it more attractive to bees, the bee species is likely to vary so as to adapt better to its changing food source.

18:   Modern geology has banished the instant excavation of great valleys by huge waves in favor of the long-term cumulative action of ordinary visible forces. So too will natural selection banish the belief that new beings are continually created or suddenly modified.

SIGMUND FREUD

The Oedipus Complex (pp. 915–925)

Paragraphs 1–2: In childhood, all human beings—whether normal or psychoneurotic—develop powerful feelings of love for one parent and hate for the other. This hypothesis is confirmed by the ancient story of King Oedipus.

3: As an infant, Oedipus is abandoned by his parents because an oracle warns that he will grow up to kill his father and marry his mother. Oedipus unknowingly fulfills this prophesy and is eventually punished for his actions.

4–5: This story, as told in Sophocles' play *Oedipus Rex,* appeals to modern readers not because it is a tragedy of destiny but because Oedipus's fate is one that, psychologically, we all share: our first sexual desire is for our mother; our first murderous impulse is toward our father. Sophocles' play shows us the fulfillment of our repressed childhood wishes.

6–7: The Oedipus story has its source in ancient dream material that embodies these repressed wishes. Shakespeare's *Hamlet* springs from the same material, but in the case of *Hamlet,* the wishes are more deeply repressed. Hamlet's delay in avenging his father's death indicates his inability to resolve unconscious feelings toward his mother and father. Shakespeare explores in his writing the impulses of his own mind, as do all creative writers.

8–9: A dream of a loved one's death directly embodies a repressed wish, without the kind of censorship or modification typical in dreams. This unusual phenomenon has two causes. Likewise, in anxiety-dreams, censorship is partly or completely absent, a fact that helps explain the purpose of censorship in dreams generally.

CARL JUNG

The Personal and the Collective Unconscious (pp. 927–941)

Paragraphs 1–3:   According to Freud, the unconscious contains only those parts of the personality that are repressed by the conscious mind. I believe, however, that the unconscious also contains other psychic material.

4:   It is ordinarily assumed that all unconscious material, including dreams and fantasies, derives from our personal experiences. But observation shows that the unconscious also contains material unrelated to personal experience.

5:   The experiences of one of my patients illustrates my point. Through psychoanalysis, this woman sought to break her emotional tie with her father and to form a relationship with a man, but her feelings remained unresolved, divided between these two male figures. During treatment, she experienced what Freud calls transference. That is, she transferred the image of both her father and her lover to me (the doctor); I became the object of her conflict. Transference often provides temporary relief for the patient.

6–7:   In successful treatments, the state of transference is temporary and leads to a cure. But my patient became locked in this state, dependent on me as a sort of savior.

8:   Unable to break the deadlock, we decided to study her dreams, hoping that they would provide a solution.

9:   Dreams contain images that we produce unconsciously, and they provide an objective picture of our psychic processes.

10–11:   My patient's dreams contained two actors, herself and her doctor. The latter usually appeared as a figure of supernatural size, often extremely old, sometimes resembling her father. At the same time, this figure was woven into nature, often associated with the wind. These dreams convinced me that in her unconscious, my patient was clinging to me as a father-lover of almost divine proportions.

12:   Even though the patient understood rationally the nature of her transference, her unconscious continued to cling stubbornly to the fantasy image it had created.

13:   What could be the purpose of this fantasy? Was the godlike figure in her dreams merely an image of a human person? Or did her dreams indicate an instinctual longing for a god, a longing deeper and stronger than any love for a human person?

14–15:   Such a possibility seems incongruous in a modern setting, and we must carefully test the hypothesis that this woman's dreams represent the longing for a god.

16:   The woman herself doubted this hypothesis. Gradually, she was able to separate herself from me. This occurred, I think, because of the guidance provided by her dreams, which were not merely fantasies but representations of her unconscious life that enabled her to escape her dependence.

17:   In her dreams, the woman had what amounts to a vision of God. Though a nonbeliever, she found comfort in a giant primordial father figure associated with the wind (or spirit). At this point, we can distinguish what may be called the personal unconscious. We gain deepened self-knowledge by bringing material from this layer of the unconscious into conscious awareness. Psychoanalysis facilitates this process, as does dream analysis.

18:   My patient derived her primitive god image not from the personal content of her unconscious but from a deeper impersonal source shared by people of various times and from various parts of the world. The god she dreamed about is an archetype, an ancient image reactivated by unconscious patterns of thought common to all humans.

19:   The preceding discussion shows that along with personal elements, the unconscious contains impersonal (or collective) elements. The latter exist in a deeper level of the unconscious called the *collective unconscious.*

RENÉ DESCARTES

Fourth Meditation: Of Truth and Error

(bedfordstmartins.com/worldofideas/epages)

Paragraph 1:   Over the past few days I have tried to detach my mind from my senses. I have seen that one can know very little about corporeal objects, but one can know many things about the human mind and even more things about God. Now I turn from sensible or material things to things that are intelligible only.

2:   The human mind is not extended in length, breadth, or depth, and it does not participate in anything connected to the body. The mind thinks, and it is more distinct than any corporeal object. The fact that I can think about a perfect and complete God is proof that God exists and that my existence depends on him; this fact is the most clear and certain thing the human mind can know. After contemplating God, I see the path to thinking about other things in the universe.

3–5:   I know, first of all, that God would not deceive me. Secondly, I know that I have received my power of judgment from God. If I use it properly, I will not be wrong. When I think only of the perfect God, I am not in error. But since I am only midway between God and nothing, and since I am not myself God, there are many things I am mistaken about. Error does not come from God; it is a defect. I can make mistakes because the power of reason God gave me is not infinite in me.

6–8:   These errors, though, appear to be a deprivation of a knowledge I *should* have. Since I am so much weaker and smaller than God, it is not surprising that there are many things I do not understand. When I contemplate the works of God, I must look upon not one thing but all things together. A thing that appears imperfect alone might appear perfect if we looked upon it as a part of a whole. I am clearly only one being among many other beings in the universe.

9:   My errors come from my power of understanding and my power of will. With understanding I conceive of things, but there are many things I cannot comprehend because my understanding is less than God's understanding. God has also given me free will, and it is limitless. All my other faculties, including understanding, I can imagine to be greater and more perfect. My understanding is very small compared to God's. But I cannot imagine that my will could be greater or more extended—thus, because of my will, I know that I resemble God and bear his image. The power of will is greater in God than in me, but this is because his knowledge and understanding are greater. When my will is weak, it is because my understanding is weak. If I always knew what was right, I would never have any trouble deciding the correct course or acting upon it.

10:   I see that my power of willing and my power of understanding are as perfect as they can be *in me.* So where do my errors come from? They come from this alone—my will is greater than my understanding. I extend my will to things I do not understand, and thus I fall into error or sinning.

11–14:   I can conceive many things clearly and know that they are true. Other things I am unsure about and cannot conceive clearly. Things that I am uncertain of I do not judge. This is right behavior. The knowledge of understanding must precede the will. The incorrect use of free will is an error. This error comes from me, but it is not a faculty I received from God, and I cannot complain about it. God did not make me perfect, but he gave me whatever perfections I have, so I should be grateful to him. The wrong use of will is simply a privation that has no need of the concurrence of God; it is not a flaw in God, but it is a flaw in me that I do not use my will perfectly.

15–17:   God could have given me perfect understanding and will. I am, however, only a part of the universe, and it is good that some parts of the universe are imperfect—indeed, God wanted them to be that way. What he has given me is the ability to never hold judgment on things I do not clearly know the truth about. With attentive thinking I can gain the habit of not falling into error. Through this meditation, I have discovered the cause of falsity and error. If I can restrain my will and not judge things I do not understand, then I will never be in error. If, however, I do see something clearly and distinctly, I know that it is real and positive and thus came from God, and then I can conclude that my judgment of it is true. I know now how to avoid error and find truth.

SUGGESTIONS FOR
FURTHER READING

KWAME ANTHONY APPIAH

Appiah, Kwame Anthony. *Cosmopolitanism: Ethics in a World of Strangers*. New York: W. W. Norton, 2006.

————. *The Ethics of Identity*. Princeton: Princeton University Press, 2005.

————. *Experiments in Ethics*. Cambridge: Harvard University Press, 2008.

————. *For Truth in Semantics*. Oxford: Blackwells, 1986.

————. *The Honor Code: How Moral Revolutions Happen*. New York: W. W. Norton, 2010.

————. *In My Father's House: Africa in the Philosophy of Culture*. New York: Oxford University Press, 1992.

————. *Thinking It Through: An Introduction to Contemporary Philosophy*. New York: Oxford University Press, 2003.

Appiah, Kwame Anthony, and Amy Gutmann. *Color Conscious: The Political Morality of Race*. Introduction by David Wilkins. Princeton, NJ: Princeton University Press, 1996.

Ignatieff, Michael. *Human Rights As Politics and Idolatry*. Edited by Amy Gutmann, with commentaries by Kwame Anthony Appiah, David Hollinger, Thomas W. Laqueur and Diane F. Orentlicher. Princeton: Princeton University Press, 2001.

Taylor, Charles. *Multiculturalism: Examining "The Politics of Recognition."* Commentary by Amy Gutmann, Kwame Anthony Appiah, Jürgen Habermas, Steven C. Rockefeller, Michael Walzer, and Susan Wolf. Princeton: Princeton University Press, 1994.

HANNAH ARENDT

Arendt, Hannah. *Between Friends: The Correspondence of Hannah Arendt and Mary McCarthy, 1949–1975*. New York: Harcourt, 1995.

————. *Between Past and Future: Six Exercises in Political Thought*. New York: Viking, 1968.

————. *The Burden of Our Time*. London: Secker & Warburg, 1951.

————. *Crises of the Republic: Lying in Politics, Civil Disobedience, on Violence, Thoughts on Politics*. New York: Harcourt, 1972.

. *Eichmann in Jerusalem: A Report on the Banality of Evil*. New York: Penguin, 1994.

————. *Essays in Understanding, 1930–1954*. Edited by Jerome Kohn. New York: Harcourt, 1994.

————. *The Human Condition*. Chicago: University of Chicago Press, 1958.

————. *The Life of the Mind*. New York: Harcourt, 1978.

————. *Men in Dark Times*. New York: Harcourt, 1968.

————. *On Revolution*. New York: Penguin, 1977.

————. *On Violence*. New York: Harcourt, 1970.

————. *The Origins of Totalitarianism*. New York: Harcourt, 1966.

Aschheim, Steven E. *Culture and Catastrophe: German and Jewish Confrontations with National Socialism and Other Crises*. New York: New York University Press, 1996.

Barnouw, Dagmar. *Visible Spaces: Hannah Arendt and the German-Jewish Experience*. Baltimore: Johns Hopkins University Press, 1990.

Birmingham, Peg. *Hannah Arendt and Human Rights: The Predicament of Common Responsibility*. Bloomington: Indiana University Press, 2006.

Gottsegen, Michael G. *The Political Thought of Hannah Arendt*. Albany: State University of New York Press, 1994.

Hill, Melvyn A. *Hannah Arendt: The Recovery of the Public World*. New York: St. Martin's Press, 1979.

Kaplan, Gisela T., and Clive S. Kessler, eds. *Hannah Arendt: Thinking, Judging, Freedom*. Sydney: Allen and Unwin, 1989.

King, Richard, and Dan Stone, eds. *Hannah Arendt and the Uses of History: Imperialism, Nation, Race, and Genocide*. New York: Berghahn Books, 2007.

Lang, Antholy, F. Jr., and John Williams. *Hannah Arendt and International Relations Readings Across the Lines.* New York: Palgrave Macmillan, 2008.

May, Larry, and Jerome Kohn, eds. *Hannah Arendt: Twenty Years Later.* Cambridge: MIT, 1996.

Parekh, Serena. *Hannah Arendt and the Challenge of Modernity: A Phenomenology of Human Rights.* New York: Routledge, 2008.

Whitfield, Stephen J. *Into the Dark: Hannah Arendt and Totalitarianism.* Philadelphia: Temple University Press, 1980.

Young-Bruehl, Elisabeth. *Hannah Arendt: For Love of the World.* New Haven: Yale University Press, 1982.

ARISTOTLE

Adler, Mortimer. *Aristotle for Everybody: Difficult Thought Made Easy.* New York: Macmillan, 1978.

Aristotle. *A New Aristotle Reader.* Edited by J. L. Ackrill. Princeton: Princeton University Press, 1987.

———. *The Nichomachean Ethics.* Translated by Martin Ostwald. Indianapolis: Bobbs-Merrill, 1962.

———. *The Pocket Aristotle.* Edited by Justin D. Kaplan. New York: Washington Square, 1982.

———. *Politics.* Rev. ed. New York: Viking, 1982.

Broadie, Sarah. *Ethics with Aristotle.* New York: Oxford University Press, 1991.

Cherniss, Harold. *Aristotle's Criticism of Plato and the Academy.* Baltimore: Johns Hopkins University Press, 1944.

Davidson, Thomas. *Aristotle and Ancient Educational Ideals.* New York: Franklin, 1969.

Edel, Abraham. *Aristotle and His Philosophy.* Chapel Hill: University of North Carolina Press, 1982.

Evans, John David Gemmill. *Aristotle.* New York: St. Martin's, 1987.

Ferguson, John. *Aristotle.* New York: Twayne, 1972.

Hardie, William. *Aristotle's Ethical Theory.* New York: Oxford University Press, 1980.

Kenny, Anthony. *Aristotle on the Perfect Life.* New York: Oxford University Press, 1992.

Keyt, David, and Fred D. Miller, Jr., eds. *Aristotle's Politics: A Critical Reader.* Cambridge: Basil Blackwell, 1991.

Lear, Jonathan. *Aristotle and Logical Theory.* London: Cambridge Unversity Press, 1980.

———. *Aristotle: The Desire to Understand.* New York: Cambridge University Press, 1988.

Leyden, Wolfgang von. *Aristotle on Equality and Justice: His Political Argument.* New York: St. Martin's, 1985.

———. *Aristotle: The Growth and Structure of His Thought.* London: Cambridge University Press, 1968.

Lloyd, Geoffrey. *Aristotelian Explorations.* New York: Cambridge University Press, 1996.

Oates, Whitney. *Aristotle and the Problem of Value.* Princeton: Princeton University Press, 1963.

Panagiotou, Spiro. *Justice, Law and Method in Plato and Aristotle.* Edmunton: Academic Print and Pub., 1987.

Rist, John M. *The Mind of Aristotle: A Study in Philosophical Growth.* Toronto: University of Toronto Press, 1989.

Robinson, Daniel N. *Aristotle's Psychology.* New York: Columbia University Press, 1989.

Shields, Christopher. *Aristotle.* New York: Routledge, 2007.

Veatch, Henry. *Aristotle: A Contemporary Appreciation.* Bloomington: Indiana University Press, 1974.

Vella, John. *Aristotle: A Guide for the Perplexed.* New York: Continuum, 2008.

FRANCIS BACON

Bacon, Francis. *The Essays.* 1597. Edited with an introduction by John Pitcher. New York: Penguin, 1986.

———. *Francis Bacon: A Selection of His Works.* Edited by Sidney Warhaft. Indianapolis: Odyssey, 1965.

———. *New Organon and Related Writings.* Edited by H. Fulton Anderson. Indianapolis: Bobbs-Merrill, 1960.

Briggs, John C. *Francis Bacon and the Rhetoric of Nature.* Cambridge: Harvard University Press, 1989.

Brighton, Andrew. *Francis Bacon.* Princeton: Princeton University Press, 2001.

Davies, Hugh Marlais. *Francis Bacon.* New York: Abbeville, 1986.

Eiseley, Loren. *The Man Who Saw Through Time.* New York: Scribner, 1973.

Epstein, Joel. *Francis Bacon: A Political Biography.* Athens: Ohio University Press, 1977.

Farrington, Benjamin. *The Philosophy of Francis Bacon.* Liverpool: Liverpool University Press, 1964.

Jardine, Lisa. *Hostage to Fortune: The Troubled Life of Francis Bacon.* London: Victor Gollancz, 1998.

Martin, Julian. *Francis Bacon, the State, and the Reform of Natural Philosophy.* New York: Cambridge University Press, 1992.

Mathews, Nieves. *Francis Bacon: The History of Character Assassination.* New Haven: Yale University Presss, 1996.

Prez-Ramos, Antonio. *Francis Bacon's Idea of Science and the Maker's Knowledge Tradition.* New York: Oxford University Press, 1988.

Rossi, Paolo. *Francis Bacon: From Magic to Science.* Translated by Sacha Rabinovitch. Chicago: University of Chicago Press, 1968.

Snider, Alvin. *Origins and Authority in Seventeenth-Century England: Bacon, Milton, Butler.* Toronto: University of Toronto Press, 1994.

Stephens, James. *Francis Bacon and the Style of Science.* Chicago: University of Chicago Press, 1975.

Urbach, Peter. *Francis Bacon's Philosophy of Science: An Account and a Reappraisal.* La Salle: Open Court, 1987.

Vickers, Brian. *Essential Articles for the Study of Francis Bacon.* Hamden: Archon, 1968.

Wallace, Karl. *Francis Bacon on Communication and Rhetoric.* Chapel Hill: University of North Carolina Press, 1943.

Whitney, Charles. *Francis Bacon and Modernity.* New Haven: Yale University Press, 1986.

Zagorin, Perez. *Francis Bacon.* Princeton: Princeton University Press, 1998.

JAMES BALDWIN

Baldwin, James. *The Devil Finds Work.* 1976. New York: Vintage International, 2011.

——. *The Fire Next Time.* New York: Dial, 1963.

——. *No Name in the Street.* New York: Dial, 1972.

——. *The Price of the Ticket: Collected Non-Fiction 1948–1985.* New York: St. Martin's Press, 1985.

Baldwin, James, and Nikki Giovanni. *A Dialogue.* Philadelphia: Lippincott, 1973.

Boyd, Herb. *Baldwin's Harlem: A Biography of James Baldwin.* New York: Atria Books, 2008.

Boyd, Herb, and Robert L. Allen, eds. *Brotherman: The Odyssey of Black Men in America—an Anthology.* New York: Ballantine Books, 1996.

Campbell, James. *Talking at the Gates: A Life of James Baldwin.* Berkeley and Los Angeles: University of California Press, 2002.

Mead, Margaret, and James Baldwin. *A Rap on Race.* Philadelphia and New York: Lippincott, 1971.

Leeming, David. *James Baldwin: A Biography.* New York: Knopf, 1994.

Porter, Horace A. *Stealing the Fire: The Art and Protest of James Baldwin.* Middletown: Wesleyan University Press, 1989.

Standley, Fred L., and Louis H. Pratt, eds. *Conversations with James Baldwin.* Jackson: University Press of Mississippi, 1989.

Weatherby, W. J. *James Baldwin: Artist on Fire.* New York: Fine, 1989.

CARL BECKER

Becker, Carl. *Beginnings of the American People.* Boston: Houghton Mifflin, 1915.

——. *Cornell University: Founders and the Founding.* Ithaca: Cornell University Press, 1943.

——. *The Declaration of Independence: A Study on the History of Political Ideas.* New York: Harcourt, Brace and Co., 1922.

——. *The Eve of the Revolution.* New Haven: Yale University Press, 1918.

——. *Everyman His Own Historian.* American Historical Review, Volume 37, Issue 2, p. 221–236.

——. *The Heavenly City of the Eighteenth-Century Philosophers.* New Haven: Yale University Press, 1932.

——. *Modern Democracy.* New Haven: Yale University Press, 1941.

——. *Progress and Power.* Stanford: Stanford University Press, 1936.

——. *The United States: An Experiment in Democracy.* New York: Harper & Brothers, 1920.

Rockwood, Raymond Oxley. *Carl Becker's Heavenly City Revisited.* Ithaca: Cornell University Press, 1958.

Smith, Charlotte Watkins. *Carl Becker: On History & the Climate of Opinion.* Ithaca: Cornell University Press, 1956.

Strout, Cushing. *The Pragmatic Revolt in American History: Carl Becker and Charles Beard.* New Haven: Yale University Press, 1958.

Wilkins, Burleigh T. *Carl Becker: A Biographical Study in American Intellectual History.* Cambridge: M.I.T. Press, 1961.

BENAZIR BHUTTO

Akhund, Iqbal. *Trial and Error: The Advent and Eclipse of Benazir Bhutto.* New York: Oxford University Press, 2000.

Bahadur, Kalim. *Democracy in Pakistan: Crises and Conflicts.* New Delhi: Har-Anand Publications, 1998.

Bhutto, Benazir. *Daughter of Destiny: An Autobiography.* 2nd ed. New York: HarperCollins, 2008.

———. *Pakistan: The Gathering Storm.* New Delhi: Vikas Publishing House, 1983.

———. *Reconciliation: Islam, Democracy, and the West.* New York: HarperCollins, 2008.

Englar, Mary. Benazir Bhutto: *Pakistani Prime Minister and Activist.* Minneapolis: Compass Point Books, 2006.

Lamb, Christina. *Waiting for Allah: Pakistan's Struggle for Democracy.* London: Penguin, 1992.

Sansevere-Dreher, Diane. *Benazir Bhutto.* Changing Our World Series. New York: Bantam Skylark, 1991.

Zakaria, Rafiq. *The Trial of Benazir Bhutto: An Insight into the Status of Women in Islam.* Pelanduk Publications, 1989.

BILL BRYSON

Bryson, Bill. *At Home: A Short History of Private Life.* London and New York: Doubleday, 2010.

———. *Bryson's Dictionary of Troublesome Words: A Writer's Guide to Getting It Right.* New York: Broadway Books, 2002.

———. *The Life and Times of the Thunderbolt Kid: A Memoir.* New York: Broadway Books, 2006.

———. *The Lost Continent: Travels in Small-Town America.* New York: HarperCollins, 1989.

———. *Made in America: An Informal History of the English Language in the United States.* New York: William Morrow, 1995.

———. *The Mother Tongue: English and How It Got That Way.* New York: William Morrow, 1990.

———, ed. *Seeing Further: The Story of Science, Discovery, and the Genius of the Royal Society.* London: HarperPress, 2010.

———. *A Short History of Nearly Everything.* New York: Broadway Books, 2003.

JUDITH BUTLER

Butler, Judith. *Bodies That Matter: On the Discursive Limits of "Sex."* New York and London: Routledge, 1993.

———. *Gender Trouble: Feminism and the Subversion of Identity.* New York and London: Routledge, 1990, 1999.

———. *Giving an Account of Oneself.* New York: Fordham University Press, 2005.

———. *Undoing Gender.* New York and London: Routledge, 2004.

Butler, Judith, and Elizabeth Weed, eds. *The Question of Gender: Joan W. Scott's Critical Feminism.* Bloomington: Indiana University Press, 2011.

Post, Robert C., Kwame Anthony Appiah, Judith Butler, Thomas C. Grey, and Reva B. Siegel. *Prejudicial Appearances: The Logic of American Antidiscrimination Law.* Durham: Duke University Press, 2002.

Singer, Linda. *Erotic Welfare: Sexual Theory and Politics in the Age of Epidemic.* New York and London: Routledge, 1993.

ANDREW CARNEGIE

Alderson, Bernard. *An American Four-in-Hand in Britain.* New York: C. Scribner's Sons, 1886.

———. *The Andrew Carnegie Reader.* Edited and with an introduction by Joseph Frazier Wall. Pittsburgh: University of Pittsburgh Press, 1992.

———. *Andrew Carnegie: The Man and His Work.* New York: Doubleday, Page & Co., 1902.

———. *Autobiography of Andrew Carnegie.* Boston: Houghton Mifflin Company, 1920.

———. *The Empire of Business.* New York: Doubleday, Page & Co., 1902.

———. *The Gospel of Wealth and Other Timely Essays.* Cambridge: Belknap Press of Harvard University Press, 1962.

———. *The Master Workers' Book.* New York: Doubleday, 1916.

———. *The Negro in America: An Address Delivered Before the Philosophical Institution of Edinburgh, 16th October 1907.* Inverness: R. Carruthers & Sons, Courier Office, 1907.

———. *Round the World.* New York: Scribner 1884.

———. *Triumphant Democracy or Fifty Years' March of the Republic.* New York: Scribner, 1887.

Harlow, Alvin F. *Andrew Carnegie.* New York: J. Messner, 1953.

Hendrick, Burton Jesse. *The Life of Andrew Carnegie.* New York: Doubleday, Doran & Company, 1932.

Judson, Clara Ingram. *Andrew Carnegie.* Chicago: Follett, 1964.

Kennedy, Gail. *Democracy and the Gospel of Wealth.* Boston: Heath, 1949.

Nasaw, David. *Andrew Carnegie.* New York: Penguin, 2006.

Swetnam, George. *Andrew Carnegie.* Boston: Twayne, 1980.

Wall, Joseph Frazier. *Andrew Carnegie.* New York: Oxford University Press, 1970.

Winkler, John Kennedy. *Incredible Carnegie: The Life of Andrew Carnegie (1835–1919).* New York: The Vanguard Press, 1931.

STEPHEN L. CARTER

Carter, Stephen L. *Civility: Manners, Morals, and the Etiquette of Democracy.* New York: Basic, 1998.

———. *The Culture of Disbelief: How American Law and Politics Trivialize Religious Devotion.* New York: Basic, 1993.

———. *The Dissent of the Governed: A Meditation on Law, Religion, and Loyalty.* Cambridge: Harvard University Press, 1998.

———. *The Emperor of Ocean Park.* New York: Knopf, 2002.

———. *God's Name in Vain: How Religion Should and Should Not Be Involved in Politics.* New York: Basic, 2000.

———. *Integrity.* New York: Basic, 1996.

———. *Reflections of an Affirmative Action Baby.* New York: Basic, 1991.

NOAM CHOMSKY

Barsky, Robert F. *The Chomsky Effect: A Radical Works Beyond the Ivory Tower.* Cambridge: MIT Press, 2007.

———. *Noam Chomsky: A Life of Dissent.* Cambridge: MIT Press, 1997.

Chomsky, Noam. *The Architecture of Language.* Edited by Nirmalangshu Mukherji, Bibudhendra Narayan Patnaik, and Rama Kant Agnihotri. New Delhi: Oxford University Press, 2000.

———. *Aspects of the Theory of Syntax.* Cambridge: MIT Press, 1965.

———. *Current Issues in Linguistic Theory.* Berlin: Mouton de Gruyter, 1970.

———. *Essays on Form and Interpretation.* North-Holland: Elsevier, 1977.

———. *Knowledge of Language: Its Nature, Origin, and Use.* New York: Praeger Publishers, 1986.

———. *Language and Mind.* New York: Harcourt Brace, 1968.

———. *Language and Problems of Knowledge.* The Managua Lectures. Cambridge: MIT Press, 1987.

———. *Language and Thought.* Wakefield: Moyer Bell, 1993.

———. *The Logical Structure of Linguistic Theory.* Chicago: University of Chicago Press, 1985.

———. *New Horizons in the Study of Language and Mind.* Cambridge: Cambridge University Press, 2000.

————. *Reflections on Language.* New York: Pantheon Books, 1975.

————. *Rules and Representations.* New York: Columbia University Press, and Oxford: Basil Blackwell, 1980.

————. *Studies on Semantics in Generative Grammar.* The Hague: Mouton, 1972. Reprint. Berlin and New York, 1980.

————. *Syntactic Structures.* The Hague: Mouton, 1957. Reprint. Berlin and New York, 1985.

Lyons, John. *Noam Chomsky.* New York: Viking Press, 1970.

Sperlich, Wolfgang B. *Noam Chomsky.* London: Reaktion Books, 2006.

MARCUS TULLIUS CICERO

Bonner, S. F. *Roman Declamation in the Late Republic and Early Empire.* Liverpool: Liverpool University Press, 1949.

Cicero, Marcus Tullius. *Selected Letters.* Translated by D. R. Shackleton Bailey. New York: Penguin, 1989.

————. *Selected Political Speeches.* Translated by Michael Grant. Baltimore: Penguin, 1969.

————. *Selected Works.* Translated by Michael Grant. Baltimore: Penguin, 1960.

Clarke, M. L. *Rhetoric at Rome.* 3rd ed. New York: Routledge, 1996.

Dorey, T. A., ed. *Cicero.* London: Routledge, 1965.

Frisch, Hartvig. *Cicero's Fight for the Republic.* Kobenhavn: Gyldendal, 1946.

Habicht, Christian. *Cicero the Politician.* Baltimore: Johns Hopkins University Press, 1989.

Haskell, H. J. *This Was Cicero.* New York: Knopf, 1942.

Holmes, T. Rice. *The Roman Republic and the Founder of the Empire.* Oxford: Clarendon, 1923.

Hunt, H. A. K. *The Humanism of Cicero.* Carlton: Melbourne University Press, 1954.

Lintott, Andrew. *Cicero as Evidence: A Historian's Companion.* Oxford: Oxford University Press, 2008.

MacKendrick, Paul. *The Speeches of Cicero.* London: Duckworth, 1995.

Mitchell, Thomas N. *Cicero: The Ascending Years.* New Haven: Yale University Press, 1979.

————. *Cicero: The Senior Statesman.* New Haven: Yale University Press, 1991.

Murrell, John. *Cicero and the Roman Republic.* Cambridge: Cambridge University Press, 2008.

Petersson, Torsten. *Cicero: A Biography.* New York: Biblo and Tannen, 1963.

Plutarch. "Life of Cicero." In *Fall of the Roman Republic.* Translated by Rex Warner. Baltimore: Penguin, 1958.

Sallust. *Conspiracy of Catiline.* Cambridge: Harvard University Press, 1963.

Scullard, H. H. *From the Gracchi to Nero.* London: Methuen, 1982.

Smith, R. E. *Cicero the Statesman.* London: Cambridge University Press, 1966.

Stockton, David. *Cicero: A Political Biography.* London: Oxford University Press, 1971.

Vasaly, Ann. *Representations: Images in the World of Ciceronian Oratory.* Berkeley: University of California Press, 1993.

Wood, Neal. *Cicero's Social and Political Thought: An Introduction.* Berkeley: University of California Press, 1991.

CHARLES DARWIN

Appleman, Philip, ed. *Darwin.* New York: Norton, 1970.

Bannister, Robert. *Social Darwinism: Science and Myth in Anglo-American Social Thought.* Philadelphia: Temple University Press, 1979.

Bowler, Peter J. *Charles Darwin the Man and His Influence.* Cambridge: Basil Blackwell, 1990.

Brown, E. J. *Charles Darwin: A Biography.* New York: Knopf, 1995.

Crook, D. P. *Darwinism, War, and History: The Debate over the Biology of War from the "Origins of Species" to the First World War.* New York: Cambridge University Press, 1994.

Darwin, Charles. *The Autobiography of Charles Darwin.* Edited by Nora Barlow. New York: Norton, 1969.

————. *Charles Darwin: Interviews and Recollections.* Edited by Harold Orel. New York: St. Martin's, 2000.

————. *The Correspondence of Charles Darwin.* Edited by Frederick Burkhardt and Sydney Smith. New York: Cambridge University Press, 1985.

————. *The Darwin Reader.* Edited by Mark Ridley. New York: Norton, 1987.

————. *The Descent of Man and Selection in Relation to Sex.* Princeton: Princeton University Press, 1981.

————. *On the Origin of Species.* Edited by J. W. Burrow. Baltimore: Penguin, 1968.

————. *The Voyage of the Beagle: Charles Darwin's Journal of Researches.* Edited with an introduction by Janet Browne and Michael Neve. New York: Penguin, 1989.

————. *The Works of Charles Darwin.* Edited by Paul H. Barrett and R. B. Freeman. New York: New York University Press, 1987.

Desmond, Adrian J. *Darwin.* New York: Warner, 1992.

Eiseley, Loren. *Darwin's Century: Evolution and the Men Who Discovered It.* Garden City: Doubleday, 1958.

Eldredge, Niles. *Darwin: Discovering the Tree of Life.* New York: W. W. Norton, 2005.

Francis, Keith. *Charles Darwin and the Origin of Species.* Westport: Greenwood Press, 2007.

Herbert, Sarah. *Charles Darwin, Geologist.* Ithaca: Cornell University Press, 2005.

Himmelfarb, Gertrude. *Darwin and the Darwinian Revolution.* Garden City: Doubleday, 1962.

Irvine, William. *Apes, Angels, and Victorians.* New York: McGraw-Hill, 1955.

Jastrow, Robert, and Kenneth Korey. *The Essential Darwin.* Boston: Little, Brown, 1984.

Mayr, Ernst. *One Long Argument: Charles Darwin and the Genesis of Modern Evolutionary Thought.* Cambridge: Harvard University Press, 1991.

Miller, Jonathan. *Darwin for Beginners.* New York: Pantheon, 1982.

Ruse, Michael. *Charles Darwin.* Malden: Blackwell, 2008.

————. *The Darwinian Revolution: Science Red in Tooth and Claw.* Chicago: University of Chicago Press, 1999.

Russett, Cynthia. *Darwin in America.* San Francisco: Freeman, 1976.

White, Michael, and John Gribben. *Darwin: A Life in Science.* New York: Dutton, 1995.

RENÉ DESCARTES

Balz, Albert G. A. *Descartes and the Modern Mind.* Hamden: Archon, 1952.

Clarke, Desmond. *Rene Descartes.* Cambridge: Cambridge University Press, 2006.

Cottingham, John, ed. *The Cambridge Companion to Descartes.* Cambridge: Cambridge University Press, 1992.

Descartes, René. *The Philosophical Works of Descartes.* Translated by Elizabeth S. Haldane and G.T.R. Ross. London: Cambridge University Press, 1955.

Gaukroger, Stephen. *Descartes: An Intellectual Biography.* New York: Oxford University Press, 1995.

Gibson, A. Boyce. *The Philosophy of Descartes.* New York: Russell & Russell, 1932.

Grayling, A. C. *Descartes: The Life and Times of a Genius.* New York: Walker & Co., 2006.

Haldane, Elizabeth. *Descartes: His Life and Times.* New York: American Scholar, 1966.

Keeling, Stanley V. *Descartes.* 2nd ed. New York: Oxford University Press, 1968.

Pearl, Leon. *Descartes.* Boston: Twayne Publishers, 1977.

Rodis-Lewis, Geneviève. *Descartes: A Biography.* Paris: Calmann-Lévy, 1995.

Smith, Norman Kemp. *New Studies in the Philosophy of Descartes: Descartes as Pioneer.* London: Macmillan, 1966.

————. *Studies in the Cartesian Philosophy.* New York: Russell & Russell, 1902.

Strathern, Paul. *Descartes in 90 Minutes.* Chicago: Ivan R. Dee, 1996.

Watson, Richard. *Cogito, Ergo Sum: The Life of René Descartes.* Boston: D. R. Godine, 2002.

JOHN DEWEY

Boydston, Jo Ann, ed. *Guide to the Works of John Dewey.* Carbondale: Southern Illinois University Press, 1970.

Brickman, William W., ed. *John Dewey: Master Educator.* New York: Society for the Advancement of Education, 1961.

Dewey, John. *American Education Past and Future.* Chicago: University of Chicago Press, 1931.

————. *Democracy and Education: An Introduction to the Philosophy of Education.* New York: Macmillan, 1963.

————. *Education and the Social Order.* New York: League for Industrial Democracy, 1934.

————. *Ethical Principles Underlying Education.* Chicago: University of Chicago Press, 1908.

————. *Moral Principles in Education.* Boston: Houghton Mifflin, 1909. [Reprint Carbondale: Southern Illinois University Press, 1975.]

————. *My Pedagogic Creed.* Washington, DC: Progressive Education Association, 1929.

————. *Philosophy of Education.* Also published as *Problems of Men.* New York: Philosophical Library, 1946.

Dewey, John, and Evelyn Dewey. *Schools of Tomorrow.* New York: Macmillan, 1915.

Edman, Irwin, ed. *John Dewey: His Contribution to the American Tradition.* Westport: Greenwood Press, 1955.

Hickman, Larry A, and Thomas M. Alexander, eds. *The Essential Dewey.* Bloomington: Indiana University Press, 1998.

Sidorsky, David, ed. *John Dewey: The Essential Writings.* New York: Harper & Row, 1977.

FREDERICK DOUGLASS

Andrews, William L., ed. *Critical Essays on Frederick Douglass.* Boston: Hall, 1991.

Bontemps, Arna. *Free at Last: The Life of Frederick Douglass.* New York: Dodd, Mead, 1971.

Colaiaco, James A. *Frederick Douglass and the Fourth of July.* New York: Palgrave Macmillan, 2007.

Douglass, Frederick. *Frederick Douglass on Women's Rights.* Edited by Philip S. Foner. Westport: Greenwood, 1976.

————. *The Frederick Douglass Papers, Series One: Speeches, Debates, and Interviews.* Vol. 1. *1841–1846.* Edited by John W. Blassingame et al. New Haven: Yale University Press, 1979.

————. *The Frederick Douglass Papers, Series Two: Autobiographical Writings.* Edited by John W. Blassingame et al. New Haven: Yale University Press, 1999.

————. *My Bondage and My Freedom.* Edited by William L. Andrews. Urbana: University of Illinois Press, 1987.

————. *Narrative of the Life of Frederick Douglass, an American Slave.* Edited with an introduction by David W. Blight. Boston: Bedford/St. Martin's, 1993.

————. *The Oxford Frederick Douglass Reader.* New York: Oxford University Press, 1996.

————. *Prose Works: Selections.* New York: Library of America, 1994.

Foner, Philip S. *Frederick Douglass.* New York: Citadel, 1964.

Gates, Henry Louis, Jr., ed. *The Classic Slave Narrative.* New York: New American Library, 1987.

Huggins, Nathan Irvin. *Slave and Citizen: The Life of Frederick Douglass.* Boston: Little, Brown, 1980.

Inge, Thomas, et al., eds. *Black American Writers: Bibliographical Essays.* Vol. 1. London: Macmillan, 1978.

Kendrick, Paul and Stephen Kendrick. *Douglass and Lincoln: How a Revolutionary Black Leader and a Reluctant Liberator Struggled to End Slavery and Save the Union.* New York: Walker & Company, 2008.

Martin, Waldo E., Jr. *The Mind of Frederick Douglass.* Chapel Hill: University of North Carolina Press, 1984.

McFreely, William S. *Frederick Douglass.* New York: Norton, 1991.

Oakes, James. *The Radical and the Republican: Frederick Douglass, Abraham Lincoln, and the Triumph of Antislavery Politics.* New York: W.W. Norton & Co., 2007.

Patterson, Frederick D. [Frederick Douglass]. *Chronicles of Faith: The Autobiography of Frederick D. Patterson.* Edited by Martia Graham Goodson with a foreword by Harry V. Richardson. Tuscaloosa: University of Alabama Press, 1991.

Quarles, Benjamin. *Frederick Douglass.* New York: Da Capo, 1997.

Sundquist, Eric J., ed. *Frederick Douglass: New Literary and Historical Essays.* New York: Cambridge University Press, 1990.

RALPH WALDO EMERSON

Bishop, Jonathan. *Emerson on the Soul.* Cambridge: Harvard University Press, 1964.

Buell, Lawrence. *Emerson.* Cambridge: Harvard University Press, 2004.

————. *Literary Transcendentalism.* Ithaca: Cornell University Press, 1973.

Carpenter, Frederic Ives. *Emerson Handbook.* New York: Hendricks House, 1953.

Conway, Moncure Daniel. *Emerson at Home and Abroad.* Boston: James R. Osgood, 1882.

Emerson, Ralph Waldo. *The Collected Works of Ralph Waldo Emerson,* 3 volumes. Cambridge: Harvard University Press, 1971.

———. *The Conduct of Life.* Boston: Ticknor & Fields, 1860.

———. *Emerson's Complete Works,* 12 volumes. London: Routledge, 1883–1894.

———. *Essays: First Series.* Boston: Munroe, 1841.

———. *Essays: Second Series.* Boston: Munroe, 1844.

———. *Orations, Lectures, and Addresses.* London: Clarke, 1844.

———. *Society and Solitude.* Boston: Fields, Osgood, 1870.

Lysaker, John T. *Emerson and Self-Culture.* Bloomington: Indiana University Press, 2008.

Richardson, Robert D. *Emerson: The Mind on Fire.* Berkeley: University of California Press, 1995.

Waggoner, Hyatt. *Emerson as Poet.* Princeton: Princeton University Press, 1975.

Whicher, Stephen E. *Freedom and Fate: An Inner Life of Ralph Waldo Emerson.* Philadelphia: University of Pennsylvania Press, 1953.

York, Maurice, and Rick Spaulding. *Ralph Waldo Emerson: The Infinitude of the Private Man.* Chicago: Wrightwood Press, 2008.

THE FOUNDING FATHERS AND THE CONSTITUTION

Allen, Steven W. *Founding Fathers: Uncommon Heroes.* Mesa: Legal Awareness Series, 2003.

Beeman, Richard. *Plain, Honest Men: The Making of the American Constitution.* New York: Random House, 2010.

Brands, H. W. *The First American: The Life and Times of Benjamin Franklin.* New York: Anchor Books, 2000.

Chernow, Ron. *Alexander Hamilton.* New York: Penguin Press, 2004.

Dahl, Robert A. *Original Meanings: Politics and Ideas in the Making of the Constitution.* 2nd ed. New Haven: Yale University Press, 2003.

Eidsmoe, John. *Christianity and the Constitution: The Faith of Our Founding Fathers.* Ada, MI: Baker Academic, 1985.

Ellis, Joseph J. *American Creation: Triumphs and Tragedies at the Founding of the Republic.* New York: Vintage Books, 2008.

———. *Founding Brothers: The Revolutionary Generation.* New York: Vintage Books, 2000.

———. *His Excellency, George Washington.* New York: Vintage Books, 2004.

Encyclopaedia Britannica. *Founding Fathers: The Essential Guide to the Men Who Made America.* Introduction by Joseph Ellis. Hoboken: Wiley, 2007.

Farrand, Max. *The Fathers of the Constitution: A Chronicle of the Establishment of the Union.* Edited by Allen Johnson. Vol. 13 in the Chronicles of America Series. New Haven: Yale University Press, 1921. Available through Project Gutenberg: www.gutenberg.org.

Grant, James. *John Adams: Party of One.* New York: Farrar, Straus and Giroux, 2005.

Holmes, David L. *The Faiths of the Founding Fathers.* New York: Oxford University Press, 2006.

Isaacson, Walter. *Benjamin Franklin: A Life.* New York: Simon & Schuster, 2003.

Lossing, B. J. *Lives of the Signers of the Declaration of Independence.* 1848. Aledo, TX: WallBuilder Press, 1995.

Lutz, Donald S. *The Origins of American Constitutionalism.* Baton Rouge: Louisiana State University Press, 1988.

Maier, Pauline. *Ratification: The People Debate the Constitution, 1787–1788.* New York: Simon & Schuster, 2010.

McClanahan, Brion. *The Founding Fathers Guide to the Constitution.* Washington, DC: Regnery Publishing, 2012.

McCullough, David G. *John Adams.* New York: Touchstone, 2001.

Rakove, Jack N. *Original Meanings: Politics and Ideas in the Making of the Constitution.* New York: Vintage Books, 1997.

Schwartz, Bernard. *The Great Rights of Mankind: A History of the American Bill of Rights.* New York: Oxford University Press, 1977.

Skousen, W. Cleon. *The Making of America: The Substance and Meaning of the Constitution.* 2nd ed. Malta, ID: National Center for Constitutional Studies, 1985.

Stahr, Walter. *John Jay: Founding Father*. New York: Continuum Books, 2005.

Wiencek, Henry. *An Imperfect God: George Washington, His Slaves, and the Creation of America*. New York: Farrar, Straus and Giroux, 2003.

Wood, Gordon S. *The Americanization of Benjamin Franklin*. New York: Penguin Press, 2004.

SIGMUND FREUD

Appignanesi, Lisa. *Freud's Women*. New York: Basic, 1992.

Arlow, Jacob. *The Legacy of Sigmund Freud*. New York: International University Press, 1956.

Badcock, Christopher R. *Essential Freud*. Cambridge: Basil Blackwell, 1992.

Balogh, Penelope. *Freud: A Biographical Introduction*. New York: Scribner, 1972.

Chodorow, Nancy. *Femininities, Masculinities, Sexualities: Freud and Beyond*. Lexington: University Press of Kentucky, 1994.

Clark, Ronald William. *Freud: The Man and the Cause*. London: Cape, 1980.

Edmundson, Mark. *The Death of Sigmund Freud: The Legacy of His Last Days*. New York: Bloomsbury, 2007.

Elliott, Anthony, ed. *Freud 2000*. New York: Routledge, 1999.

Fine, Reuben. *Freud: A Critical Reevaluation of His Theories*. New York: McKay, 1962.

Freeman, Lucy. *Freud Rediscovered*. New York: Arbor House, 1980.

Freud, Sigmund. *The Complete Correspondence of Sigmund Freud and Ernest Jones, 1908–1939*. Cambridge: Belknap, 1993.

———. *Freud on Women: A Reader*. Edited by Elisabeth Young-Bruehl. New York: Norton, 1990.

———. *The Freud Reader*. Edited by Peter Gay. New York: Norton, 1989.

———. *General Selection from the Works of Sigmund Freud*. Garden City: Doubleday, 1957.

———. *New Introductory Lectures in Psychoanalysis*. Edited by James Strachey. New York: Norton, 1965.

———. *Outline of Psychoanalysis*. Edited by James Strachey. New York: Norton, 1970.

———. *The Psychopathology of Everyday Life*. Edited by James Strachey. New York: Norton, 1971.

———. *Three Contributions to the Theory of Sex*. Translated by A. A. Brill. New York: Dutton, 1962.

Fromm, Erich. *The Crisis of Psychoanalysis*. New York: Holt, Rinehart and Winston, 1970.

Gay, Peter. *Freud: A Life of Our Time*. New York: Norton, 1988.

Gelfend, Toby, and John Kerr, eds. *Freud and the History of Psychoanalysis*. Hillsdale: Analytic, 1992.

Hughes, Judith M. *From Freud's Consulting Room: The Unconscious in a Scientific Age*. Cambridge: Harvard University Press, 1994.

Jones, Ernest. *The Life and Work of Sigmund Freud*. Edited by Lionel Trilling and Steven Marcus. New York: Basic, 1961.

Lear, Jonathan. *Freud*. New York: Routledge, 2005.

Masson, J. Moussaieff. *The Assault on Truth: Freud's Suppression of the Seduction Theory*. New York: Farrar, Straus and Giroux, 1984.

Meissner, W. W. *Freud and Psychoanalysis*. Notre Dame: University of Notre Dame Press, 2000.

Neu, Jerome, ed. *The Cambridge Companion to Freud*. New York: Cambridge University Press, 1991.

Noland, Richard. *Sigmund Freud Revisited*. New York: Twayne, 1999.

Petocz, Agnes. *Freud, Psychoanalysis and Symbolism*. Cambridge: Cambridge University Press, 1999.

Reiff, Philip. *Freud: The Mind of the Moralist*. Garden City: Doubleday, 1961.

Robinson, Paul A. *Freud and His Critics*. Berkeley: University of California Press, 1993.

Rosenfeld, Israel. *Freud: Character and Consciousness*. New York: New York University Press, 1970.

Stevens, Richard. *Sigmund Freud: Examining the Essence of His Contribution*. New York: Palgrave Macmillan, 2008.

Stoodley, Bartlett. *The Concepts of Sigmund Freud*. Glencoe: Glencoe Free Press, 1959.

Storr, Anthony. *Freud*. New York: Oxford University Press, 1989.

Thurschwell, Pamela. *Sigmund Freud*. London: Routledge, 2000.

Weber, Samuel M. *The Legend of Freud*. Stanford: Stanford University Press, 2000.

Welsh, Alexander. *Freud's Wishful Dream Book*. Princeton: Princeton Unversity Press, 1994.

MILTON AND ROSE FRIEDMAN

Butler, Eamonn. *Milton Friedman: A Guide to His Economic Thought.* New York: Universe Books, 1985.

Frazer, William Johnson. *Power and Ideas: Milton Friedman and the Big U-Turn.* Gainesville: Gulf/Atlantic Publishing, 1988.

Friedman, Milton. *Capitalism and Freedom.* Chicago: University of Chicago Press, 1982.

———. Dollars and Deficits: *Living With America's Economic Problems.* Englewood Cliffs: Prentice-Hall, 1968.

———. *The Essence of Friedman.* Edited by Kurt R. Leube. Stanford: Hoover Institution Press, 1987.

———. *From Galbraith to Economic Freedom.* London: Institute of Economic Affairs, 1977

———. *Monetary Mischief: Episodes in Monetary History.* New York: Harcourt Brace Jovanovich, 1992.

———. *Money and Economic Development.* New York: Praeger, 1973.

———. *There's No Such Thing as a Free Lunch.* La Salle, IL: Open Court Press, 1974.

Friedman, Milton, and Rose Friedman. *Free to Choose: A Personal Statement.* New York: Harcourt Brace Jovanovich, 1980.

———. *Two Lucky People: Memoirs.* Chicago: University of Chicago Press, 1998.

Friedman, Milton, and Anna Jacobson Schwartz. *A Monetary History of the United States, 1867–1960.* Princeton: Princeton University Press, 1963.

Friedman, Milton, et al. *Politics and Tyranny: Lessons in the Pursuit of Freedom.* Edited by David Theroux. San Francisco: Pacific Institute for Public Policy Research, 1984.

Friedman, Rose. *Poverty: A Definition and Perspective.* Washington, DC: American Enterprise Institute for Public Policy Research, 1965.

Hammond, J. Daniel. *Theory and Measurement: Causality Issues in Milton Friedman's Monetary Economics.* Cambridge: Cambridge University Press, 1965.

Hirsch, Abraham. *Milton Friedman: Economics in Theory and Practice.* Ann Arbor: University of Michigan Press, 1989.

Rayack, Elton. *Not So Free to Choose: The Political Economy of Milton Friedman and Ronald Reagan.* New York: Praeger. 1988.

JOHN KENNETH GALBRAITH

Bowles, Samuel, et al., eds. *Unconventional Wisdom: Essays on Economics in Honor of John Kenneth Galbraith.* Boston: Houghton Mifflin, 1989.

Galbraith, John Kenneth. *The Affluent Society.* Boston: Houghton Mifflin, 1978.

———. *The Age of Uncertainty.* Boston: Houghton Mifflin, 1977.

———. *Almost Everyone's Guide to Economics.* Boston: Houghton Mifflin, 1978.

———. *Ambassador's Journal.* 1969. New York: Paragon House, 1988.

———. *The Anatomy of Power.* Boston: Houghton Mifflin, 1983.

———. *A Contemporary Guide to Economics, Peace, and Laughter.* Boston: Houghton Mifflin, 1971.

———. *The Culture of Contentment.* Boston: Houghton Mifflin, 1992.

———. *The Galbraith Reader.* Edited by the editors of Gambit. Ipswich: Gambit, 1977.

———. *A Journey Through Economic Time: A Firsthand View.* Boston: Houghton Mifflin, 1994.

———. *The Nature of Mass Poverty.* Cambridge: Harvard University Press, 1979.

———. *A Short History of Financial Euphoria.* New York: Whittle, 1993.

Gambs, John S. *John Kenneth Galbraith.* Boston: Twayne, 1975.

Lamson, Peggy. *Speaking of Galbraith: A Personal Portrait.* New York: Ticknor & Fields, 1991.

Laperche, Blandine, and Dimitri Uzunidis. *John Kenneth Galbraith and the Future of Economics.* New York: Palgrave Macmillan, 2005.

Okroi, Loren J. *Galbraith, Harrington, Heilbroner: Economics and Dissent in the Age of Optimism.* Princeton: Princeton University Press, 1988.

Parker, Richard. *John Kenneth Galbraith: His Life, His Politics, His Economics.* New York: Farrar, Straus and Giroux, 2005.

Reisman, David A. *Galbraith and Market Capitalism.* New York: New York University Press, 1980.

Sharpe, Myron E. *John Kenneth Galbraith and the Lower Economics*. White Plains: International Arts and Sciences, 1974.

Stanfield, J. Ron. *John Kenneth Galbraith*. New York: St. Martin's, 1996.

Waligorski, Conrad. *John Kenneth Galbraith: The Economist as Political Theorist*. Lanham, MD: Rowman & Littlefield, 2006.

HOWARD GARDNER

Berube, Maurice. *Eminent Educators: Studies in Intellectual Influence*. Westport: Greenwood Press, 2000.

Gardner, Howard. *Art, Mind, and Brain: A Cognitive Approach to Creativity*. New York: Basic, 1982.

————. *The Arts and Human Development: A Psychological Study of the Artistic Process*. New York: Wiley, 1973.

————. *Changing Minds: The Art of Changing Our Own and Other People's Minds*. Boston: Harvard Business School Press, 2006.

————. *Creating Minds: An Anatomy of Creativity Seen through the Lives of Freud, Einstein, Picasso, Stravinsky*. New York: Basic, 1993.

————. *Developmental Psychology: An Introduction*. Boston: Little, Brown, 1978.

————. *The Disciplined Mind: What All Students Should Understand*. New York: Simon & Schuster, 1999.

————. *Extraordinary Minds: Portraits of Exceptional Individuals and an Examination of Our Extraordinariness*. New York: Basic, 1997.

————. *Five Minds for the Future*. Boston: Harvard Business School Press, 2006.

————. *Frames of Mind: The Theory of Multiple Intelligences*. New York: Basic, 1983.

————. *Intelligence Reframed: Multiple Intelligences for the 21st Century*. New York: Basic, 1999.

————. *The Mind's New Science: A History of the Cognitive Revolution*. New York: Basic, 1985.

————. *Multiple Intelligences: The Theory in Practice*. New York: Basic, 1993.

————. *The Shattered Mind: The Person After Brain Damage*. New York: Knopf, 1975.

————. *To Open Minds: Chinese Clues to the Dilemma of Contemporary Education*. New York: Basic, 1989.

————. *The Unschooled Mind: How Children Think and How Schools Should Teach*. New York: Basic, 1991.

Gardner, Howard, and Emma Laskin. *Leading Minds: An Anatomy of Leadership*. New York: Basic, 1995.

Schaler, Jeffrey A., ed. *Howard Gardner Under Fire: The Rebel Psychologist Faces His Critics*. Peru, IL: Carus, 2006.

MICHAEL GAZZANIGA

Gazzaniga, Michael S. *The Ethical Brain: The Science of Our Moral Dilemmas*. New York: Dana Press, 2005.

————. *Human: The Science behind What Makes Us Unique*. New York: HarperCollins, 2008.

————. *Mind Matters: How Mind and Brain Interact to Create Our Conscious Lives*. Boston: Houghton Mifflin, 1988.

————. *The Mind's Past*. Berkeley: University of California Press, 1998.

————. *Nature's Mind: Biological Roots of Thinking, Emotions, Sexuality, Language, and Intelligence*. New York: Basic Books, 1992.

————. *The Social Brain: Discovering the Networks of the Mind*. New York: Basic Books, 1985.

————. *Who's In Charge? Free Will and the Science of the Brain*. New York: HarperCollins, 2011.

Gazzaniga, Michael, Tamara Russell, and Carl Senior, eds. *Methods in Mind (Cognitive Neuroscience)*. Cambridge: MIT Press, 2009.

GERMAINE GREER

Edwards, Tim. *Cultures of Masculinity*. New York: Routledge, 2006.

Greer, Germaine. *Daddy, We Hardly Knew You*. New York: Viking Penguin, 1989.

————. *The Change: Women, Ageing, and the Menopause*. New York: Ballantine, 1993.

————. *The Female Eunuch*. New York: Bantam, 1971.

———. *Sex and Destiny: The Politics of Human Fertility.* New York: Harper & Row, 1984.

———. *Shakespeare's Wife.* New York: Harper, 2008.

———. *The Whole Woman.* New York: A. A. Knopf, 1999.

Plante, David. *Difficult Women: A Memoir of Three.* New York: Atheneum, 1983.

Wallace, Christine. *Germaine Greer: Untamed Shrew.* Boston: Faber and Faber, 1998.

KAREN HORNEY

Horney. Karen. *Feminine Psychology.* New York: Norton, 1967.

———. *Final Lectures.* Edited by Douglas H. Ingram. New York: Norton, 1987.

———. *Neurosis and Human Growth.* New York: Norton, 1950.

———. *The Neurotic Personality of Our Time.* New York: Norton, 1942.

———. *New Ways in Psychoanalysis.* Reprint ed. New York: Norton, 1964.

———. *Self-Analysis.* New York: Norton, 1937.

Kelman, Harold. *Helping People: Karen Horney's Psychoanalytic Approach.* New York: Science House, 1971.

Paris, Bernard J. *Karen Horney: A Psychoanalyst's Search for Self-Understanding.* New Haven: Yale University Press, 1994.

———. *The Unknown Karen Horney: Essays on Gender, Culture, and Psychoanalysis.* New Haven: Yale University Press, 2000.

Quinn, Susan. *A Mind of Her Own: The Life of Karen Horney.* New York: Summit, 1987.

Rubin, Jack. *Karen Horney: Gentle Rebel of Psychoanalysis.* New York: Dial, 1978.

Sayers, Janet. *Mothers of Psychoanalysis: Helene Deutsch, Karen Horney, Anna Freud, Melanie Klein.* New York: Norton, 1991.

Westkott, Marcia. *The Feminist Legacy of Karen Horney.* New Haven: Yale University Press, 1986.

HSÜN TZU

Ames, Roger T., and Henry Rosemont Jr., trans. *The Analects of Confucius: A Philosophical Translation.* New York: Random House, 1998.

Chin, Annping. *The Authentic Confucius: A Life of Thought and Politics.* New York: Scribner, 2007.

Gardner, Daniel K. *The Four Books: The Basic Teachings of the Later Confucian Tradition.* Indianapolis: Hackett, 2007.

Hagen, Kurtis. *The Philosophy of Xunzi: A Reconstruction.* Peru, IL: Carus, 2007.

Hsün Tzu. *Hsün Tzu: Basic Writings.* Trans. Burton Watson. New York: Columbia University Press, 1963, 1996.

Kline, T. C., and Philip J. Ivanhoe, eds. *Virtue, Nature and Moral Agency in the Xunzi.* Indianapolis: Hackett, 2000.

Stalnaker, Aaron. *Overcoming Our Evil: Human Nature and Spiritual Exercises in Xunzi and Augustine.* Washington, DC: Georgetown University Press, 2006.

Yao, Xinzhong. *An Introduction to Confucianism.* Cambridge: Cambridge University Press, 2000.

THOMAS JEFFERSON

Appleby, Joyce. *Thomas Jefferson.* New York: Times Books, 2003.

Bailey, Jeremey D. *Thomas Jefferson and Executive Power.* Charlottesville: University of Virginia Press, 2007.

Becker, Carl L. *The Declaration of Independence: A Study in the History of Political Ideas.* Rev. ed. New York: Knopf, 1966.

Bedini, Silvio A. *Thomas Jefferson: Statesman of Science.* New York: Macmillan, 1990.

Bernstein, Richard B. *Thomas Jefferson.* New York: Oxford University Press, 2003.

Bober, Natalie. *Thomas Jefferson: Draftsman of a Nation.* Charlottesville: University of Virginia Press, 2007.

Brodie, Fawn M. *Thomas Jefferson: An Intimate History.* New York: Norton, 1974.

Crawford, Allen Pell. *Twilight at Monticello: The Final Years of Thomas Jefferson.* New York: Random House, 2008.

Cunningham, Noble E., Jr. *In Pursuit of Reason: The Life of Thomas Jefferson.* Baton Rouge: Louisiana State University Press, 1987.

Dewey, Frank L. *Thomas Jefferson, Lawyer.* Charlottesville: University Press of Virginia, 1986.

Fliegelman, Jay. *Declaring Independence: Jefferson, Natural Language and the Culture of Performance.* Stanford: Stanford University Press, 1993.

Hitchens, Christopher. *Thomas Jefferson: Author of America.* New York: Atlas Books/HarperCollins, 2005.

Huddleston, Eugene L. *Thomas Jefferson, A Reference Guide.* Boston: Hall, 1982.

Jefferson, Thomas. *Notes on the State of Virginia.* Edited with an introduction and notes by William Peden. New York: Norton, 1972.

———. *A Summary View of the Rights of British America.* 1774. Introduction by Lawrence W. Towner. A facsimile of the 1st ed. as amended by the author in his own hand. Chicago: Caxton Club, 1976.

———. *The Viking Portable Thomas Jefferson.* Edited by Merrill D. Peterson. New York: Viking, 1977.

———. *Writings.* The Library of America 17. New York: Viking, 1984.

Malone, Dumas. *Jefferson and His Time.* 6 vols. Boston: Little, Brown, 1948–1981.

Matthews, Richard K. *The Radical Politics of Thomas Jefferson: A Revisionist View.* Lawrence: University Press of Kansas, 1984.

Mayer, David N. *The Constitutional Thought of Thomas Jefferson.* Charlottesville: University Press of Virginia, 1994.

McLaughlin, Jack. *To His Excellency Thomas Jefferson: Letters to a President.* New York: Norton, 1991.

Onuf, Peter S. *The Mind of Thomas Jefferson.* Charlottesville: University of Virginia Press, 2007.

Peterson, Merrill D., ed. *Thomas Jefferson: A Reference Biography.* New York: Scribner, 1986.

Randall, Willard Sterne. *Thomas Jefferson: A Life.* New York: Holt, 1993.

Risjord, Norman K. *Thomas Jefferson.* Madison: Madison House, 1994.

Sheldon, Garrett Ward. *The Political Philosophy of Thomas Jefferson.* Baltimore: Johns Hopkins University Press, 1991.

Shuffelton, Frank. *Thomas Jefferson: A Comprehensive Annotated Bibliography of the Writings about Him.* New York: Garland, 1983.

Wills, Garry. *Inventing America: Jefferson's Declaration of Independence.* Garden City: Doubleday, 1978.

CARL JUNG

Aziz, Robert. *C. G. Jung's Psychology of Religion and Synchronicity.* Albany: State University of New York Press, 1990.

Bair, Deirdre. *Jung: A Biography.* New York: Little Brown, 2003.

Bennet, E. A. *What Jung Really Said.* Introduction by Anthony Storr. New York: Pantheon, 1983.

Clarke, John J. *In Search of Jung: Historical and Philosophical Enquiries.* New York: Routledge, 1992.

Dunne, Claire. *Carl Jung: Wounded Healer of the Soul.* New York: Parabola, 2000.

Dyer, Donald. *Cross-Currents of Jungian Thought: An Annotated Bibliography.* Boston: Shambhala, 1991.

Fordheim, Frieda. *An Introduction to Jung's Psychology.* Baltimore: Penguin, 1954.

Hall, Calvin Springer. *A Primer of Jungian Psychology.* New York: New American Library, 1973.

Hannah, Barbara. *Jung: His Life and Work.* New York: Putnam, 1976.

Jung, Carl. *Aspects of the Feminine.* Translated by R. F. C. Hull. Princeton: Princeton University Press, 1982.

———. *The Essential Jung.* Princeton: Princeton University Press, 1983.

———. *The Gnostic Jung.* Princeton: Princeton University Press, 1992.

———. *Man and His Symbols.* New York: Dell, 1968.

———. *Memories, Dreams, Reflections.* New York: Random House, 1965.

———. *The Viking Portable Jung.* Edited by Joseph Campbell. New York: Viking, 1976.

McLynn, Frank. *Carl Gustave Jung: A Biography.* New York: St. Martin's Press, 1997.

Moreno, Artorio. *Jung, God, and Modern Man.* Notre Dame: University of Notre Dame Press, 1970.

Papadopoulos, Renos K., ed. *The Handbook of Jungian Psychology: Theory, Practice and Applications.* New York: Routledge, 2006.

Pauson, Marian L. *Jung the Philosopher: Essays in Jungian Thought.* New York: Lang, 1988.

Prograff, Ira. *Jung's Psychology and Its Social Meaning.* New York: Dialogue House Library, 1985.

Robertson, Robin. *C. G. Jung and the Archetypes of the Collective Unconscious.* New York: Lang, 1987.

Sanford, John. *The Invisible Partners: How the Male and Female in Each of Us Affects Our Relationships.* New York: Paulist, 1980.

Smith, Curtis D. *Jung's Quest for Wholeness: A Religious and Historical Perspective.* Albany: State University of New York Press, 1990.

Stevens, Anthony. *On Jung.* New York: Routledge, 1990.

Ulanov, Ann Bedford. *The Feminine in Jungian Psychology and in Christian Theology.* Evanston: Northwestern University Press, 1971.

Wehr, Gerhard. *Carl Gustav Jung.* Boston: Shambhala, 1987.

MARTIN LUTHER KING JR.

Albert, Peter J., and Ronald Hoffman, eds. *We Shall Overcome: Martin Luther King, Jr., and the Black Freedom Struggle.* New York: Pantheon, 1990.

Branch, Taylor. *America in the King Years.* New York: Simon & Schuster, 1988.

———. *Parting the Waters.* New York: Simon & Schuster, 1988.

Bruns, Roger. *Martin Luther King: A Biography.* Westport: Greenwood Press, 2006.

Downing, Frederick L. *To See the Promised Land: The Faith Pilgrimage of Martin Luther King, Jr.* Macon: Mercer University Press, 1986.

Erskine, Noel Leo. *King Among the Theologians.* Cleveland: Pilgrim, 1994.

King, Martin Luther Jr. *I Have a Dream: Writings and Speeches That Changed the World.* Edited by James Melvin Washington. San Francisco: Harper, 1992.

———. *I've Been to the Mountaintop.* San Francisco: Harper, 1994.

———. *The Papers of Martin Luther King, Jr.* Edited by Clayborne Carson et al. Berkeley: University of California Press, 1992.

———. *Strength to Love.* Philadelphia: Fortress, 1981.

———. *A Testament of Hope: The Essential Writings of Martin Luther King, Jr.* Edited by James M. Washington. New York: Harper & Row, 1986.

———. *Where Do We Go from Here: Chaos or Community?* Boston: Beacon, 1968.

———. *Why We Can't Wait.* New York: New American Library, 1965.

———. *The Wisdom of Martin Luther King, Jr.* Edited by Alex Ayers. New York: Meridian, 1993.

Lewis, David. *King: A Critical Biography.* New York: Praeger, 1970.

Lyght, Ernest Shaw. *The Religious and Philosophical Foundations in the Thought of Martin Luther King.* New York: Vantage, 1972.

Martin Luther King Jr. Papers Project. *A Guide to Research on Martin Luther King, Jr., and the Modern Black Freedom Struggle.* Stanford: Stanford University Libraries, 1989.

Miller, Keith D. *Voice of Deliverance: The Language of Martin Luther King, Jr., and Its Sources.* New York: Free, 1992.

Oates, Stephen B. *Let the Trumpet Sound: The Life of Martin Luther King, Jr.* New York: Harper & Row, 1982.

Ramachandram, G., and T. K. Mahadevan. *Nonviolence after Gandhi: A Study of Martin Luther King.* New Delhi: Gandhi Peace Foundation, 1968.

Walton, Hanes. *The Political Philosophy of Martin Luther King.* Westport: Greenwood, 1971.

Zepp, Ira G. *The Social Vision of Martin Luther King, Jr.* Brooklyn: Carlson, 1989.

JONATHAN KOZOL

DeLeon, David. *Leaders from the 1960s: A Biographical Sourcebook of American Activism.* Westport: Greenwood Press, 1994.

Kozol, Jonathan. *Alternative Schools: A Guide for Educators and Parents.* New York: Continuum Books, 1980.

———. *Amazing Grace: The Lives of Children and the Conscience of a Nation.* New York: Crown Publishers, 1995.

———. *Death at an Early Age: The Destruction of the Hearts and Minds of Negro Children in the Boston Public Schools.* New York: Penguin, 1967.

———. *Free Schools.* Boston: Houghton Mifflin, 1972.

———. *Illiterate America.* New York: Penguin, 1986.

————. *Letters to a Young Teacher.* New York: Three Rivers Press, 2007.

————. *On Being a Teacher.* 1981. Rockport, MA: Oneworld Publications, 2009.

————. *Prisoners of Silence: Breaking the Bonds of Adult Illiteracy in the United States.* New York: Continuum Books, 1980.

————. *Savage Inequalities: Children in America's Schools.* New York: HarperCollins, 1991.

————. *The Shame of the Nation: The Restoration of Apartheid Schooling in America.* New York: Three Rivers Press, 2005.

SUSANNE K. LANGER

Innis, Robert E. *Susanne Langer in Focus: The Symbolic Mind.* Bloomington: Indiana University Press, 2009.

Langer, Susanne K. *Feeling and Form: A Theory of Art.* 1953. Prentice Hall, 1977.

————. *Mind: An Essay on Human Feeling.* 3 vols. Baltimore: Johns Hopkins University Press, 1967–1982.

————. *Philosophical Sketches: A Study of the Human Mind in Relation to Feeling, Explored through Art, Language, and Symbol.* Baltimore: Johns Hopkins University Press, 1962.

————. *Philosophy in a New Key: A Study in the Symbolism of Reason, Rite, and Art.* 1942. 3rd ed. Cambridge, MA: Harvard University Press, 1957.

————. *Problems of Art: Ten Philosophical Lectures.* New York: Scribner, 1957

LAO-TZU

Finazzo, Giancarlo. *The Notion of Tao in Lao-tzu and Chuang Tzu.* Taipei: Mei Ya, 1968.

Heider, John. *The Tao of Leadership: Lao-tzu's Tao te Ching Adapted for a New Age.* Atlanta: Humanics New Age, 1985.

Ho-Shang-Kung. *Commentary on Lao-tzu.* Translated by Eduard Erkes. Ascona: Artibus Asiae, 1958.

Kaltenmark, Max. *Lao-tzu and Taoism.* Translated by Roger Greaves. Stanford: Stanford University Press, 1969.

Kohn, Livia, and Michael LaFargue, eds. *Lao-Tzu and the Tao-Te-Ching.* Albany: State University of New York Press, 1998.

LaFargue, Michael. *Tao and Method: A Reasoned Approach to the Tao te Ching.* Albany: State University of New York Press, 1994.

Lagerway, John. *Taoist Ritual in Chinese Society and History.* New York: Macmillan, 1987.

Lao-tzu. *Hua Hu Ching.* Translated by Brian Walker. Livingston: Clark City, 1992.

————. *Tao te Ching.* Translated by Ni Hua-Ching. Santa Monica: Sevenstar Communications Group, 1993.

————. *Tao te Ching.* Translated with an introduction by D. C. Lau. Baltimore: Penguin, 1964.

————. *Tao te Ching: The Classic Book of Integrity and the Way.* New York: Bantam, 1990.

Liu, Hsiao-kan. *Classifying the Zhuangzi Chapters.* Ann Arbor: University of Michigan Press, 1994.

Maspero, Henri. *Taoism and Chinese Religion.* Translated by Frank A. Kierman Jr. Amherst: University of Massachusetts Press, 1981.

McNaughton, William. *The Taoist Vision.* Ann Arbor: University of Michigan Press, 1971.

Mitchell, Stephen, trans. *Tao te Ching.* New York: Harper & Row, 1988.

Welch, Holmes. *Taoism: The Parting of the Way.* Rev. ed., 1964. Boston: Beacon, 1957.

Wing, R. L., trans. and ed. *The Tao of Power: A Translation of the Tao te Ching.* Garden City: Doubleday, 1986.

NICCOLÒ MACHIAVELLI

Althusser, Louis. *Machiavelli and Us.* New York: Verso, 1999.

Anglo, Sydney. *Machiavelli: A Dissection.* New York: Harcourt, 1970.

Bock, Gisela, et al., eds. *Machiavelli and Republicanism.* New York: Cambridge University Press, 1990.

Bondanella, Peter. *Machiavelli and the Art of Renaissance History.* Detroit: Wayne State University Press, 1973.

Butterfield, Herbert. *The Structure of Machiavelli.* New York: Collins, 1962.

Hulliung, Mark. *Citizen Machiavelli.* Princeton: Princeton University Press, 1983.

Jay, Anthony. *Management and Machiavelli: An Inquiry into the Politics of Corporate Life.* New York: Holt, 1968.

Jensen, De Lamar. *Machiavelli: Cynic, Patriot or Political Scientist?* Lexington: Heath, 1960.

Kahn, Victoria Ann. *Machiavellian Rhetoric: From the Counter-Reformation to Milton.* Princeton: Princeton University Press, 1994.

Machiavelli, Niccolò. *The Prince: A Revised Translation, Backgrounds, Interpretations, Marginalia.* New York: Norton, 1992.

———. *The Viking Portable Machiavelli.* Edited and translated by Peter Bondanella and Mark Musa. New York: Viking, 1979.

Olschki, Leonard. *Machiavelli the Scientist.* Berkeley: Gallick, 1945.

Parel, Anthony. *The Machiavellian Cosmos.* New Haven: Yale University Press, 1992.

———, ed. *The Political Calculus: Essays on Machiavelli's Philosophy.* Toronto: University of Toronto Press, 1972.

Pearce, Edward. *Machiavelli's Children.* London: Victor Gollancz, 1993.

Procock, John. *The Machiavellian Moment.* Princeton: Princeton University Press, 1974.

Ridofi, Roberto. *The Life of Machiavelli.* Translated by Cecil Grayson. Chicago: University of Chicago Press, 1963.

Ridowski, Victor Anthony. *The Prince: A Historical Critique.* New York: Twayne, 1992.

Ruffo-Fiore, Silvia. *Niccolò Machiavelli: An Annotated Bibliography of Modern Criticism and Scholarship.* New York: Greenwood, 1990.

Viroli, Maurizio. *Niccolo's Smile: A Biography of Machiavelli.* Translated by Antony Shugaar. New York: Hill and Wang, 2002.

JAMES MADISON

Ketcham, Ralph. *James Madison: A Biography.* Newtown, CT: American Political Biography Press, 2003.

Labunski, Richard. *James Madison and the Struggle for the Bill of Rights.* Oxford: Oxford University Press, 2008.

Larson, Edward J., and Michael P. Winship. *The Constitutional Convention: A Narrative History from the Notes of James Madison.* New York: Modern Library, 2005.

Madison, James. *James Madison: Writings 1772–1836.* New York: Library of America, 1999.

———. *Letters and Other Writings of James Madison.* Philadelphia: J. B. Lippincott & Co., 1865.

———. *Notes of Debates in the Federal Convention of 1787.* Introduction by Adrienne Koch. Athens: Ohio University Press, 1966.

McCoy, Drew R. *The Last of the Fathers: James Madison & The Republican Legacy.* Cambridge: Cambridge University Press, 1989.

Rakove, Jack. *James Madison and the Creation of the American Republic.* 3rd ed. New York: Pearson/Longman, 2007.

Sheehan, Colleen A. *James Madison and the Spirit of Republican Self-Government.* New York: Cambridge University Press, 2009.

Vile, John R., William D. Pederson, and Frank J. Williams, eds. *James Madison: Philosopher, Founder, and Statesman.* Athens: Ohio University Press, 2008.

Willis, Garry. *James Madison.* The American Presidents Series. Edited by Arthur M. Schlesinger. New York: Times Books, 2002.

KARL MARX

Adamson, Walter L. *Marx and the Disillusionment of Marxism.* Berkeley: University of California Press, 1985.

Avineri, Schlomo. *The Social and Political Thought of Karl Marx.* London: Cambridge University Press, 1968.

Berman, Marshall. *Adventures in Marxism.* New York: Verso, 1999.

Callinicos, Alex. *Marxism and Philosophy.* New York: Oxford University Press, 1983.

Carver, Terrell, ed. *The Cambridge Companion to Marx.* New York: Cambridge University Press, 1991.

Clarke, Simon. *Marx's Theory of Crisis.* London: Macmillan, 1994.

Conway, David. *A Farewell to Marx: An Outline and Appraisal of His Theories.* New York: Penguin, 1987.

Cowling, Mark, and Lawrence Wilde. *Approaches to Marx.* Philadelphia: Open University Press, 1989.

Dupre, Louis. *The Philosophical Foundations of Marxism.* New York: Harcourt, 1966.

Elster, John. *An Introduction to Karl Marx.* New York: Cambridge University Press, 1986.

Felix, David. *Marx as Politician.* Carbondale: Southern Illinois University Press, 1983.

Fetscher, Irving. *Marx and Marxism.* New York: Herder and Herder, 1971.

Forbes, Ian. *Marx and the New Individual.* Boston: Unwin Hyman, 1990.

Gottlieb, Roger S. *Marxism, 1844–1990: Origins, Betrayal, Rebirth.* New York: Routledge, 1992.

Graham, Keith. *Karl Marx: Our Contemporary.* New York: Harvester Wheatsheaf, 1992.

Lichtheim, George. *Marxism: An Historical and Critical Study.* New York: Praeger, 1961.

Lukacs, Gyorgy. *History and Class Consciousness: Studies in Marxist Dialectics.* Cambridge: MIT, 1971.

Marx, Karl. *Capital.* 3 vols. New York: International, 1976.

———. *The Communist Manifesto.* Edited by A. J. Taylor. Baltimore: Penguin, 1968.

———. *Karl Marx, a Reader.* Edited by John Elster. New York: Cambridge University Press, 1986.

Marx, Karl, and Friedrich Engels. *The Communist Manifesto.* Translated by Samuel Moore. Edited and annotated by Friedrich Engels. Chicago: Kerr, 1978.

Mazlish, Bruce. *The Meaning of Karl Marx.* New York: Oxford University Press, 1984.

McLellan, David. *Karl Marx: A Biography.* New York: Palgrave Macmillan, 2006.

Meister, Robert. *Political Identity: Thinking through Marx.* Cambridge: Basil Blackwell, 1991.

Meszaros, Istvan. *Marx's Theory of Alienation.* New York: Harper & Row, 1972.

Ollman, Bertell. *Alienation: Marx's Conception of Man in Capitalist Society.* New York: Cambridge University Press, 1976.

Parkinson, G. H. R. *Marx and Marxisms.* New York: Cambridge University Press, 1982.

Rigby, S. H. *Marxism and History: A Critical Introduction.* New York: St. Martin's, 1998.

Rubel, M., and M. Mamale. *Marx without Myth: A Chronological Study of His Life and Work.* New York: Harper & Row, 1975.

Shortall, Felton C. *The Incomplete Marx.* Aldershot: Avebury, 1994.

Thomas, Paul. *Alien Politics: Marxist State Theory Retrieved.* New York: Routledge, 1994.

Tucker, Robert C. *The Marxian Revolutionary Idea.* New York: Norton, 1968.

Van den Berg, Axel. *The Immanent Utopia: From Marxism on the State to the State of Marxism.* Princeton: Princeton University Presss, 1988.

Wheen, Francis. *Karl Marx.* New York: Norton, 1999.

Wood, Allen. *Karl Marx.* New York: Routledge, 2004.

MARGARET MEAD

Banner, Lois. *Intertwined Lives: Margaret Mead, Ruth Benedict, and Their Circle.* New York: Vintage, 2003.

Bateson, Mary Catherine. *With a Daughter's Eye: A Memoir of Margaret Mead and Gregory Bateson.* New York: Morrow, 1984.

Bowman-Kruhm, Mary. *Margaret Mead: A Biography.* Westport: Greenwood, 2003.

Cassidy, Robert. *Margaret Mead: A Voice for the Century.* New York: Universe, 1982.

Freeman, Derek. *Margaret Mead and Samoa: The Making and Unmaking of an Anthropological Myth.* New York: Penguin, 1986.

Goodman, Richard A. *Mead's Coming of Age in Samoa, A Dissenting View.* Oakland: Pipperine, 1983.

Gordon, Joan, *Margaret Mead: The Complete Bibliography.* The Hague: Mouton, 1976.

Howard, Jane. *Margaret Mead: A Life.* New York: Simon & Schuster, 1984.

Mead, Margaret, *Anthropology, a Human Science: Selected Papers, 1939–1960.* Princeton: Van Nostrand, 1964.

———. *Blackberry Winter: My Early Years.* 1972. Gloucester: Peter Smith, 1989.

———. *Coming of Age in Samoa: A Psychological Study of Primitive Youth for Western Civilization.* 1961. Foreword by Franz Boas. Gloucester: Peter Smith, 1973.

———. *Growing Up in New Guinea: A Comparative Study of Primitive Education.* Reprint. New York: Morrow, 1975.

————. *Letters from the Field, 1925–1975.* New York: Harper & Row, 1977.

————. *The School in American Culture,* Cambridge: Harvard University Press, 1951.

————. *Some Personal Views.* Edited by Rhoda Metraux. New York: Walker, 1979.

Mead, Margaret, and Ken Heyman. *Family.* New York: Macmillan, 1965.

Mead, Margaret, and Martha Wolfenstein, eds. *Childhood in Contemporary Cultures.* Text ed. Chicago: University of Chicago Press, 1963.

JOHN STUART MILL

Capaldi, Nicholas. *John Stuart Mill: A Biography.* Cambridge: Cambridge University Press, 2004.

Ellery, John B. *John Stuart Mill.* New York: G. K. Hall & Co., 1999.

Goehlert, Robert. *John Stuart Mill: A Bibliography.* Monticello: Vance Bibliographies, 1982.

Mill, John Stuart. *Autobiography.* Boston: Houghton Mifflin, 1969.

————. *On Liberty.* 1859. New York: Norton, 1975.

————. *On Liberty and Other Essays.* Edited with an introduction and notes by John Gray. Oxford: Oxford University Press, 1998.

————. *On Liberty; Representative Government; The Subjection of Women: Three Essays by John Stuart Mill.* 1921. Introduction by Millicent Garrett Fawcett. London: Oxford University Press, 1933.

————. *The Subjection of Women.* 1869. Cambridge: M.I.T. Press, 1970.

————. *Utilitarianism.* Edited by Roger Crisp. Oxford: Oxford University Press, 1998.

Mill, John Stuart, and Harriet Taylor Mill. *Essays on Sex Equality.* Edited and with an introductory essay by Alice S. Rossi. Chicago: University of Chicago Press, 1970.

Packe, Michael St. John. *The Life of John Stuart Mill.* New York: Macmillan, 1954.

Reeves, Richard. *John Stuart Mill.* New York: Overlook, 2008.

Ryan, Alan. *J. S. Mill.* New York: Routledge, 1974.

Skorupski, John, ed. *The Cambridge Companion to Mill.* Cambridge: Cambridge University Press, 1998.

————. *Why Read Mill Today?* New York: Routledge, 2006.

Wollstonecraft, Mary. *The Rights of Women.* 1792. New York: E. P. Dutton & Co., 1929.

MARIA MONTESSORI

Hainstock, Elizabeth, ed. *The Essential Montessori.* New York: Plume, 1997.

Montessori, Maria. *The Advanced Montessori Method.* New York: Frederick A. Stokes, 1917.

————. *The Child in the Church: Essays on the Religious Education of Children and the Training of Character.* Edited by Mortimer Standing. London: Sands, 1929.

————. *The Montessori Method: Scientific Pedagogy as Applied to Child Education in "The Children's Houses."* Translated by Anne E. George. New York: Frederick A. Stokes, 1912.

————. *The Secret Childhood.* London, New York: Longmans, 1936.

————. *To Educate the Human Potential.* Madras: Kalakshetra, 1967.

Rambusch, Nancy McCormick. *Learning How to Learn: An American Approach to Montessori.* Baltimore: Helicon, 1962.

Standing, E. Mortimer. *Maria Montessori: Her Life and Work.* London: Hollis & Carter, 1957.

————. *The Montessori Method: A Revolution in Education.* Fresno: Academy Library Guild, 1962.

IRIS MURDOCH

Antonaccio, Maria, and William Schweiker. *Iris Murdoch and the Search for Human Goodness.* Chicago: University of Chicago Press, 1996.

Conradi, Peter J. *Iris Murdoch: A Life.* New York: Norton, 2001.

Murdoch, Iris. *Acastos: Two Platonic Dialogues.* New York: Viking, 1987.

————. *An Accidental Man.* New York: Viking, 1971.

————. *The Bell.* New York: Viking, 1958.

————. *The Black Prince.* New York: Viking, 1973.

————. *The Book and the Brotherhood.* New York: Viking, 1987.

————. *Bruno's Dream.* New York: Viking, 1969.

————. *Existentialists and Mystics: Writings on Philosophy and Literature.* New York: Viking, 1998.

———. *A Fairly Honorably Defeat.* New York: Viking, 1970.

———. *The Fire and the Sun: Why Plato Banished the Artists.* New York: Viking, 1990.

———. *The Green Knight.* New York: Viking, 1994.

———. *Metaphysics as a Guide to Morals: Philosophical Reflections.* New York: Penguin, 1993.

———. *The Nice and the Good.* New York: Viking, 1968.

———. *Nuns and Soldiers.* New York: Viking, 1980.

———. *The Philosopher's Pupil.* New York: Viking, 1983.

———. *The Red and the Green.* New York: Viking, 1965.

———. *The Sacred and Profane Love Machine.* New York: Viking, 1974.

———. *The Sandcastle.* New York: Viking, 1957.

———. *Sartre: Romantic Rationalist.* New Haven: Yale University Press, 1953.

———. *The Sea, the Sea.* New York: Viking, 1978.

———. *A Severed Head.* New York: Viking, 1954.

———. *The Sovereignty of Good over Other Concepts.* New York: Schocken, 1983.

———. *Under the Net.* New York: Viking, 1954.

Spear, Hilda. *Iris Murdoch.* New York: St. Martin's Press, 1995.

Widdows, Heather. *The Moral Vision of Iris Murdoch.* Burlington: Ashgate, 2005.

FRIEDRICH NIETZSCHE

Clark, Maudmarie. *Nietzsche on Truth and Philosophy.* New York: Cambridge University Press, 1990.

Conway, Daniel W. *Nietzsche: Critical Assessments.* New York: Routledge, 1998.

Danto, Arthur C. *Nietzsche as Philosopher.* New York: Macmillan, 1965.

Emden, Christian. *Friedrich Nietzsche and the Politics of History.* Cambridge: Cambridge University Press, 2008.

Gillespie, Michael Allen, and Tracy B. Strong, eds. *Nietzsche's New Seas: Explorations in Philosophy, Aesthetics, and Politics.* Chicago: University of Chicago Press, 1988.

Heller, Erich. *The Importance of Nietzsche: Ten Essays.* Chicago: University of Chicago Press, 1988.

Heller, Otto. *Prophets of Dissent.* New York: Knopf, 1918.

Hollingdale, R. J. *Nietzsche: The Man and His Philosophy.* Baton Rouge: Louisiana State University Press, 1965.

Jaspers, Karl. *Nietzsche and Christianity.* Translated by E. B. Ashton. Chicago: Regnery, 1961.

Kaufmann, Walter A. *Nietzsche: Philosopher, Psychologist, Antichrist.* Princeton: Princeton University Press, 1950.

Makarushka, Irena S. M. *Religious Imagination and Language in Emerson and Nietzsche.* New York: St. Martin's, 1994.

Nietzsche, Friedrich. *The Viking Portable Nietzsche.* Edited by Walter A. Kaufmann. New York: Viking, 1977.

Pfeffer, Rose. *Nietzsche: Disciple of Dionysus.* Lewisburg: Bucknell University Press, 1972.

Safranski, Reudiger. *Nietzsche: A Philosophical Biography.* New York: W. W. Norton, 2003.

Salter, William. *Nietzsche the Thinker.* London: Cecil, Palmer, and Hayward, 1917.

Schacht, Richard. *Nietzsche.* London: Routledge, 1983.

Schrift, Alan D. *Why Nietzsche Still? Reflections on Drama, Culture, Politics.* Berkeley: University of California Press, 2000.

Solomon, Robert C., and Kathleen M. Higgins, eds. *Reading Nietzsche.* New York: Oxford University Press, 1988.

Staten, Henry. *Nietzsche's Voice.* Ithaca: Cornell University Press, 1990.

Strong, Tracy B. *Freidrich Nietzsche and the Politics of Transfiguration.* Urbana: University of Illinois Press, 2000.

Tanner, Michael. *Nietzsche.* Oxford: Oxford University Press, 1994.

Westphal, Merold. *Suspicion and Faith: The Religious Uses of Modern Atheism.* Grand Rapids: Eerdmans, 1993.

Wilcox, John. *Truth and Value in Nietzsche.* Ann Arbor: University of Michigan Press, 1974.

Zeitlin, Irving M. *Nietzsche: A Re-examination.* Cambridge: Polity, 1994.

JULIUS K. NYERERE

Chachage, Chambi, and Annar Cassam, eds. *Africa's Liberation: The Legacy of Nyerere*. Nairobi: Pambazuka Press, and Kampala: Fountain Publishers, 2010.

Nyerere, Julius K. *Crusade for Liberation*. Introduction by the Press Office, State House, Dar es Salaam. Dar es Salaam: Oxford University Press, 1978.

―――. *Freedom and Development (Uhuru na Maendeleo): A Selection from the Writings and Speeches, 1968–1973*. London: Oxford University Press, 1973.

―――. *Freedom and Socialism (Uhuru na Ujama): A Selection from Writings and Speeches, 1965–1967*. Dar es Salaam: Oxford University Press, 1968.

―――. *Freedom and Unity (Uhuru na Umoja): A Selection from Writings and Speeches, 1952–1965*. London: Oxford University Press, 1967.

―――. *Man and Development*. Dar es Salaam: Oxford University Press, 1974.

―――. *Our Leadership and the Destiny of Tanzania*. Harare, Zimbabwe: African Pub. Group, 1995.

Russian Academy of Sciences Institute for African Studies. *Julius Nyerere. Humanist, Politician, Thinker*. Dar es Salaam: Mkuki na Nyota Publishers, 2005.

MARIO PEI

Pei, Mario. *All About Language*. Philadelphia: Lippincott, 1954.

―――. *Double-Speak in America*. New York: Hawthorn Books, 1973.

―――. *English: A World-Wide Tongue*. New York: S. F. Vanni, 1944.

―――. *The Geography of Language*. New York: S. F. Vanni, 1944.

―――. *How to Learn Languages and What Languages to Learn*. New York: Harper & Row, 1966.

―――. *Invitation to Linguistics: A Basic Introduction to the Science of Language*. Garden City: Doubleday, 1965.

―――. *The Many Hues of English*. New York: Knopf, 1967.

―――. *One Language for the World*. New York: Devin-Adair, 1958.

―――. *The Story of Language*. 1949. Revised ed. London: Allen & Unwin, 1966.

―――. *Voices of Man: The Meaning and Function of Language*. 1962. New York: AMS Press, 1972.

―――. *Weasel Words: The Art of Saying What You Don't Mean*. New York: Harper & Row, 1978.

―――. *What's in a Word? Language: Yesterday, Today, and Tomorrow*. New York: Hawthorn Books, 1968.

―――. *Words in Sheep's Clothing: How People Manipulate Opinion by Distorting Word Meanings*. New York: Hawthorn Books, 1969.

PLATO

Barrow, Robin. *Plato, Utilitarianism, and Education*. London: Routledge, 1975.

Blackburn, Simon. *Plato's Republic: A Biography*. London: Atlantic, 2006.

Brickhouse, Thomas C. *Plato's Socrates*. New York: Oxford University Press, 1994.

Brumbaugh, Robert Sherrick. *Plato for the Modern Age*. New York: Crowell-Collier, 1962.

Clegg, Jerry. *The Structure of Plato's Philosophy*. Lewisburg: Bucknell University Press, 1976.

Cornford, Francis MacDonald. *Before and After Socrates*. Cambridge: Cambridge University Press, 1958.

Fine, Gail, ed. *Plato*. New York: Oxford University Press, 2000.

Fox, Adam. *Plato for Pleasure*. London: Westhouse, 1945.

Grube, Georges. *Plato's Thought*. Boston: Beacon, 1958.

Gulley, Norman. *Plato's Theory of Knowledge*. New York: Barnes and Noble, 1962.

Kraut, Richard, ed. *The Cambridge Companion to Plato*. New York: Cambridge University Press, 1992.

McCrone, John. *The Myth of Irrationality: The Science of the Mind from Plato to Star Trek*. London: Macmillan, 1993.

Melling, David J. *Understanding Plato*. Oxford: Oxford University Press, 1987.

Neheman, Alexander. *Virtues of Authenticity: Essays on Plato and Socrates*. Princeton: Princeton University Press, 1999.

Plato. *The Dialogues of Plato.* Edited by Justin D. Kaplan. New York: Washington Square, 1982.

————. *Plato's Sophist.* Translated by William S. Cobb. Savage: Rowan & Littlefield, 1990.

————. *The Republic of Plato.* Translated by Allan Bloom. New York: Basic, 1991.

————. *The Viking Portable Plato.* Edited by Scott Buchanan. New York: Viking, 1977.

Rankin, H. D. *Plato and the Individual.* New York: Barnes and Noble, 1964.

Rowe, C. J. *Plato.* New York: St. Martin's, 1984.

Taylor, Alfred. *Plato: The Man and His Work.* London: Methuen, 1960.

Tuana, Nancy, ed. *Feminist Interpretations of Plato.* University Park: Pennsylvania State University Press, 1994.

Vlastos, Gregory. *Plato's Universe.* Seattle: University of Washington Press, 1975.

Williams, Bernard Arthur Owen. *Plato.* New York: Routledge, 1999.

Zeitlin, Irving M. *Plato's Vision: The Classical Origins of Social and Political Thought.* Englewood Cliffs: Prentice-Hall, 1993.

ALEXANDER POPE

Brower, Reuben Arthur. *Alexander Pope: The Poetry of Allusion.* Oxford: Clarendon Press, 1959.

Brownell, Morris R. *Alexander Pope and the Arts of Georgian England.* Oxford: Clarendon Press, 1978.

Erskine-Hill, Howard. *The Social Milieu of Alexander Pope: Lives, Example, and the Poetic Response.* New Haven: Yale University Press, 1975.

Fraser, George Sutherland. *Alexander Pope.* London: Routledge and Paul, 1978.

Knight, George Wilson. *The Poetry of Pope, Laureate of Peace.* New York: Barnes and Noble, 1965.

Mack, Maynard. *Alexander Pope: A Life.* New Haven: Yale University Press, 1985.

————. *Collected in Himself: Essays Critical, Biographical, and Bibliographical on Pope.* Newark: University of Delaware Press, 1982.

————. *Essential Articles for the Study of Alexander Pope.* Hamden, CT: Archon Books, 1964.

Nicolson. Marjorie Hope, and G. S. Rousseau. *"This Long Disease, My Life": Alexander Pope and the Sciences.* Princeton: Princeton University Press, 1968.

Parkin, Rebecca Price. *The Poetic Workmanship of Alexander Pope.* New York: Octagon Books, 1966.

Pope, Alexander. *Correspondence.* Oxford: Clarendon Press, 1956.

————. *The Dunciad.* Edited by James Runcieman Sutherland. London: Methuen, 1943.

————. *An Essay on Man* Twickenham ed. London: Methuen 1951.

————. *The Poems of Alexander Pope.* Twickenham ed. Edited by John Butt. London: Routledge, 1993.

————. *The Prose Works of Alexander Pope.* Edited by Norman Ault. Oxford: Blackwell, 1936.

————. *The Rape of the Lock and Other Poems.* Twickenham ed. Edited by Geoffrey Tillotson. New York: Oxford University Press, 1942.

Rogers, Pat. *An Introduction to Pope.* London: Methuen, 1975.

Russo, John Paul. *Alexander Pope: Tradition and Identity.* Cambridge: Harvard University Press, 1972.

Spacks, Patricia Ann Meyer. *An Argument of Images: The Poetry of Alexander Pope.* Cambridge: Harvard University Press, 1971.

Tillotson, Geoffrey. *On the Poetry of Pope.* Oxford: Clarendon Press, 1938.

————. *Pope and Human Nature.* Oxford: Clarendon Press, 1958.

NEIL POSTMAN

Postman, Neil. *Amusing Ourselves to Death: Public Discourse in the Age of Show Business.* 20th anniversary ed. New York: Penguin Books, 2006.

————. *Conscientious Objections: Stirring Up Trouble about Language, Technology, and Education.* New York: Knopf, 1988.

————. *Crazy Talk, Stupid Talk: How We Defeat Ourselves by the Way We Talk and What to Do about It.* New York: Delacorte Press, 1976.

————. *The Disappearance of Childhood.* New York: Delacorte Press, 1982.

————. *Technopoly: the Surrender of Culture to Technology.* New York: Knopf, 1992.

Postman, Neil, and the Committee on the Study of Television of the National Council of Teachers of English. *Television and the Teaching of English.* New York: Appleton-Century-Crofts, 1961.

Postman, Neil, and Charles Weingartner. *Linguistics: A Revolution in Teaching*. New York: Delacorte Press, 1966.
Postman, Neil, Charles Weingartner, and Terence P. Moran. *Language in America*. New York: Pegasus, 1969.

ROBERT B. REICH

Henkoff, Ronald. "An Interview with Robert Reich." *Fortune* 127 (1993): 11.
Litchfield, Randall. "New Dealer: Interview with Robert B. Reich." *Canadian Business* 66 (1993): 38–39.
Magaziner, Ira C., and Robert B. Reich. *Minding America's Business: The Decline and Rise of the American Economy*. 1982. New York: Vintage, 1983.
Reich, Robert B. *American Competitiveness and American Brains*. New York: Baruch College, City University of New York, 1993.
———. *Education and the Next Economy*. Washington, D.C.: National Education Association, 1988.
———. *The Future of Success: Working and Living in the New Economy*. New York: Vintage Books, 2000.
———. *I'll Be Short: Essentials for a Decent Working Society*. Boston: Beacon Press, 2002.
———. *Locked in the Cabinet*. New York: Knopf, 1997.
———. *The Next American Frontier*. New York: Viking, 1984.
———, ed. *The Power of Public Ideas*. 1988. Cambridge: Harvard University Press, 1990.
———. *The Resurgent Liberal: And Other Unfashionable Prophecies*. 1989. New York: Vintage, 1991.
———. *Supercapitalism: The Transformation of Business, Democracy, and Everyday Life*. New York: Alfred A. Knopf, 2007.
———. *The Work of Nations: Preparing Ourselves for Twenty-first-Century Capitalism*. New York: Knopf, 1991.
Warsh, David. *Economic Principals: Masters and Mavericks of Modern Economics*. New York: Free Press, 1993.

JEAN-JACQUES ROUSSEAU

Blanchard, William. *Rousseau and the Spirit of Revolt*. Ann Arbor: University of Michigan Press, 1967.
Broome, Jack Howard. *Rousseau: A Study of His Thought*. New York: Barnes and Noble, 1963.
Cassirer, Ernst. *The Question of Jean-Jacques Rousseau*. Translated and edited by Peter Gay. New York: Columbia University Press, 1954.
Chapman, John William. *Rousseau: Totalitarian or Liberal?* New York: Columbia University Press, 1956.
Damrosch, Leo. *Jean-Jacques Rousseau: Restless Genius*. Boston: Houghton Mifflin, 2005.
Dent, N. J. II. *A Rousseau Dictionary*. Cambridge: Blackwell, 1992.
Dobinson, Charles Henry. *Jean-Jacques Rousseau: His Thought and Its Relevance Today*. London: Methuen, 1969.
Fermon, Nicole. *Domesticating Passions: Rousseau, Woman, and Nation*. Hanover: University Press of New England, 1997.
Friedlander, Eli. *Jean-Jacques Rousseau: An Afterlife of Words*. Cambridge: Harvard University Press, 2004.
Gauthier, David. *Rousseau: The Sentiment of Existence*. New York: Cambridge University Press, 2006.
Grimsley, Ronald. *Jean-Jacques Rousseau*. Totowa: Barnes and Noble, 1983.
Huizinga, Jacob Herman. *Rousseau: The Self-Made Spirit*. New York: Grossman, 1976.
Kelly, Christopher. *Rousseau as Author: Consecrating One's Life to Truth*. Chicago: University of Chicago Press, 2003.
Masters, Roger. *The Political Philosophy of Rousseau*. Princeton: Princeton University Press, 1968.
Morgenstern, Mira. *Rousseau and the Politics of Ambiguity: Self, Culture, and Society*. University Park: Pennsylvania State University Press, 1996.
Murry, John Middleton. *Heroes of Thought*. New York: J. Messner, 1938.
O'Hagen, Timothy. *Rousseau*. New York: Routledge, 1999.

Orwin, Clifford, and Nathan Tarcov. *The Legacy of Rousseau.* Chicago: University of Chicago Press, 1997.

Perkins, Merle. *Jean-Jacques Rousseau on the Individual and Society.* Lexington: University Press of Kentucky, 1974.

Riesenberg, Peter N. *Citizenship in the Western Tradition: Plato to Rousseau.* Chapel Hill: University of North Carolina Press, 1992.

Reisert, Joseph R. *Jean-Jacques Rousseau: A Friend of Virtue.* Ithaca: Cornell University Press, 2003.

Rousseau, Jean-Jacques. *The Annotated Social Contract.* Edited by Charles M. Sherover. New York: New American Library, 1974.

———. *Confessions.* Translated by John M. Cohen. Baltimore: Penguin, 1953.

———. *Emile.* Introduction, translation, and notes by Allan Bloom. New York: Basic Books, 1979.

Wokler, Robert. *Rousseau.* Oxford: Oxford University Press, 1995.

ADAM SMITH

Aspromourgos, Tony. *On the Origins of Classical Economics: Distribution and Value from William Petty to Adam Smith.* London: Routledge, 1996.

Brown, Vivienne. *Adam Smith's Discourse: Canonicity, Commerce, and Conscience.* London: Routledge, 1994.

Buchan, James. *The Authentic Adam Smith: His Life and Ideas.* New York: W. W. Norton, 2006.

Campbell, Thomas Douglas. *Adam Smith's Science of Morals.* London: Allen and Unwin, 1971.

Copley, Stephen, and Kathryn Sutherland, eds. *Adam Smith's Wealth of Nations: New Interdisciplinary Essays.* Manchester: Manchester University Press, 1995.

Fitzgibbons, Athol. *Adam Smith's System of Liberty, Wealth, and Virtue: The Moral and Political Foundations of the Wealth of Nations.* Oxford: Clarendon, 1995.

Fry, Michael. *Adam Smith's Legacy: His Place in the Development of Modern Economics.* London: Routledge, 1992.

Göçmen, Dogan. *The Adam Smith Problem: Human Nature and Society in The Theory of Moral Sentiments and The Wealth of Nations.* New York: Palgrave Macmillan, 2007.

Haakonssen, Knud. *The Cambridge Companion to Adam Smith.* Cambridge: Cambridge University Press, 2006.

Henderson, Willie. *Evaluating Adam Smith: Creating the Wealth of Nations.* New York: Routledge, 2006.

Lindgren, J. Ralph. *The Social Philosophy of Adam Smith.* The Hague: Marinus Nijhoff, 1973.

Macfarlane, Alan. *The Riddle of the Modern World: Of Liberty, Wealth and Equality.* New York: St. Martin's, 2000.

Minowitz, Peter. *Profits, Priests, and Princes: Adam Smith's Emancipation of Economics from Politics.* Stanford: Stanford University Press, 1993.

Montes, Leonidas, and Eric Schliesser. *Voices on Adam Smith.* New York: Routledge, 2006.

Muller, Jerry Z. *Adam Smith in His Time and Ours: Designing the Decent Society.* New York: Free Press, 1993.

Rae, John. *Life of Adam Smith.* New York: Kelley, 1965.

Smith, Adam. *The Early Writings of Adam Smith.* Edited by J. Ralph Lindgren. New York: Kelley, 1967.

———. *The Essential Adam Smith.* Edited by Robert L. Heilbroner. New York: Norton, 1986.

———. *An Inquiry into the Nature and Cause of the Wealth of Nations: A Selected Edition.* Oxford: Oxford University Press, 1993.

———. *Lectures on Jurisprudence.* Edited by R. L. Meek, D. D. Raphael, and P. G. Stein. Indianapolis: Liberty Classics, 1982.

———. *The Theory of Moral Sentiments.* Edited by D. D. Raphael and A. L. Macfie. Indianapolis: Liberty Classics, 1982.

ELIZABETH CADY STANTON

Banner, Lois. *Elizabeth Cady Stanton: A Radical for Women's Rights.* Boston: Little, Brown, 1980.

Davis, Sue. *The Political Thought of Elizabeth Cady Stanton: Women's Rights and the American Political Traditions.* New York: New York University Press, 2008.

DuBois, Ellen Carol. *The Elizabeth Cady Stanton and Susan B. Anthony Reader: Correspondence, Writings, and Speeches.* Chicago: Northeastern University Press, 1999.

DuBois, Ellen, and Richard Candida Smith. *Elizabeth Cady Stanton, Feminist as Thinker: A Reader in Documents and Essays.* New York: New York University Press, 2007.

Griffith, Elizabeth. *In Her Own Right: The Life of Elizabeth Cady Stanton.* New York: Oxford University Press, 1984.

Lutz, Alma. *Created Equal.* New York: John Day, 1940.

Oakley, Mary Anne B. *Elizabeth Cady Stanton.* Old Westbury: Feminist Press, 1972.

Pellauer, Mary. *Towards a Tradition of Feminist Theology: The Religious Social Thought of Elizabeth Cady Stanton, Susan B. Anthony, and Anna Howard Shaw.* Brooklyn: Carlson, 1991.

Sigerman, Harriet. *Elizabeth Cady Stanton: The Right Is Ours.* New York: Oxford University Press, 2001.

Stanton, Elizabeth Cady. *Eighty Years and More (1815–1897): Reminiscences of Elizabeth Cady Stanton.* New York: Source Book, 1970.

——. *Elizabeth Cady Stanton as Revealed in Her Letters.* New York: Harper, 1922.

——. *Elizabeth Cady Stanton, Susan B. Anthony: Correspondence, Writings, Speeches.* Edited by Ellen Carol DuBois. New York: Schocken, 1981.

——. *The Selected Papers of Elizabeth Cady Stanton and Susan B. Anthony.* Edited by Ann D. Gordon and Tamara Gaskell Miller. New Brunswick: Rutgers University Press, 1997.

——. *The Woman's Bible.* Amherst: Prometheus, 1999.

Stanton, Elizabeth Cady, Susan B. Anthony, and Matilda Joslyn Gage, eds. *History of Woman Suffrage.* Salem: Ayer, 1985.

Waggenspack, Beth Marie. *The Search for Self-Sovereignty: The Oratory of Elizabeth Cady Stanton.* New York: Greenwood, 1989.

Ward, Geoffrey C. *Not for Ourselves Alone: The Story of Elizabeth Cady Stanton and Susan B. Anthony: An Illustrated History.* New York: Knopf, 1999.

HENRY DAVID THOREAU

Bloom, Harold, ed. *Henry David Thoreau.* New York: Bloom's Literary Criticism, 2007.

Borst, Raymond. *Henry David Thoreau: A Reference Guide.* Boston: Hall, 1987.

Derleth, August William. *Concord Rebel: A Life of Henry David Thoreau.* Philadelphia: Cholton, 1962.

Fink, Steven. *Prophet in the Marketplace: Thoreau's Development as a Professional Writer.* Princeton: Princeton University Press, 1992.

Gayet, Claude. *The Intellectual Development of Henry David Thoreau.* Stockholm: Almqvist and Wikseu, 1981.

Hamilton, Franklin W. *Thoreau on the Art of Writing.* Flint: Walden, 1967.

Harding, Walter Roy. *Henry David Thoreau: A Profile.* New York: Hill and Wang, 1971.

Milder, Robert. *Reimagining Thoreau.* New York: Cambridge University Press, 1995.

Myerson, Joel, ed. *The Cambridge Companion to Henry David Thoreau.* New York: Cambridge University Press, 1995.

Richardson, Robert D., Jr. *Henry Thoreau: A Life of the Mind.* Berkeley: University of California Press, 1986.

Salt, Henry. *Life of Henry David Thoreau.* Urbana: University of Illinois Press, 1993.

Sattelmeyer, Robert. *Thoreau's Reading: A Study in Intellectual History.* Princeton: Princeton University Press, 1988.

Sayre, Robert F., ed. *New Essays on Walden.* New York: Cambridge University Press, 1992.

Schneider, Richard J. *Henry David Thoreau.* Boston: Twayne, 1987.

Thoreau, Henry David. *The Annotated Walden: Walden, or Life in the Woods.* New York: Potter, Crown, 1970.

——. *The Best of Thoreau's Journal.* Edited by Carl Bode. Carbondale: Southern Illinois University Press, 1971.

——. *Collected Poems.* Edited by Carl Bode. Baltimore: Johns Hopkins University Press, 1964.

——. *The Thoreau Log: A Documentary Life of Henry David Thoreau.* Compiled by Raymond Borst. New York: Hall, 1992.

——. *Walden.* Edited by J. Lyndon Shanley. Princeton: Princeton University Press, 1971.

——. *Walden and Resistance to Civil Government.* Edited by William Rossi. New York: Norton, 1992.

——. *A Week on the Concord and Merrimack Rivers.* Edited by Carl Howde. Princeton: Princeton University Press, 1980.

ALEXIS DE TOCQUEVILLE

Gannett, Robert T., Jr., *Tocqueville Unveiled: The Historian and His Sources for the Old Regime and the Revolution*. Chicago: University of Chicago Press, 2003.

Jardin, Andre. *Tocqueville: A Biography*. New York: Farrar, Straus and Giroux, 1989.

Lamberti, Jean-Claude. *Tocqueville and the Two Democracies*. Translated by Arthur Goldhammer. Cambridge: Harvard University Press, 1989.

Nolla, Eduardo, ed. *Liberty, Equality, Democracy*. New York: New York University Press, 1996.

Schleifler, James T. *The Making of Tocqueville's* Democracy in America. 2nd ed. Indianapolis: Liberty Fund, 1999.

Tocqueville, Alexis de. *Democracy in America*. 1835. Translated by Arthur Goldhammer. New York: Library of America, 2004.

———. *Journey to America*. Translated by George Lawrence. Edited by J. P. Mayer. Rev. and augmented ed. in collaboration with A. P. Kerr. Westport: Greenwood Press, 1981.

———. *Recollections*. 1893. Translated by George Lawrence. Edited by J. P. Mayer and A. P. Kerr. Introduction by J. P. Mayer. Garden City: Doubleday, 1970.

Zunz, Oliver. *Alexis de Tocqueville and Gustave de Beaumont in America: Their Friendship and Their Travels*. Translated by Arthur Goldhammer. Charlottesville: University of Virginia Press; 2011.

MARY WOLLSTONECRAFT

Bouter, Jacob. *Mary Wollstonecraft and the Beginnings of Female Emancipation in France and England*. Philadelphia: Porcupine, 1975.

Detre, Jean. *A Most Extraordinary Pair: Mary Wollstonecraft and William Godwin*. Garden City: Doubleday, 1975.

Franklin, Caroline. *Mary Wollstonecraft: A Literary Life*. New York: Palgrave, 2004.

Godwin, William. *Godwin & Mary: Letters of William Godwin and Mary Wollstonecraft*. Edited by Ralph M. Wardle. Lincoln: University of Nebraska Press, 1966.

———. *Memoirs of the Author of A Vindication of the Rights of Woman*. New York: Garland, 1974.

Gordon, Lyndall. *Mary Wollstonecraft: A New Genus*. New York: Little Brown, 2004.

Jacobs, Diane. *Her Own Woman*. New York: Simon & Schuster, 2001.

Johnson, Claudia. *Cambridge Companion to Mary Wollstonecraft*. New York: Cambridge University Press, 2002.

Kelly, Gary. *Revolutionary Feminism: The Mind and Career of Mary Wollstonecraft*. New York: St. Martin's, 1992.

Lorch, Jennifer. *Mary Wollstonecraft: The Making of a Radical Feminist*. New York: Berg/St. Martin's, 1990.

Todd, Janet. *Mary Wollstonecraft: A Revolutionary Life*. New York: Columbia University Press, 2000.

Wollstonecraft, Mary. *Collected Letters of Mary Wollstonecraft*. Edited by Ralph M. Wardle. Ithaca: Cornell University Press, 1979.

———. *Letters Written During a Short Residence in Sweden, Norway, and Denmark*. Edited by Carol H. Poston. Lincoln: University of Nebraska Press, 1976.

———. *Maria or The Wrongs of Woman*. New York: Norton, 1975.

———. *Political Writings*. Edited by Janet Todd. Toronto: University of Toronto Press, 1933.

———. *Thoughts on the Education of Daughters*. Oxford: Woodstock, 1994.

———. *A Vindication of the Rights of Men*. Amherst: Prometheus, 1996.

———. *A Vindication of the Rights of Woman: An Authoritative Text, Backgrounds, and Criticism*. Edited by Carol H. Poston. New York: Norton, 1975.

CARTER G. WOODSON

Goggin, Jacqueline. *Carter G. Woodson: A Life in Black History*. Baton Rouge: Louisiana State University Press, 1997.

Greene, Lorenzo Thomas. *Selling Black History for Carter G. Woodson: A Diary, 1930-1933*. Columbia: University of Missouri Press, 1996.

Jimison, Linda S. *Carter G. Woodson: Views on History and Education*. Indianapolis: LifeStar Enterprises, 1994.

Woodson, Carter G. *A Century of Negro Migration.* 1918. New York: AMS Press, 1970.

———. *The History of the Negro Church.* 1921. CreateSpace, 2011.

———. *The Mind of the Negro as Reflected in Letters Written during the Crisis, 1800–1860.* 1927. New York: Russell & Russell, 1969.

———. *The Mis-Education of the Negro.* 1933. New York: AMS Press, 1977.

———. *The Education of the Negro Prior to 1861.* 1915. Foreword by John Henrik Clarke. Brooklyn: A&B Publishers Group, 1999.

VIRGINIA WOOLF

Beer, Gillian. *Virginia Woolf: The Common Ground.* Ann Arbor: University of Michigan Press, 1996.

Bell, Quentin. *Virginia Woolf: A Biography.* New York: Harcourt, 1973.

Bishop, Edward. *Virginia Woolf.* New York: St. Martin's, 1991.

Briggs, Julie. *Virginia Woolf: An Inner Life.* New York: Harcourt, 2005.

Cuddy-Keane, Melba. *Virginia Woolf, the Intellectual, and the Public Sphere.* Cambridge: Cambridge University Press, 2003.

Fernald, Anne. E. *Virginia Woolf: Feminism and the Reader.* New York: Palgrave Macmillan, 2006.

Goldman, Jane. *The Cambridge Introduction to Virginia Woolf.* Cambridge: Cambridge University Press, 2006.

Gordon, Lyndall. *Virginia Woolf: A Writer's Life.* London: Oxford University Press, 1984.

Gorsky, Susan Rubinow. *Virginia Woolf.* Boston: Twayne, 1989.

Hussey, Mark. *Virginia Woolf A to Z: A Comprehensive Reference for Students, Teachers, and Common Readers to Her Life, Work, and Critical Reception.* New York: Facts on File, 1995.

King, James. *Virginia Woolf.* London: Norton, 1995.

Leaska, Mitchell Alexander. *Granite and Rainbow: The Hidden Life of Virginia Woolf.* London: Picador, 1998.

Lee, Hermione. *Virginia Woolf.* New York: Knopf, 1997.

Nicholson, Nigel. *Virginia Woolf.* New York: Viking, 2000.

Poole, Roger. *The Unknown Virginia Woolf.* Cambridge: Cambridge Univesity Press, 1995.

Reid, Panthea. *Art and Affection: A Life of Virginia Woolf.* New York: Oxford University Press, 1996.

Rose, Phyllis. *A Woman of Letters: The Life of Virginia Woolf.* New York: Oxford University Press, 1981.

Webb, Ruth. *Virginia Woolf.* New York: Oxford University Press, 2000.

Whitworth, Michael. *Virginia Woolf.* Oxford: Oxford University Press, 2005.

Woolf, Virginia. *The Captain's Deathbed and Other Essays.* New York: Harcourt, 1950.

———. *The Death of the Moth and Other Essays.* New York: Harcourt, 1942.

———. *Moments of Being: Unpublished Autobiographical Works.* Edited by Jeanne Schulkind. New York: Harcourt, 1973.

———. *Night and Day.* New York: Harcourt, 1973.

Wussow, Helen. *New Essays on Virginia Woolf.* Dallas: Contemporary Research, 1995.

APPENDIX

Two Student Papers

Bedford/St. Martin's asked instructors who used a previous edition of *A World of Ideas* to submit student essays written in response to selections in the book. Here we offer two of those essays.[1] The first writer applies Lao-tzu's principles to the government of the family; the second examines Martin Luther King Jr.'s use of emotion as a persuasive tool. You may use these actual student papers in any way you wish. The assignments for these essays are also shown.

[1] I want to thank Michael Hennessy, Professor of English at Southwest Texas State University, who submitted the following assignments and essays.

Assignment 1

Take any group structure within our society—family, classroom, workplace, community, and so on—and imagine that the leader of that particular group is a Taoist. How could Lao-tzu's principles of government be applied to the group? How would the leader have to adapt those principles to fit contemporary circumstances?

Paul Nelson   Nelson 1

Professor Michael Hennessy

English 1320.264

7 February 2005

Losing Control: Good Family Advice

The ancient Chinese philosopher Lao-tzu writes: "The people are difficult to govern: It is because those in authority are too fond of action." I see this as Lao-tzu's assertion that too much government control will breed resentment in the people and thus make them difficult to handle. The act of controlling suddenly brings about uncontrollability, much to the leader's surprise. John Wayne might express this idea differently: "Pull the reins too tight--horse'll buck!" This lesson also lends itself readily to the "government" of a family. Picture the "leaders" as the mother and father (or either one separately) and the "people" they govern as the children, whether one child or many. When a parent exerts too much control over a child, the action initiates a pattern of resentment, which can create distance between the two and eventually leave the relationship devoid of respect and love.

I believe that people, for the most part, do not like being told what to do. Lao-tzu seems to think so too. He explains that he prefers people in their simple, unmeddled-with form, like that of an "uncarved block." For him, people in this form are truer to their nature and perhaps closer to a basic goodness; it is when people are continually acted upon or "controlled" that they exhibit undesirable behaviors. "Win the empire by not being meddlesome," advises Lao-tzu. He also writes, "The better known the laws and edicts, the more thieves and robbers there are." I translate this as, "More control results in uncontrollability." One could argue, of course, that children not only need but also feel more comfortable with some predetermined boundaries. Perhaps this is true of adults as well. We feel safer knowing that all of our desires will not be permitted to run recklessly through the world in a laissez-faire fashion. Therefore, I think it is important to clarify that "less" control does not necessarily mean a complete absence of control, rather that a little personal freedom must be granted to individuals in order to bring about healthy behaviors in them. To give credibility to this statement, I can cite a personal experience.

When I moved to Texas three years ago, I began a relationship with a woman who already had a young son. After a year or so, we began living together and operating as a family. Both the child and I had no idea how we were going to begin our relationship, but I knew I wanted to be the father, and I knew I wanted him to listen to me. At first I observed a respectful distance between us, hoping to give birth slowly to a long and beautiful friendship. I thought to myself, "Pretty soon this kid will be crazy about me and will do all the things I ask out of profound admiration and undying love." After a while I realized the foolish error of my reasoning and then made my second mistake. To get the cooperation I wanted out of this six-year-old-boy, I tried to control him with a host of rules, close observation, and timely punishment, which I regret included a few spankings. I found that not only did I start a pattern of fear and resentment, but that I was less happy with myself. I sought absolute power and felt the by-product of corruption eating away at my own well-being. To paraphrase Lao-tzu, I lost the empire with too much meddling. I took the "uncarved block" and whittled an angry, frustrated, rebellious figure. Lao-tzu teaches that people will be hard to govern if those in authority are too fond of action. It was only after I realized the mess I helped create that I made the decision to do less. I reasoned that constant action implies constant fixing, which is not only bothersome but unnecessary.

I have given up a great deal of desire to control. By accepting my stepson, now eight, as he is, I discovered that he's quite a wonderful person, and by not telling him what to do so often, I have discovered that most of the time he *knows* what to do and takes pride in doing it. He now enjoys a little bit of personal freedom. This personal freedom has manifested itself as self-esteem, which in turn has generated respect for me and inspired a little bit of love. Our relationship has strengthened considerably, and the family is happier.

As I suggested earlier, I believe the desire to control someone tends to make that person more uncontrollable. It happened with my stepson. History is also full of good examples: England tried to control the religious practices of its people and ended up in a revolution; Prohibition was an attempt to control the use of alcohol, and we found that the cure was more problematic than the problem. These situations more than likely could have been avoided. By decreasing the amount of control over our children, perhaps we can become parents whom they love and respect. Love and respect may be the masks of what Lao-tzu considered the "second best ruler," but I believe they make a first-rate parent.

Assignment 2

Martin Luther King Jr. uses both reason and emotion to make his ideas convincing. Locate a key passage in the letter that is primarily rational and one that is primarily emotional. Briefly discuss the two passages, focusing on why you think each is or is not effective. In general, are people today more easily persuaded by appeals to reason or appeals to emotion? Cite examples and explain.

Angie Calder   Calder 1
Professor Michael Hennessy
English 1310.264
7 February 2005

The Use of Emotion in Martin Luther King Jr.'s

"Letter from Birmingham Jail"

Through the media and in our daily interaction with others, we are bombarded by a steady stream of "arguments" persuading us to adopt a political position, to follow a certain course of action, or to buy a particular brand of car or deodorant. These arguments are both reasonable and emotional, but I believe that people are more responsive to arguments that appeal to their emotions than those that appeal to their reason. When someone backs a position for emotional reasons, he or she is more likely to have a strong commitment to that position. Politicians know this and make heavy use of emotional appeals to sway voters and constituents. However, in terms of emotional intensity, today's political battles pale in comparison to those of the civil rights struggles of the 1960s. At the most stirring points in the classic "Letter from Birmingham Jail," for example, Martin Luther King Jr. uses emotion to point out the horror of segregation and to explain why it must be ended immediately. Although King uses sound reason to make many of his points, his most moving arguments persuade by triggering his audience's emotions.

In King's "Letter," he rationally makes the point that he and the members of the Southern Christian Leadership Conference (SCLC) have tried everything possible, within reason, to end segregation. To King, public demonstrations are the last resort. He says, "In any nonviolent campaign there are four basic steps: collection of the facts to determine whether injustices exist; negotiation; self-purification; and direct action." King assures his audience that he and the other sit-in participants have gone through these steps. He states that the number of unsolved bombings of African American homes and churches in Birmingham is higher than in any other city in the United States. Clearly, he and his colleagues have done their research. In the next few paragraphs of his "Letter," King recounts how he and the SCLC attempted to negotiate with city officials, how this failed, and how he and the other protesters underwent a process of self-purification in order to be ready for direct action: the planned sit-ins. Here King clearly and rationally states his views, his actions, and his reasons for his actions. This method of making his case is effective in communicating facts and clarifying opinions. Reasonable argument aptly carries King's points; however, it alone does not move people to action the way that emotional argument might.

King is indeed very talented at evoking the kinds of emotions that do move people to action. In paragraph 14, where he describes in vivid detail what segregation is like and what it means to be oppressed, he transports the reader into his life and the life of everyone who has ever felt oppressed. King draws on emotions that many people try to ignore, such as fear, hate, pity, frustration--the emotions that go along with oppression. King explains why it is so difficult for African Americans to wait for equality when faced with what they must live through. He tells of watching "vicious mobs lynch . . . mothers and fathers at will"; of trying "to explain to [a] six-year-old daughter why she can't go to the public amusement park . . . and see[ing] tears well up in her eyes when she is told that Funtown is closed to colored children"; of trying to find "an answer for a five-year-old son who is asking 'Daddy, why do white people treat colored people so mean?'"; and of feeling humiliated "when your first name becomes 'nigger,' your middle name becomes 'boy' (however old you are) and your last name becomes 'John,' and your wife and your mother are never given the respected title 'Mrs.'" These insults that King and other African Americans have had to endure are horrible. These horrors, more powerful and compelling than arguments based solely on reason, have the ability to arouse strong emotions in his audience.

I believe it to be as true today as it was when King wrote: emotion is generally more powerful than logic and reason. In today's politics, appeals to people's emotions form the basis of most effective political debates. One has simply to look at any of Newt Gingrich's or Rush Limbaugh's speeches to see how emotion is used to influence the public. Further, many current and controversial political questions concern emotionally charged issues such as abortion, morality, the homeless, and health care; issues such as foreign affairs, the national debt, and the constitutionality of government policies, on the other hand, are often left to the lawmakers and their various committees. In the past, emotions played a much stronger role than logic in stirring public reaction. Many of the most influential people in history relied almost entirely on the power of emotions, and for the most part they were successful in persuading people to follow them. For example, Joan of Arc convinced the French to follow her because of the strong emotions--religious and patriotic--with which she spoke of her cause. Four centuries later, Adolf Hitler succeeded in part because of his ability to whip a crowd into an emotional frenzy. With such overwhelming examples, how can one argue the power of the emotional argument?

Martin Luther King Jr. was well aware of the appeal of emotion. I believe he was wise to use emotion in his "Letter" because of its power to persuade. However, King also knew when to be reasonable and rational. Had he not known how to use emotion and reason in balance, not only in his "Letter" but in his entire campaign, the American civil rights struggle might have turned out very differently. King was willing to fight for what he believed in because of his emotions, and he appealed to this side of his audience in searching for help in his struggle for equality. Most stirring debates, past and present, have been fought on deeply felt emotional, not logical, grounds. When logic is no longer useful, people turn to emotional tactics. I doubt that this will change in the future; after all, think about what persuades you to adopt a political position, follow a certain course of action, or buy a particular product. I believe that Martin Luther King Jr. knew that he had to touch people's emotions in order to persuade his audience and win his battle for civil rights.